MUSIC

HIGHWAYS AND BYWAYS

Edited by

OSBOURNE McCONATHY
Formerly Director of the Department of Public School Music
Northwestern University

JOHN W. BEATTIE
Dean of the School of Music
Northwestern University

RUSSELL V. MORGAN
Directing Supervisor of Music, Cleveland Public Schools
Professor of Music
Western Reserve University

SILVER BURDE

ACKNOWLEDGMENTS

The editors and publishers wish to express their appreciation to the following:

The Beacon Press for the first stanza of "Morning Praise" from their publication *The Beacon Song and Service Book;* Dodd, Mead & Company for the eight lines from *The Joys of the Road,* by Bliss Carman, which were used by permission of the publishers, Dodd, Mead & Company, Inc.; E. P. Dutton & Co., Inc., for the words, "The Night Will Never Stay," taken from *Gypsy and Ginger* by Eleanor Farjeon, published and copyrighted by E. P. Dutton & Co., Inc., New York; Miss Mary Wood Hinman for her version of the melody, "Korobushka" from *Group Dances,* Vol. IV, published by A. S. Barnes and Company, New York; Mr. Hugh Lofting for the poem, "The Kitchen Kalendar" from *Porridge Poetry,* published by F. A. Stokes Company; Miss Andronike Mekelatos for the selection and arrangement of the characteristic Hellenic (Greek) folk songs and the accompanying descriptive notes; Mr. Fred Sonnen for the harmonica notation in Unit IX; Dr. Eugene Sturchio for permission to reproduce the paintings "Festa Campestre" and "The Blind Violinist" by Vincenzo Irolli; The University Society for permission to use "Tu" from *La Mejor Música del Mundo;* Mr. Ross C. Whitmire for his assistance in the selection of the melodies for Unit IX and for typical Western incidents described in the dialogue; and to the boys of the William H. Seward School, Chicago, whose enthusiasm, ingenuity, and eager performance contributed to the successful working out of Mrs. Alice Gideon Whitmire's playlet, "Roundup Camp at Night"; Miss Dixie Willson for the poem, "The Mist and All" from *Child Life,* published by Rand McNally and Company; the poem "Highways and Byways," by John Vanderbilt from Daringer-Eaton's *The Poet's Craft,* copyright 1935 by World Book Company, Yonkers-on-Hudson, New York;. Mr. Alfred Howell, Directing Supervisor of Art, Cleveland Public Schools, for his advice in the the selection of pictures; the R C A Manufacturing Company, Inc., for assistance in listing correlated recorded selections and for invaluable cooperation in the making of records of songs from this book.

Stella Marek Cushing, author of "Trips Abroad," wishes to express her sincere appreciation to the many persons who have aided her in interpreting the culture and folk music of the countries represented, and especially to the following:

For advice in the selection of authentic and characteristic folk songs:
  Sweden: Mrs. Eric Scherstram and Reverend C. A. Gavert
  Russia: Helena Ettinger, Academy of Science, Kiev; and Constantin Shvedoff
  Poland: Dr. Alexander Guttry, Warsaw, Poland
  Czechoslovakia: Milos Lichard, Užhorod, Ruthenia
  Yugoslavia: Dr. Bogdan Njemčić, Zagreb, Yugoslavia; Ivan Mladineo; and Rudolf Matz
  Bulgaria: Raina Katžarova, Sofia, Bulgaria
  Italy: Maria M. Alliegro
  China: Dr. T. Z. Koo
  Japan: Marguerite Haven

For accuracy of detail in the correct interpretation of the customs depicted in the plays:
  Sweden: Alpha Bostrom
  Poland: Mrs. Stephen J. Zand, Consulate of Poland, New York City
  Czechoslovakia: Dr. Josef Hanč, Czechoslovakia Vice-Consul, New York City
  Yugoslavia: M. S. Stanojević
  Italy: Nicola Latorraca and Dr. Carlo de Franchis, Italian Vice-Consul, Newark, New Jersey
  China: Li Jenkung
  Japan: Takeshi Haga

For assistance in directing the national groups which sang for the Victor recordings of the folk songs in "Trips Abroad":
  Sweden: Gustav V. Lindgren
  Russia: Ukrainian songs: Leo Bezruchko
  Poland: H. Zimnoch and E. Hynes
  Czechoslovakia: Robert Mokrejš
  Yugoslavia: Emil Blažević
  Italy: Maestro Sandro Benelli
  China: Li Jenkung
  Japan: Takeshi Haga

For dance directions as indicated throughout the book:
  Michael Herman, consultant on folk dancing for the Folk Festival Council of New York City

CONTENTS

ILLUSTRATIONS

BEETHOVEN AND NATURE

And this our life, exempt from public haunt,
Finds tongues in trees, books in the running brooks,
Sermons in stones, and good in every thing.

As You Like It — Shakespeare

UNIT I: THE OPEN ROAD

Now the joys of the road are chiefly these:
A crimson touch on the hard-wood trees;

A shadowy highway cool and brown,
Alluring up and enticing down

From rippled water to dappled swamp,
From purple glory to scarlet pomp;

These are the joys of the open road —
For him who travels without a load.

Couplets from "The Joys of the Road"
by Bliss Carman
from *Songs of Vagabondia*

Highways and Byways

John Vanderbilt   William G. Hammond

1

by - way, A rut - ted,— nar - row by - way, A
turn - ing, wood - ed by - way,— For my - self.

Morning Praise

First stanza: Author unknown
Second stanza: WILLIAM WALSHAM HOW

LUDWIG VAN BEETHOVEN (1770–1827)

Love is to hu - man hearts What sun - shine is to flow'rs; And
We give Thee but Thine own, What - e'er the gift may be; All

friend - ship is the fair - est thing In this great world of ours.
that we have is Thine a - lone, A trust, O Lord, from Thee!

TONE BLENDING DRILL

I IV I V I

The Folk Song

From the German, by
Phyllis McGinley

German Folk Song

What is a folk song? These beautiful verses, set to an old German tune, tell in a fanciful way how a folk song grows. No one knows the source of a true folk song. Someone was inspired to sing a melody. Others liked it and repeated it until it took on the characteristics of all those who loved and sang it. That is why we can often tell to what country or race a folk song belongs even without knowing its name.

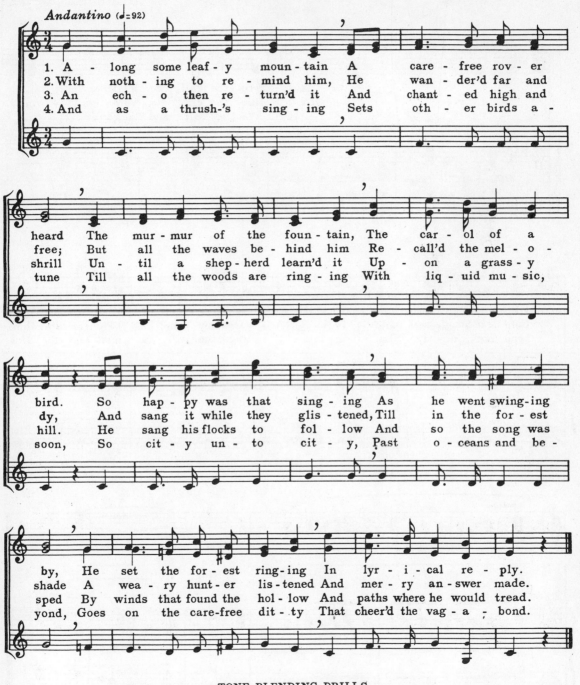

TONE BLENDING DRILLS

The Mist and All

DIXIE WILLSON   NOBLE CAIN

The classic masters wrote melodies chiefly in scalewise progressions and harmonized them largely with the primary triads and seventh chords. Here is a song with modern effects, such as we frequently hear over the radio. Observe that both melody and harmony are chromatic, which gives the song its distinctive tang.

Sing the "Whoo's" and the "hum's" *legato;* sing the "Ho's" with a soft *staccato.* Divide the last chord equally.

The brief chromatic passage, measures 8–10, may be used as Tone Blending Drill.

Morning Song

Anna Mary Mealand   Anna Mary Mealand

By means of changes of key, the composer secures variety of tonal effects.   This is called Modulation.   By means of phrase repetitions and contrasts, the composer secures structural balance and proportion, which we call Musical Form.

1. A - wake and greet the morn-ing fair, A - wake for life stirs ev-'ry-where, The clouds are ros - y with the dawn, A lark is sing - ing in the morn. And he wish - es you good morn - ing, And he wish - es you good morn - ing.

2. The sun is mount-ing in the blue, The ros - es glis - ten with the dew, A breeze is stir - ring through the trees, And faint - ly sounds the hum of bees. And they wish us all good morn - ing, And they wish us all good morn - ing.

3. The wak - ing woods are fresh and sweet, All things do now the morn-ing greet. Come let us too our voic - es raise And swell this joy - ous song of praise. As we sing a glad good morn - ing, As we sing a glad good morn - ing.

Modulation: Bridge tones

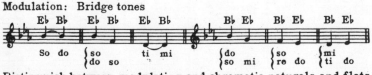

Distinguish between modulating and chromatic naturals and flats.

The letters above the staff indicate the key into which the song has modulated, capital letters for major keys and small letters for minor keys.

The Night Will Never Stay

ELEANOR FARJEON

HECTOR MACCARTHY

UNIT II: TRIPS ABROAD—SWEDEN

by STELLA MAREK CUSHING

Before the days of recorded history Scandinavian peoples occupied the Northlands of Europe. These tall, fair-haired, blue-eyed adventurous "men of the north," called Vikings from the Norse word "warrior," carried their civilization by conquest to the east, south, and west. In the second century, the Northmen swept to the south to attack the Roman Empire. To the west we find them in the ninth century forcing Alfred the Great to acknowledge them as the masters of northern England. To the east, they gave the name Rusland to Russia where they occupied territory from the Baltic to the Black Sea.

Unlike the warlike conquests in the Age of the Vikings, the Scandinavians came peaceably to help settle America in the nineteenth century, bringing with them their distinctive music and culture and the same virility, enduring courage, and noble qualities of character that have re-vitalized other civilizations.

Today these northern peoples are known as Danes (in Denmark), Norwegians (in Norway), and Swedes (in Sweden). Originally they were one race with a common language, which in time became three distinct languages as the peoples set up separate kingdoms. No foreign power has ever ruled over these three kingdoms of the north, which have lived peaceably together for more than one hundred and twenty-five years. They have remained neutral during many wars in Europe, thus challenging all peoples today to effect peaceful settlements of international disputes.

Spring

Vårvindar friska

(Recorded)

From the Swedish of JULIA NYBERG.
Based on a translation by C. A. GAVERT
and versified by VIRGINIA CLEAVELAND

SWEDISH FOLK SONG

After the long darkness of winter, it is easy to understand the joy of the northern peoples at the coming of spring. Green grasses and flowers suddenly arise beside the melting snowbanks. Flocks again graze on the hills and the farmer sows the fertile fields. This song reflects the moods of springtime.

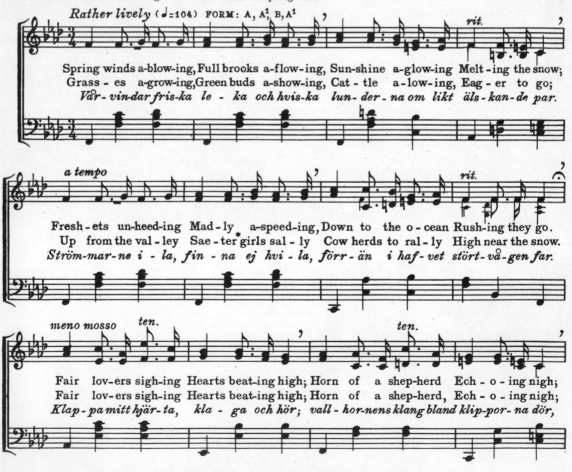

Spring winds a-blow-ing, Full brooks a-flow-ing, Sun-shine a-glow-ing Melt-ing the snow;
Grass-es a-grow-ing, Green buds a-show-ing, Cat-tle a-low-ing, Eag-er to go;
Vår-vindar fris-ka le-ka och hvis-ka lun-der-na om likt äls-kan-de par.

Fresh-ets un-heed-ing Mad-ly a-speed-ing, Down to the o-cean Rush-ing they go.
Up from the val-ley Sae-ter girls sal-ly Cow herds to ral-ly High near the snow.
Ström-mar-ne i-la, fin-na ej hvi-la, förr-än i haf-vet stört-vå-gen far.

Fair lov-ers sigh-ing Hearts beat-ing high; Horn of a shep-herd Ech-o-ing nigh;
Fair lov-ers sigh-ing Hearts beat-ing high; Horn of a shep-herd, Ech-o-ing nigh;
Klap-pa mitt hjär-ta, kla-ga och hör; vall-hor-nens klang bland klip-por-na dör,

Scale of F Minor, Melodic Form, by Tetrachords

*See p. 226

8

Gay car-ol swell-ing, Sor-row dis-pel-ling, O'er dale and moun-tain flow.
Gay car-ol swell-ing, Sor-row dis-pel-ling, O'er dale and moun-tain flow.
ström-kar-len spe-lar, sor-ger-na de-lar va-kan kring berg och dal.

My Homeland

Till Österland
(Recorded)

Translated from the Swedish

SWEDISH FOLK SONG

No doubt the text of this song originated after someone had returned from a long journey, because it is filled with the solemn joy of homecoming. It is a very popular song among Swedish people living in America.

1. I jour-ney east-ward at sun-set For there is the land of my soul,
   The home that shel-ter'd my child-hood, The land of my birth is the goal.
2. I'll build a hut in the mead-ow 'Mid grass-es and trees ev-er green,
   Where crys-tal clear flow-ing riv-ers, Will mois-ten the roots all un-seen.
3. A foun-tain rip-ples be-yond it, And sweet smelling herbs scent the air,
   Ripe ber-ries hang there in clus-ters, And fruit trees their full rich-es bear;

Till Ös-ter-land vill jag fa-ra, där bor all-ra kä-res-tan min;

O-ver moun-tain, through deep val-ley Past green lin-den trees on the knoll.
And be-side my hut a gar-den With flow'rs blooming fair and se-rene.
To my fa-ther-land I'll has-ten, The home of my child-hood so fair.

Bor-tom berg och dju-pa da-lar allt un-der så grö-nan en lind.

Scale of A Minor, Melodic Form, by Tetrachords

Buxom Lassies

Flickorna de små uti dansen de gå

(*Recorded*)

From the Swedish

SWEDISH FOLK GAME

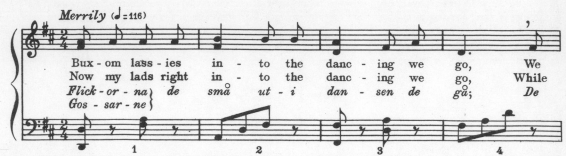

Bux - om lass - ies in - to the danc - ing we go, We
Now my lads right in - to the danc - ing we go, While
Flick - or - na de små ut - i dan - sen de gå; De
Gos - sar - ne

Formation: Any number of couples form two circles, all facing center; girls in the inner circle with hands joined; boys in outer circle, hands on hips.

PART I. Measures 1-8. Girls drop hands and face left. Beginning with left foot, they walk clockwise,

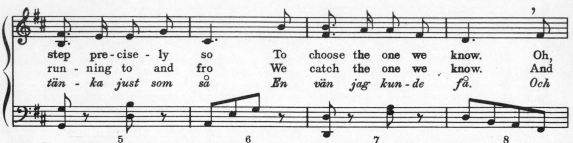

step pre - cise - ly so To choose the one we know. Oh,
run - ning to and fro We catch the one we know. And
tän - ka just som så En vän jag kun - de få. Och

taking two steps to each measure, pretending to hunt for a partner among the boys, who stand still.

if I am sure that you my part - ner will be Then
as I am sure that you my part - ner will be Then
om du vill blif - va all - ra kä - res - tan min, så

Measures 9-16. Girl chooses partner by taking right hand of chosen boy on her left. Beginning with the outside

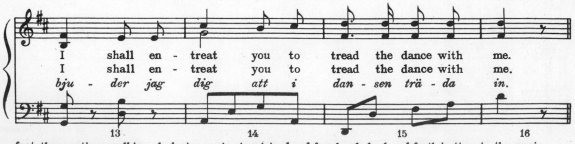

I shall en - treat you to tread the dance with me.
I shall en - treat you to tread the dance with me.
bju - der jag dig att i dan - sen trä - da in.

foot, they continue walking, clockwise, swinging joined and free hands back and forth in time to the music.

PART II. A. Measures 17-23. Partners take waltz position and all couples take 14 slides following each

other clockwise.

Measure 24. Count 1, pause.
Count 2, couples reverse
positions, boys now inside
circle.

Measures 25-31. Couples take 14 slides, counter clockwise, back to places.

Measure 32. Count 1, pause.
Count 2, boy takes girl's left
hand in his right.

Dance directions by Michael Herman

PART II. B. Measures 17-28. All couples walk in a circle, counter clockwise, as if in promenade.
Measures 29-31. Partners face each other, join right hands and swing them from side to side 6 times.
Measure 32. Partners drop hands, placing them on hips. Girl curtsies with left toe back of right heel. Boy bows from the hips.

PARTS III and IV. The whole dance is now repeated; boys, beginning on the inside of circle, now walk around counter clockwise, looking for a partner as the girls did in Part I. Part IV is same as Part II with positions and directions reversed.

Note: To vary Part II, the Polka Step may be used, turning right about continuously and moving forward in circle clockwise; then reverse counter clockwise.

A FESTIVAL PROCESSION IN SWEDEN

Neptune

Näcken
(Recorded)

From the Swedish

SWEDISH FOLK SONG

In Norse mythology Freja (frāy-ya) was the goddess of love and beauty. Although in this song she is smiling and gay, many of the old folk tales picture her as the fair, weeping goddess. Neptune's hopeless love for Freja is one of the most popular of northern legends.

This song may be sung in several ways: 1. Voices in Unison, with piano accompaniment; 2. Sopranos and Altos, accompanied or unaccompanied; 3. Sopranos, Altos, and Basses, accompanied or unaccompanied; 4. Or the Bass part may be sung by Altos, an octave higher, thereby making a three-part song for unchanged voices, accompanied or unaccompanied. The piano plays the large notes.

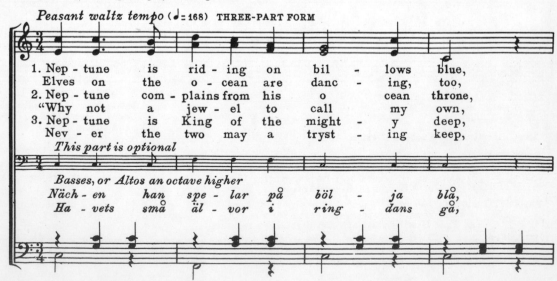

Peasant waltz tempo (♩=168) THREE-PART FORM

1. Nep - tune   is   rid - ing   on   bil - lows   blue,
Elves   on   the   o - cean   are   danc - ing,   too,
2. Nep - tune   com - plains from   his   o   cean   throne,
"Why   not   a   jew - el   to   call   my   own,
3. Nep - tune   is   King   of   the   might - y   deep,
Nev - er   the   two   may   a   tryst - ing   keep,

This part is optional

Basses, or Altos an octave higher

Näch - en   han   spe - lar   på   böl - ja   blå,
Ha - vets   små   äl - vor   i   ring - dans   gå,

UNIT III: STEPHEN COLLINS FOSTER

by JOHN TASKER HOWARD *

Every American boy and girl knows some of Stephen Foster's songs, but not everyone who sings "My Old Kentucky Home" and "Old Folks at Home" stops to think that it was he who wrote these songs. Neither do many of us realize that Foster was a typical American who lived and worked in mid-nineteenth-century surroundings similar to those of millions of his fellow countrymen. His music has now become such a familiar part of American life that we accept it as a matter of course, just as we accept many of the other splendid things which we have inherited from our forefathers. Nevertheless, among the many composers of music that our country has produced, Stephen Collins Foster stands forth as the writer of songs whose music expresses most truly the spirit of America. Although his musical training was limited, his simple melodies achieve greatness because they voice universal sentiments — the thoughts and feelings of people in every walk of life, not only in America but throughout the world.

The several types of songs that Foster composed show the typically American influences which surrounded him in his childhood and youth. Many of his works were the so-called Ethiopian, or Negro songs. These were not actual Negro melodies, but rather imitations of Negro songs written for the black-faced minstrel shows which came into popularity during Foster's childhood. Some of these songs were lively nonsense songs — "Oh! Susanna," "Camptown Races," "Lou'siana Belle"; and others were sentimental songs in Negro dialect — "Old Uncle Ned," "Old Folks at Home," and others.

Whatever knowledge Foster may have had of the singing of Negroes was gained principally in the North rather than in the South, for he lived most of his life in the neighborhood of Pittsburgh, Pennsylvania, where he was born on the Fourth of July, 1826. When he was a little boy he was often taken to a Negro church by a servant in the Foster family. There Stephen first heard the songs of the Negro. They made a great impression on him and he later used snatches of melody heard in that church in two songs of his own — "Oh! Boys, Carry Me 'Long," and "Hard Times, Come Again No More."

Pittsburgh lies at the head of the Ohio River. In Foster's boyhood it was the end of a long journey for steamboats that came all the way from New Orleans. The deck hands on these boats were Negroes from the South and Stephen must have heard them sing their songs on the wharves of Pittsburgh. He probably heard them in Cincinnati, also, where he spent four years as a bookkeeper for his brother. These experiences were typical of America, and they influenced the songs of Stephen Foster. They made Foster's songs far more characteristic of our country than were the works of composers in the older cities along the Atlantic coast, who were trained largely under foreign influence. Their compositions were more in the style of German music even though written by Americans in America.

Although Foster's music showed the influences that had surrounded him, he was no mere copyist or imitator. He absorbed the spirit of his environment, yet his creative genius enabled him to bring forth songs that were stamped with his own individuality. The best of Foster's songs are those which express the emotions deepest in his own nature. Stephen loved his home and his greatest songs were home songs — "Old Folks at Home," "My Old Kentucky Home," "Massa's in the Cold Ground," "Old Black Joe," and others of their kind. The love of home is shared by millions of people, and because Foster was able to tell so simply and faithfully of this feeling common to all mankind, his songs have been translated into almost every language throughout the world.

There was another side to Stephen Foster's nature which also was reflected in his music. In his youth and early manhood he loved the company of his friends. Often these companions would gather to sing the rollicking songs Stephen had written for serenading parties and other jovial times. Thus were produced "Lou'siana Belle" and "Oh! Susanna," a song which became the marching song of the "forty-niners" on their way to California during the gold rush of that year.

Foster wrote both the words and the music for most of his songs. He possessed a rare gift for wedding words and music so that they seem inseparable. In his early Ethiopian songs the poet-composer used a crude dialect which he abandoned in his later works. It is interesting to note that in "Old Folks at Home," Foster begins with "Way down upon de Swanee ribber," while in "Old Black Joe," published in 1860 (Foster died January 13, 1864), he uses pure English rather than attempting to imitate the speech of the plantation Negro. In this unit we have followed Foster's later practice.

Everybody knows the more familiar Foster songs — "Old Folks at Home" (Swanee River), "My Old Kentucky Home," "Old Black Joe," "Massa's in the Cold Ground," "Oh! Susanna," "Come Where My Love Lies Dreaming," "Old Dog Tray," "Hard Times, Come Again No More," etc. These will be found in innumerable inexpensive song collections and for that reason are not given in this unit. It seems preferable to offer here some of the fine songs which are not so universally known.

The songs in this book together with those just mentioned show Foster in all his moods and make possible a wide variety of interesting programs for school and community activities. These may take the form of tableaux, operettas, minstrels, recitals with biographical and appreciative comments, and other forms of creative entertainment which the pupils can develop.

During Foster's lifetime his melodies were widely sung, though few people then imagined that they were destined to be accepted as our choicest folk songs and that their composer would be hailed as typifying the voice of America.

* Author of *Stephen Collins Foster, America's Troubadour*, published by Thomas Y. Crowell Company, New York.

Jeanie with the Light Brown Hair

STEPHEN COLLINS FOSTER   STEPHEN COLLINS FOSTER

"Jeanie with the Light Brown Hair" is one of the few successful love songs written by Foster. Generally he did not achieve his best expression in this type of song, yet "Jeanie" is truly beautiful. Stephen's wife was named Jane and it may be that he was thinking of her when he wrote this song and the other "Jenny" songs he composed later — "Jenny's Coming O'er the Green," "Little Jenny Dow," "Jenny June." The melody is tender and wistful and deserves to rank with some of the world's great love songs, such as "Annie Laurie," "How Can I Leave Thee," "The Last Rose of Summer," "Drink to Me Only with Thine Eyes," "Juanita."

Tenderly (♩=60)   FORM: A,B,A,C,D,E,A,F

1. I dream of Jean-ie with the light brown hair,
2. I long for Jean-ie with the day dawn smile,
3. I sigh for Jean-ie but her light form stray'd,

dream, I dream
long, I long
sigh, I sigh

Borne, like a va - por, on the sum-mer air; I
Ra - diant in glad - ness, warm with win - ning guile; I
Far from the fond hearts 'round her na - tive glade; Her

see her trip - ping where the bright streams play, I
hear her mel - o - dies, like joys gone by,
smiles have van - ish'd and her sweet songs flown,

see, I see
hear, I hear
smiles, her smiles

C

Hap-py as the dai - sies that dance on her way.
Sigh-ing 'round my heart o'er the fond hopes that die.
Flit-ting like the dreams that have cheer'd us and gone.

F

Man-y were the wild notes her
Sigh-ing like the night wind and
Now the nod-ding wild flow'rs may

TONE BLENDING DRILLS

a.   b.   c.

Diminished—seventh chords.   Chords on vii of the scale.

mer - ry voice would pour, Man - y were the blithe birds that
sob - bing like the rain, Wail - ing for the lost one that
with - er on the shore, While her gen - tle fin - gers will

ad lib.

war - bled them o'er. I dream of Jean - ie with the
comes not a - gain. I long for Jean - ie and my
cull them no more. I sigh for Jean - ie, with the

dream, I dream
long, I long
sigh, I sigh

light brown hair, Float - ing, like a va - por, on the soft sum - mer air.
heart bows low, Nev - er more to find her where the bright wa - ters flow.
light brown hair, Float - ing, like a va - por, on the soft sum - mer air.

Nelly Bly

STEPHEN COLLINS FOSTER   STEPHEN COLLINS FOSTER

"Nelly Bly" is one of Foster's most whimsical songs. Its words are humorous but they are not of the boisterous type found in "The Camptown Races" or in "Oh! Susanna." "Nelly Bly" was published in 1850 when Stephen was achieving his first success as a composer. It is still widely sung, yet few associate the song with the name of Stephen Foster or realize that it was written by the composer of "Old Folks at Home." Such is the case with many of Foster's works; they have become a part of American life without regard to their origin. Whenever a song becomes an expression of the spirit of a people it gradually takes on the characteristics of a folk song. The song itself becomes more important than the composer. In this way Foster's songs are now recognized as truly American folk music.

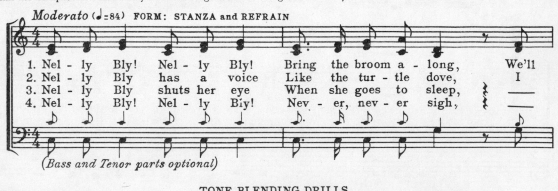

Moderato (♩=84) FORM: STANZA and REFRAIN

1. Nel - ly Bly! Nel - ly Bly! Bring the broom a - long, We'll
2. Nel - ly Bly has a voice Like the tur - tle dove, I
3. Nel - ly Bly shuts her eye When she goes to sleep,
4. Nel - ly Bly! Nel - ly Bly! Nev - er, nev - er sigh,

(Bass and Tenor parts optional)

TONE BLENDING DRILLS

a.   b.   c.   d.   e.   f.   g.

I _ _ _ I IV I I IV I I IV I I IV I I IV I I IV I

sweep the kitch-en clean, my dear, And have a lit-tle song.
hear it in the mead-ow, And I hear it in the grove: The__
When she wak-ens up a-gain Her eyes be-gin to peep: The__
Nev-er bring the tear-drop To the cor-ner of your eye. For the

Poke the wood, my la-dy love, And make the fire burn, And__
Nel-ly Bly__ has a heart__ Warm as cup of tea, And__
way she walks, she lifts her foot, And then she brings it down, And__
pie is made of pump-kin And the mush is made of corn, And there's

while I take the ban-jo down, Just give the mush a turn.
big-ger than the sweet po-ta-to Down in Ten-nes-see.
when it lights there's mu-sic there In that part of the town.
corn and pump-kins plen-ty, love, A-ly-ing in the barn.

REFRAIN

Heigh! Nel-ly, Ho! Nel-ly, lis-ten, love, to me, I'll

sing for you, play for you, A dul-cem mel-o-dy. Heigh! Nel-ly, Ho! Nel-ly,

lis-ten, love, to me, I'll sing for you, play for you, A dul-cem mel-o-dy.

The Camptown Races

STEPHEN COLLINS FOSTER   STEPHEN COLLINS FOSTER

"The Camptown Races" has rivalled Foster's "Oh! Susanna" in popularity. It was a favorite in Negro minstrel shows for many years and is still widely sung as a comic song. The melody of the refrain is similar to the opening phrase of the Negro spiritual, "Couldn't Hear Nobody Pray." It is possible that Foster patterned his song on the spiritual, yet "The Camptown Races" is so characteristic of its composer that it is equally likely that the spiritual was based upon Foster's song. Another similarity to "Camptown Races" is found in the refrain of "A Capital Ship," the widely known college song. Who can tell where these bits of melody really originated.

CHORUS

go back— home with a pock-et full of tin, Oh! doo-dah - day!
Can't touch the bot-tom with a ten - foot pole, Oh! doo-dah - day!
Run-ning a race with a shoot - ing star, Oh! doo-dah - day!
keep my— mon-ey in an old— tow - bag, Oh! doo-dah - day!

REFRAIN

Goin' to run all night! Goin' to run all day! I'll—

bet my mon-ey on the bob-tail nag, Some-bod-y bet on the bay!

TONE BLENDING DRILLS

I - - -   I IV I$_4^6$ V I

Ring, Ring the Banjo

STEPHEN COLLINS FOSTER   STEPHEN COLLINS FOSTER

This is one of Foster's lively songs composed for the minstrel shows of his day. "Ring, Ring the Banjo" was first published in 1851 when Foster was providing songs for Edwin P. Christy, one of the most famous American minstrels. Although we seldom see the old-time minstrel shows, they were the most individual contribution America has made to the theater. With songs and jokes in imitation of the Negro, the black-faced comedians presented a caricature of the Negro's eccentricities that was highly amusing and entertaining in spite of its obvious exaggeration.

All the actors and singers in the minstrel shows appeared in absurd costumes except the white interlocutor, or master of ceremonies, who sat in sedate and dignified fashion in the middle of the row formed by the other players. The end men, the principal comedians, addressed their remarks to the interlocutor, who always answered in serious vein. Songs, dances, and other specialties formed an indispensable part of the entertainment. Some of the greatest comedians of the American stage made their first appearances as black-faced song and dance men in the old-time minstrel shows.

Moderato (♩=104)   FORM: STANZA and REFRAIN

1. The time is nev-er drear-y, If the dark-y nev-er groans; The ladies nev-er wea-ry With the rat-tle of the bones; Then come a-gain, Su-san-na, By the gas-light of the moon; We'll

2. Oh! nev-er count the bub-bles While there's wa-ter in the spring: The dark-y has no trou-bles While he's got this song to sing. The beau-ties of cre-a-tion Will nev-er lose their charm, While I

3. Once I was so luck-y, My mas-sa set me free, I went to old Ken-tuck-y To see what I could see: I could not go no far-ther, I turn to mas-sa's door, Old

4. Ear-ly in the morn-ing Of a love-ly, sum-mer day, My mas-sa sent me warn-ing He'd like to hear me play. On the ban-jo tap-ping, I come with dul-cem strain; I'll

5. My love, I'll have to leave you While the riv-er's run-ning high; But I nev-er can de-ceive you, So don't you wipe your eye. I'm goin' to make some mon-ey; But I'll come a-noth-er day, I'll

strum the old pi - an - o   When the ban-jo's out of tune.
roam the old plan - ta - tion   With my true love on my arm.
love him all the hard - er,   I'll___ go a - way no more.
mas - sa fall a - nap - ping   He'll nev - er wake a - gain.
come a - gain my hon - ey,   If I have to work my way.

REFRAIN

Ring, ring the ban - jo!   I like that good old song,

Come a - gain my true love,   Oh! where you been so long?

TONE BLENDING DRILLS

a.   *b.*

I IV I   I IV I$_4^6$ - V$_7$ I

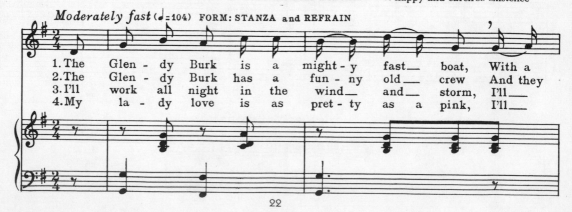

THE

Glendy Burk

A

Plantation Melody

Written and Composed by

STEPHEN C. FOSTER.

Cover Design of the Original Edition

The 'Glendy Burk'

STEPHEN COLLINS FOSTER   STEPHEN COLLINS FOSTER

This song is about a steamboat, the *Glenn D. Burk*, which for many years plied the waters of the Ohio River. The Negroes called it the "Glendy Burk," and Foster used this nickname for one of his jolliest songs. The river boats of those days were among the most picturesque sights of the Old South. The song is supposed to be sung by the Negro roustabouts who carried the freight on and off the boats and lived a strenuous but happy and carefree existence

Moderately fast (♩=104) FORM: STANZA and REFRAIN

1. The Glen - dy Burk is a might-y fast__ boat, With a
2. The Glen - dy Burk has a fun - ny old__ crew And they
3. I'll work all night in the wind__ and__ storm, I'll__
4. My la - dy love is as pret - ty as a pink, I'll__

mighty fine cap - tain,— too; He— sits up there on the
sing— the boat - man's song, They burn the pitch and the
work— all day in the rain, Till I find my - self on the
meet— her on the— way, I'll— take her back to the

hur - ri - cane roof And he keeps his eye on the crew. I
pine— knot, too, For to shove the boat a - long. The
lev - y - dock In— New Or - leans a - gain. They
sun - ny old south And— there I'll make her— stay. So

can't stay here, for the work's too hard; I'm—
smoke goes up and the en - gine roars, And the
make me mow in the hay field here And—
don't you fret, my— hon - ey dear, Oh!—

bound to leave this— town; I'll take my— duds and—
wheel goes 'round and— 'round, So fare you— well! for I'll
knock my head with the flail, I'll go where they work with the
don't you fret, Miss— Brown, I'll take you— back 'fore the

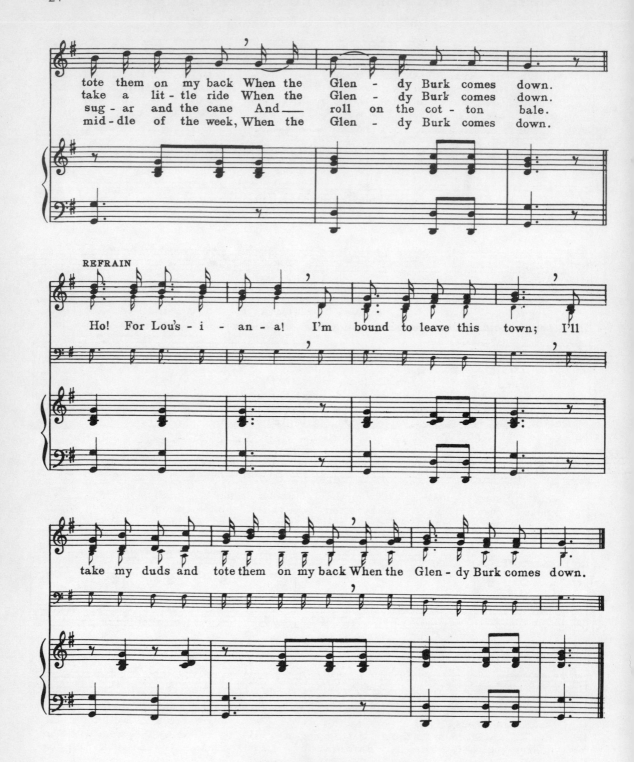

tote them on my back When the Glen - dy Burk comes down.
take a lit - tle ride When the Glen - dy Burk comes down.
sug - ar and the cane And roll on the cot - ton bale.
mid - dle of the week, When the Glen - dy Burk comes down.

REFRAIN

Ho! For Lou's - i - an - a! I'm bound to leave this town; I'll

take my duds and tote them on my back When the Glen - dy Burk comes down.

TONE BLENDING DRILL

I   IV   V   I

UNIT IV: TRIPS ABROAD—RUSSIA AND UKRAINE

by STELLA MAREK CUSHING

THE SLAVONIC PEOPLES

In the early Christian centuries, while the Roman legions were straining to hold back the hordes of barbarians pressing their northern frontiers, Slavs from beyond the Baltic Sea entered the eastern borders of the Roman Empire and settled in the valley of the Dnieper River. Here they found all the necessities of life. The great stream provided water, fish in abundance, and a means of transportation. The dense forests afforded game and lumber. The high cliffs in the vicinity of Kiev, their principal settlement, were natural protecting fortresses. From this fertile valley the Slavs also spread to the north, south, and west. Later, other nomadic tribes from the east, kinsmen of the Huns, swept into this territory and intermingled with the Slavs.

Do you know where the Slavonic peoples are to be found now? Look at the map on p. 50. They populate a vast territory and number almost 200 million people in the following countries:

Russia: Total population is 147 million. There are 169 ethnic groups living within these borders; 90 million are Slavs, divided as follows: Great Russians, 78 million; Ukrainians, 7 million; White Russians, 5 million.

Ukraine: Total population 30 million, divided as follows: Ukrainians, 25 million; Russians, 2 million; other nationalities, 3 million.

Poland: Total population is 31 million: Poles, 17 million; Ukrainians, 7 million; other nationalities, 7 million.

Czechoslovakia: Total population is 15 million, of whom 12 million are Slavs (Czech and Slovak).

Yugoslavia: Total population is 13 million, Serbs, Croats, and Slovenes.

Bulgaria: Total population is 11 million, mostly Bulgarians.

Each branch of the Slavonic race is proud of its own distinctive characteristics, but all trace their ancestry to the early nomadic tribes. As civilization advanced, this race was divided, changed, and developed into many different patterns; yet all the languages have common root words, and folk lore, folk music, and folk dance reveal the same cultural heritage.

Stage Setting by Sergei Soudeikine for the Metropolitan Opera Company

THE FAIR OF SOROCHINTZY — COMIC OPERA BY M. MOUSSORGSKY

RUSSIA

The early historical background of Russia is similar to that of all Slavs. Recorded knowledge of the Russians begins with the rise to power of the Muscovites, a mixture of Slav, Finn, and Mongol. By the tenth century, they had patterned their civilization and adopted Christianity from the Greeks of the Eastern Roman Empire. The Great Russian Empire was formed in the last half of the fifteenth century.

Since then we read most frequently about the reigns of three rulers: Ivan the Terrible, Peter the Great, and Catherine the Great. Under them Russia was changed from a little-known country to one of the great European powers. The government was remodeled along the lines of other European states. Industry was encouraged. The half-Oriental customs of the people were gradually changed by contacts with western Europe. These rulers and their successors were absolute monarchs.

After the French Revolution, many Russians became inspired by the new ideas of "Liberty, Equality, and Fraternity." Those who proposed economic and political reforms had to do so in secret, and were often arrested and cruelly exiled to Siberia. Nevertheless, the unrest in the country continued. Finally the Tsar, Alexander the Second, emancipated the serfs in 1861 and planned other reforms. However, the new changes proved unsuccessful and reaction against reforms set in. After the Russo-Japanese War in 1904, an attempt was made to extend representative government through an elected assembly, but it was too late. The defeat of Russia in the World War touched off the discontent, and the revolution of 1917 deposed the ruling house of Romanoff and confiscated the lands of the nobles.

During the nineteenth century, music, art, drama, and literature flourished. Ancient lore and customs are preserved in the inexhaustibly rich folk music. The great composers, Rimsky-Korsakov, Moussorgsky, and Tschaikowsky have frequently used folk melodies as the basis of many of their own compositions. The styles of Russian songs are as varied as the remote sections of this vast country are different from each other.

The Peddler's Pack

Korobushka

Translated from the Russian

RUSSIAN FOLK SONG

This is an old song, but the dance originated among the Russian exiles in America near the close of the World War.

With vigor (♩=126) FORM: A,B,C,B,C¹,B

1. Full to the brim is my fine ko - ro-bush-ka Pack'd with cot - ton, silk, and
2. Much have I paid, for the goods are cost-ly,___ Bar - gain not nor stin-gy
3. I shall be stand-ing up - on the high-way,___ Till the night-fall I shall

(The basses may sing the bass notes to the syllable, "pom, pom," etc. in imitation of the pluck-ing of the bass viol.)

lace; Glad am I to be young and lust-y, Shoul-ders strong and stur-dy
be; See, my dove, all that I can of - fer, Clos - er come and sit by
wait; When you come, then be - fore your dark eyes Spread my wares and learn my

Dance directions by Michael Herman

FORMATION: Any number of couples form two lines facing each other, boys in one line and girls in the other. Partners join both hands. (When danced, the music is in strict tempo.) Partners join both hands.

FIGURE I.

Meas. 1–2. Count 1, 2, 1. Beginning with left foot, boy takes three walking steps forward; beginning with right foot, partner does same backward. Count 2, Meas. 2. Boy hops on left foot; girl on right.

Meas. 3–4. Count 1, 2, 1. Beginning with right foot, boy takes three walking steps backward; beginning with left foot, partner does same forward. Count 2, Meas. 4. Boy hops on right foot; partner on left.

Meas. 5–6. Repeat Meas. 1–2.

Meas. 7. Count 1. Boy takes one step backward with right foot; partner forward with left. Count 2. Point free foot to the side.

Meas. 8. Count 1. Bring heels together. Pause on count 2.

FIGURE II.

A. Meas. 9–10. Count 1, 2, 1. Partners drop hands. All fold arms. Beginning with right foot, all moving in straight lines, take three steps to right, away from partner. Count 2, Meas. 10. Hop on right foot, swing left forward over right.

Meas. 11–12. Count 1, 2, 1. Beginning with left foot, return to place. Count 2, Meas. 12. Hop on left foot, swing right forward over left.

Meas. 13. Count 1. Partners join right hands, balance forward toward each other with right foot, raising joined hands. Pause on count 2.

Meas. 14. Count 1. Balance backward with left foot, lowering hands. Pause on count 2.

Meas. 15. Partners take two steps forward, changing places.

Meas. 16. Count 1. Face each other, bring heels together. Pause on count 2; drop hands.

B. Meas. 17–24. Repeat Figure II, A, ending in original position.

(Entire dance should be repeated several times.)

pace, Glad am I to be young and lust-y, Shoul-ders strong and stur-dy pace.
me, See, my dove, all that I can of-fer, Clos - er come and sit by me.
fate, When you come, then be-fore your dark eyes Spread my wares and learn my fate.

Flow, River, Flow

Подле реку

Translated from the Russian

RUSSIAN FOLK SONG

So many folk songs when translated are apt to lose the spirit of the original language. In this translation great care has been taken to retain the mood as well as to fit the words to the Russian musical phrases. For example, you will note that the first phrase closes at the end of the second measure; the second phrase closes after the first beat of the fourth measure, etc., as is the case in the original Russian. This ancient song, apparently in G minor, is really in the *la* mode, as is shown by the absence of a leading tone (*si*) and by the nature of the final cadence.

It is of interest to know that this song comes from a collection used today by boys and girls in the schools of Russia.

Flow, riv - er, flow, _____ Flow, riv - er, flow Gen - tly
Mur - mur - ing low, _____ Mur - mur - ing low Where im -
Под - ле ре - ку, _____ Под - ле ре - ку, На кру -

lap - ping the shore As you pass by my door. _____
pris - oned is heard The sad call of a bird.
том бе - ре - гу, на кру - том бе - ре - гу. _____ гу.

THE DNIEPER RIVER FROM THE CLIFFS ABOVE KIEV

UKRAINE

You will remember that the Slavs settled in the valley of the Dnieper, and it is this section that is known as Ukraine. Although the Ukrainians are not now united in a country of their own, they comprise the second largest Slavonic racial group. According to the best authorities, they have retained the most pure characteristics of the Slavonic race, especially in their language. Kiev, now the heart of Ukraine, has always been the center of Ukrainian culture. The first federation of Slavic tribes was formed there in the third and fourth centuries, showing an early desire for unity.

Ukrainian contribution to civilization is the rich folk lore, the handcrafts, folk music, and folk dance which express so vividly a freedom-loving, high-spirited race. The men have lived in the saddle since early childhood, inheriting the daring and courage from their Cossack forefathers. The women indulge their taste for artistic expression by beautifying every garment, utensil, and article of furniture in skilful fashion. Their songs are among the most beautiful and expressive in the world and the vigor of their dances (which have been called visible music) reveal the spirit and character of their vitality. Folk song has played a profound part in the life of the people, for Ukrainians must sing at all times to express themselves at work or play, in joy or grief.

In My Garden Is a Hazel Tree

На городі калинонька

(*Recorded*)

UKRAINIAN FOLK SONG

Translated from the Ukrainian

Arranged by CONSTANTIN SHVEDOFF, Op. 27

This song is in the melancholy mood of so many Slavonic folk songs. Although the tempo is fast, the words express the sorrow of one who sees in the withering of the hazel tree a symbol of his own sadness.

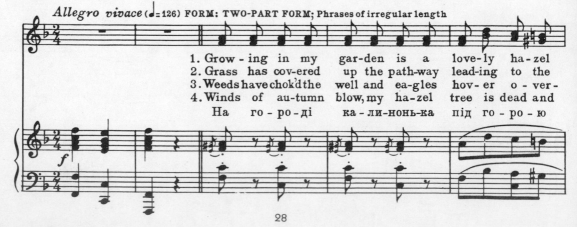

28

My Friend

Ой важу я, важу
(Recorded)

Translated from the Ukrainian

Ukrainian Folk Song

Arranged by Constantin Shvedoff, Op. 27

This vigorous song, with its boisterous humor, shows its Slavic origin in the accent on the second beat of many of the measures and especially in the unusual rhythm with which the final cadence closes.

Allegro (♩=92)   FORM: A, A¹, B, C, B, C

1. Of my friend I thought one morn-ing So de-part-ed with-out warn-ing,
2. Quick-ly down the path-way walk-ing Soon up-on his door I'm knock-ing,
3. Through the house the noise re-sound-ing Ech-oes loud my heav-y pound-ing,
Ой ва-жу я, ва-жу на ту дів-чи-ну вра-жу

Out of doors with ea-ger feel-ing, Soft-ly to his door-way steal-ing.
No one seems to hear my greet-ing Can it be they all are sleep-ing?
Noth-ing an-swers but his snor-ing, Home I go, 'tis much too bor-ing.
ме-не ма-ти не пус-ка-э, я ві ко-неч-ком вда-жу.

CHORUS — briskly

Out of doors with ea-ger feel-ing, Soft-ly to his door-way steal-ing.
No one seems to hear my greet-ing Can it be they all are sleep-ing?
Noth-ing an-swers but his snor-ing, Home I go, 'tis much too bor-ing.
ме-не ма-ти не пус-ка-э, я ві ко-неч-ком вда-жу.

Anna's Rosy Cheeks

(Recorded)

Adapted from the Ukrainian

UKRAINIAN FOLK SONG

This song was selected by a teacher in the city of Kiev who wanted to acquaint American school pupils with the beautiful music of her people. It is an extremely gay song with characteristic broad retards and holds and sudden return to the brisk tempo. In spite of the far-reaching changes going on in the Soviet Union today, the ancient folk culture remains dear to the hearts of the people.

Intervals: Analyze intervals between soprano and alto voices, giving *numerical* and *specific* names.

Hopak

(Recorded)

From the Ukrainian

UKRAINIAN FOLK SONG

When Ukrainian young people get together for an evening of jollity and fun they call it "*Vechernitsi*." The girls make fancy cakes of all kinds and the boys eat them! Games are played and songs are sung, and of course no Ukrainian evening would be complete without dancing. The girls step into the circle to the vigorous clapping of the boys, and then one of the most agile boys leaps into the *Kozachok* which requires very nimble feet and strong muscles. This is the dance with the squatting step, in which the men bend their knees down to the ground and leap up with feet flung outward. This step is done only by the men as an evidence of their agility and strength. The girls are never permitted to attempt it. After the solo exhibitions everyone joins in the familiar Hopak, which grows more and more spirited and stops only when the dancers are thoroughly exhausted. That is how the "Hopak" should be done.

High, high, leap-ing light-ly, Danc-ing, glanc-ing, pranc-ing, bright-ly,

Fly, fly, step-ping spright-ly, To the lilt-ing mel-o-dy.

1. Hear the song, gai-ly sing-ing Hap-py shouts and laugh-ter ring-ing.
2. Mer-ry girls gar-lands bear-ing Flow-ers in their hair are wear-ing.

Loud and long, right-ly bring-ing, Ev-'ry heart in tune-ful key.
Laugh-ing boys, maid-ens dar-ing, Ev-'ry-one in har-mo-ny.

Dance directions by Michael Herman

This dance has many figures of which five are given here. Additional ones are often improvised.

FORMATION: All partners face counter-clockwise in a circle.

POSITION: Boy places right arm around partner, extends left arm forward at shoulder level, palm up. Girl places right hand on hip, and places left hand, palm down, on boy's left hand. With weight on left foot, both place right foot across left.

FIGURE I. PAS DE BASQUE

(Step begins on count "and" of preceding measure.)

On "and," beginning with right foot, all leap side-wise to right, swinging right foot forward in a semicircle, without bending knee.

Meas. 1. Count 1. Place right foot down firmly.

PEASANT DANCE AT A TYPICAL VECHERNITSI
By the Famous Ukrainian Painter, ILJA (ELIAS) J. REPIN

On "and" touch left toe in front of right, weight on left toe.

Count 2. Stamp in place with right foot. On "and" leap to left.

Meas. 2. Repeat Meas. 1 with opposite feet.

Meas. 3–8. Continue same step, moving forward in the circle, counter-clockwise.

FIGURE II. CHANGE STEP

Partners drop left hands; boy places his on hip; girl places hers over heart or holds her necklace in place, elbow should be high.

On "and," beginning with right foot, all leap forward onto right.

Meas. 9. Count 1. Place right foot down firmly.

On count "and 2," take two short running steps forward.

On "and," beginning with left foot, all leap forward onto left.

Meas. 10–16. Repeat instructions of Meas. 9 to left and right, alternately.

FIGURE III. SIDE STEP

Partners face each other; hold right hands, left hands on hips. They move sidewise in a circle, clockwise.

A. Meas. 1. Count 1. Boy steps on left foot, girl on right foot.

On "and" boy taps with right toe, girl with left toe.

Count 2. Boy steps on left foot, girl on right foot.

On "and" boy taps with right toe, girl with left toe.

Meas. 2–8. Repeat Meas. 1.

B. Meas. 9–16. Repeat Figure II.

FIGURE IV. PRISHEEDKA AND SOLO TURN

Partners drop hands, face each other. Boy folds arms girl places left hand over heart, palm down, right hand on hip.

Boy's step. (The Prisheedka, or squatting step, is never done by a girl; it is a Cossack man's step.)

Meas. 1. Count 1. With a spring, boy comes down on both toes, heels together, in a full knee bend, keeping knees wide apart and back perfectly straight.

Count 2. Boy comes to half standing position, hops on left foot and swings right leg forward straight, pointing toes.

Meas. 2. Same as Meas. 1 except that on count 2, he hops on right foot.

Meas. 3–8. Repeat Meas. 1 and 2.

Girl's step. (Solo Turn. Step similar to Figure III.)

Meas. 1–8. Count 1. Girl leaps on right foot. On "and" taps with left beside right, using left as pivot in the turn.

Count 2. Step on right foot. On "and" tap with left beside right. (Turn left about in place throughout.)

Meas. 9–16. Repeat Figure II.

FIGURE V.

A. Meas. 1–8. Repeat Figure I.

B. Meas. 9–16. Repeat Figure II, Change Step.

(When performing the dance, use measures 1–8 an 9–16 without repeat.)

UNIT V: TRIPS ABROAD — POLAND AND CZECHOSLOVAKIA

by STELLA MAREK CUSHING

POLAND

Poland's days of glory were from the fourteenth to the sixteenth centuries when she commanded a strong position as a world power. As late as 1683, it was a king of Poland who defeated the Turkish army at the very gates of Vienna. But misfortunes quickly followed because weak rulers and selfish lords so crippled the government that it could not cope with the heavy onslaughts of neighboring powers who coveted the rich plains and high mountains. Gradually Poland lost its strength and by the end of the eighteenth century was overwhelmed and finally partitioned between three rulers, the Tsar of Russia, Frederick the Great of Prussia, and Maria Theresa of Austria. For more than a hundred years Poland disappeared from the map of Europe.

During the nineteenth century and at the beginning of the twentieth century, the wave of nationalism that swept the whole of Europe caught fire among the Polish people and a new struggle for freedom began. Poland emerged from the World War with its borders restored, an independent republic, a united nation of 30 million people with Warsaw as its capital.

We honor Poland for giving to the world many men of genius. Chief among the musicians are Chopin, Wieniawski, and Paderewski. The latter, the great pianist and statesman of our time, who has thrilled the world with his musical genius, is revered because he was willing to sacrifice his musical career by assuming the Presidency of his country in its hour of need.

A visit to Krakow, still a center of culture and learning, gives evidences of its early grandeur. Overlooking the Vistula River stands the Wawel Cathedral and Castle of early kings. In the square is the Old Cloth Hall (bazaar), the Town Hall Tower, and the Church of Our Lady Mary. It is in the tower of this church that for five hundred years the trumpet call has sounded every hour saying, "All is well." Read Eric Kelly's *The Trumpeter of Krakow* where he tells about this melody sounding clear and commanding over the housetops.

Trumpet call, the "Heynal," *i. e.,* "Hymn to Our Lady," which the trumpeter takes a solemn oath to sound each hour of the day and night from a little balcony high up on the front of the Church of Our Lady Mary, in Krakow, Poland.

Clanking Spurs

Kiedym Jechoł Od Dziewecki

(*Recorded*)

Translated from the Polish

POLISH FOLK SONG

This song suggests the rough and hearty abandon of a carefree Polish soldier on his way to seek adventure wherever it may lead him. It is in the $\frac{3}{4}$ *mazur* (mazurka) tempo, with a primary accent on the first beat and a secondary accent on the third beat of the measure.

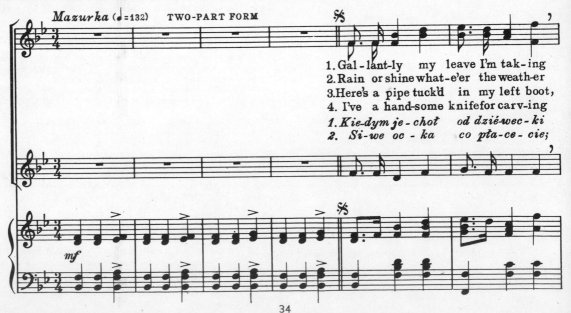

34

F

What a noise my spurs are mak - ing, Clank-ing high, clank-ing low,
On my cap a jaun - ty feath - er, See my coat, red and gray,
Now it's left but then it's right boot. Best of friends, day or night,
With it I shall not be starv-ing; Wheth - er meat, cheese, or bread,

Brzę - ka - ły mi pod - kó-wec - ki Brzę - ka - ły, brzę - ka - ły,
Kiej mnie wid-ziec nie bę-dzie - cie Na wie - ki, na wie - ki,

1.

While a - long the road I go, road I go.
I'm a wan - d'ring fel - low gay, fel - low gay.
Blow - ing smoke is my de - light, my de - light.
Mat - ters not what I am fed, I am fed.

Si - we oc - ka pła - ka - ły. pła - ka - ty.
Bom jo chło - piec da - le - ki. da - le - ki.

2. D.S. 𝄋

TONE BLENDING DRILLS

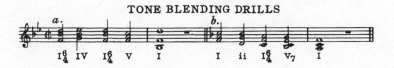

a. b.

I_4^6 IV I_4^6 V I   I ii I_4^6 V_7 I

Krakowiak

(Recorded)

Translated from the Polish

POLISH FOLK DANCE

The Krakowiak is a dance which originated in Krakow. It is in the characteristic ⅔ syncopated rhythm, and expresses in its vigor the spirit of the Polish people. The words of the song are little more than a nonsense jingle and show how completely the Polish peasants were able to forget their sorrows and grave political problems in singing and dancing.

1. Lis-ten to my sto-ry, One of Kra-kow glo-ry,
2. Once a Kra-kow lad-die Sev-en hors-es had he,
3. Sil-ly Kra-kow maid-en Was with sor-row la-den,

It will take the ban-ner In the Kra-kow man-ner.
When he went to bat-tle On-ly one could sad-dle.
Till a wax-en dol-ly Cured her of her fol-ly.

Dance directions by Michael Herman

POSITION: Double circle, partners facing each other; boy in inner circle, back to center, right arm around girl's waist, left arm held straight up in air; girl in outer circle, facing center, left hand on boy's right shoulder, holding skirt with right hand.

FIGURE I. SLIDING STEP

Meas. 1–8. Boy begins with left foot, girl with right foot. All take 16 slides sidewise around the circle, counter-clockwise (two slides to each measure).

FIGURE II. TURNING STEP

(Beginning on "and" beat of preceding measure.)
Boy's step.
On "and" boy swings left foot around and back of right foot and hops on right foot.
Meas. 9. Count 1. Places both feet down at the same time, left behind right.
On "and" pivots on left foot in ½ turn, counter-clockwise, as he lifts right foot.
Count 2. Stamps on right foot and lifts left foot.
Meas. 10–16. Continue same as Meas. 1.
Girl's step.
On "and" girl swings right foot forward and hops on left foot.
Meas. 9. Count 1. Places both feet down at the same time, right foot across left.
On "and" pivots on right foot, counter-clockwise and lifts left foot.

Count 2. Stamps on left foot and lifts right foot.
Meas. 10–16. Continue same as Meas. 1.

FIGURE III. SLIDING STEP

Meas. 1–8. Repeat Figure I — 16 slides.
Meas. 9–16. Continue same as Figure I. When Couple 1 reach center back of room or platform they slide down center followed by others, all making a straight line, facing front — 16 slides.

FIGURE IV. SLIDING STEP

A. Meas. 1–4. Beginning with outside foot, partners take 7 slides away from each other; stamp with outside foot and pause.
Meas. 5–8. Beginning with inside foot, partners repeat Meas. 1–4, coming toward each other; stamp with inside foot.
B. Meas. 9–12. Beginning with inside foot, partners take 8 slides, passing each other, boys behind girls.
Meas. 13–16. Repeat Meas. 9–12 back to place.

FIGURE V. SLIDING STEP AND TURNING STEP

A. Meas. 1–8. Couple 1 leading, all take 16 slides in a circle, counter-clockwise, forming original circle.
B. Meas. 9–16. Repeat Figure II, Turning Step.

(For the dance four stanzas are required, therefore repeat first stanza. Entire dance may be repeated several times.)

Do not be im-pa-tient / For my sto-ry an-cient,
Sev-en years of cruis-ing / Nev-er sa-ber us-ing,
Such a stu-pid ac-tion / No-where else could hap-pen,

Of the brav-est lad-die / And a weep-ing lass-ie.
With-out use it rust-ed, / Shin-ing sword he trust-ed.
It will take the ban-ner / In the Kra-kow man-ner.

Hurry Up, Fellows

Chorwacka polka

(Recorded)

Translated from the Polish

As sung in Poland, probably of Croatian origin

The polka is the most popular of all rhythms in folk dances and is found in almost all figure dances throughout Europe. It is a gay and spirited dance with a characteristic little hop and accent on the final eighth note of the measure.

Polka tempo (♩=112) **THREE-PART FORM**

Hur-ry up, fel-lows, make a cir-cle, Dance to the tune with spir-it gay,
Hur-ry up, fel-lows, all to-geth-er, Step with a hop and round a-bout,

Da-lej-że chłop-cy da-lej wko-ło, Pij-my i tańcz-my i - le sit

Fid - dler, fid - dle mer - ry mu - sic, How man - y zlo - tys* is your pay?
Fid - dler, fid - dle, fast - er, fast - er, On with a laugh and hap - py shout.
a ty nam graj - ku graj we - so - ło Da - my ci wi - na bę - dziesz pił.

Swing a part - ner ver - y frisk - y, Nim - bly like a squir - rel hop,
Plą - saj lub - ko kręć się wko - ło zwiń - nie jak wie - wiór - ka krąż

Melody

Ev - 'ry - one is danc - ing brisk - ly, On and nev - er stop, Hey!
Hej! ros - jaś - nij bia - łe czo - ło Patrz mi wo - czy wciąż Hej!

* Pronounced zwot-ys, equivalent to about twenty cents.

TONE BLENDING DRILLS

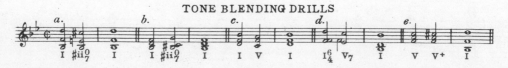

I #ii°7 I   I #ii°7 I   I V I   I6/4 V7 I   I V V+ I

CZECHOSLOVAKIA

While the peoples of western Europe were warring with each other in the early Middle Ages, the Czechs, who had settled in central Europe about the fifth century and adopted Christianity in the ninth century, became united and formed the first Bohemian Dynasty in the tenth century.

Before William the Conqueror ended Saxon rule in England in 1066, while what we know as France and Germany were still the Carolingian Empire founded by Charlemagne, while Italy was a group of city states unrelated to each other, the Duchy of Bohemia comprised an organized people and enjoyed a civilization and culture of extraordinary power. As the Kingdom of Bohemia it was long a part of the Holy Roman Empire. Its capital, Prague, is the site of one of the oldest universities in Europe.

A hundred years before the Luther Reformation in 1517, Jan Hus, who was connected with the University of Prague, had declared his beliefs regarding religious freedom. Thereupon followed years of conflict, including what is known as the "Thirty Years' War." Bohemia endeavored to establish itself again as an independent kingdom.

The year of 1620 — such a significant year for the future hope of America — was a dark one in Prague, for it was the beginning of Hapsburg rule and the subsequent suppression of Czech culture for three hundred years, while the Slovaks since the tenth century had been ruled by the Magyars, or Hungarians.

Through these years of oppression, the spirit of the Czech and Slovak people was kept alive by their folk lore and music. The World War proved to be the opportunity for which the people had been preparing for three centuries. Freedom once more was theirs, and the great leader, Thomas Garrigue Masaryk, was proclaimed President of the Republic of Czechoslovakia.

The prominence of Smetana and Dvořák, Czechoslovakia's best known composers, comes not only from their outstanding genius, but also from their use of the folk music of their native land in building their masterpieces.

The Goose Girl

Andulko
(*Recorded*)

Translated from the Czech

CZECH FOLK SONG

There is a marked difference between typical Czech and Slovak songs; the words and music of Czech songs are gayer and the melodies flow more smoothly.

Many folk stories and fairy tales tell about the goose girl, who, in this song is named, "Andulko." Practically every European farm has its flock of geese and it is the duty of one of the girls to watch over them.

Intervals: Analyze intervals between all voices in Part II. Observe flow of *thirds* and *sixths* in Part I. Work for purity of intonation, particularly in Part II.

No Is My Answer

Nechod' knám, synécku

(Recorded)

Translated from the Slovak

SLOVAK FOLK SONG

This popular melody illustrates the free rhythm and absence of metrical feeling found in many Slovak folk songs. The atmosphere of the song is slow and rather melancholy and yet there is a very distinct sense of humor in the words.

Imagine a simple peasant home near the town of Uhérské Hradiště, Moravia, the bed in one corner, table in another. Between the bed and table is the cymbalum. Hanging on a peg on the wall is the violin and over in the corner stands a bass viol available for anyone happening in who can play. Everyone seems to be able to play an instrument of some kind. After a repast of fresh, dark bread and soft homemade cheese and butter, and the fresh juice of the grapes that have been pressed that day, all sit down to an evening of singing and dancing.

Harmonic Analysis: Reduce chords throughout this selection to their fundamental series of thirds, spell them, and name them.

Ah, Lovely Meadows

Aj, lúčka, lúčka široká

(Recorded)

Translated from the Czech

CZECH FOLK SONG

During the World War the American Red Cross sent out a call for volunteer American-Czech doctors to enlist with the Czechoslovak Legionnaires in Siberia. One of the many who responded to this call tells us that "Ah, Lovely Meadows" was one of the most popular songs sung by these soldiers so far from their homeland. A significant feature of this happy march is that, instead of choosing songs of battle, the Legionnaires preferred to sing of the peaceful scenes of their homeland.

In march tempo (♩=116) FORM: STANZA and REFRAIN

1. Ah, love-ly mead-ows, green and wide,
2. Loud-ly the bar-on blows his horn,
3. Har-ness your horse, the hours are few,
   Aj, lúč-ka, lúč-ka ši-ro-ká,

Grass-es are grow-ing, grass-es are grow-ing,
Wake up, my stew-ard, wake up, my stew-ard,
Work-ing to-geth-er, work-ing to-geth-er,
ros-te na ni trá-va, ros-te na ni trá-va.

Ah, love-ly mead-ows, green and wide,
Reap-ing be-gins at ear-ly morn,
Off to the fields of gold-en hue,
Aj, lúč-ka lúč-ka ši-ro-ká,

Grow-ing so high on ev-'ry side. (Hey!)
Wake up, my stew-ard, day is born.
Gath-er the grain ere falls the dew.
ros-te na ni trá-va vy-so-ká. (Hej!)

CHORUS

Wa - ter from moun-tain flows, Melt - ed from win - ter snows,
Te - če vo - da z ho - ra, čis - tá je ja - ko já,

Bass optional; may be sung by Altos an octave higher.

Turn - ing it gai - ly goes, Cir - cling the ma - ple tree,—
to - či se do ko - la, o - ko - lo ja - vo - ra;

Wa - ter from moun-tain flows, Melt - ed from win - ter snows,
te - če vo - da z ho - ra, čis - tá je ja - ko já,

Turn - ing it gai - ly goes, Call - ing to me. (Hey!)
to - či se do ko - la, o - ko - lo mňa. (Hej!)

TONE BLENDING DRILLS

a. *b.* *c.*

I - - - I IV I I V₇ I

Obžínky (Harvest in Czechoslovakia)

A Peasant Home in Poland

Trumpeter, Blow

Jakú som si frajírenku

(Recorded)

Words adapted to the mood of the music

SLOVAK FOLK SONG

The important feature of this song is its marked accent, so characteristic of the way in which the peasants sing. It is sung with an exaggerated quickness of the short notes, the longer notes being sustained almost beyond the beat. The second part is sung a little more *legato* than the first part. The holds between the measures, as indicated, are very important.

In the original Slovak, this is a love song. The English words have been adapted to the mood of the music and bring out the spirit of the Sokol, which likewise fits into the nature of the music.

In singing the song one should aim to realize the quality of the music as an expression of the undaunted spirit of a people who have maintained their integrity through centuries of vicissitudes.

Beseda

Translated from the Czechoslovak

NATIONAL DANCE OF CZECHOSLOVAKIA

The Beseda is generally considered to be one of the most beautiful of all folk dances because of the great variety of its dance figures and its many changes in rhythm, mood, tempo, and melody. It is danced to a series of popular folk songs. Only the first four figures are given here.

INTRODUCTION (moderato, ♩=60)

Broth-ers, sis-ters, join in the Bes-e-da, Broth-ers, sis-ters,
Bra-tři bra-tři bud-me jen ve-se-li bra-tři bra-tři

SOUSEDSKA (tempo di menuetto, ♩=100) Figure 1

join in the dance. I'll tell,— I'll tell, How you are teas-ing me
rad-uj-me se Poč-kej— po-vim žes na mně lou-di-val

I'll tell,— I'll tell, You're teas-ing me. Bright blos-soms, gen-tly sway-ing,
poč-kej— po-vim že jsi lou-dil vzahrádce ky-tič-ku

Reproduced by permission of the copyright owners, A. L. Maresh Music Company, Cleveland, Ohio.

Dance directions edited by Michael Herman

Note. This dance is considered to be one of the most interesting of all folk dances because of the variety of melody and dance figures. The entire dance is in thirteen figures. The following descriptions are for the first four figures.

 BOY   ⃝ GIRL

FORMATION: Four couples in square formation required for each set; all facing the center; Couple 1 "face the music," *i.e.*, stand so that they can see the musicians.

INTRODUCTION: POSITION: All join hands in a large circle.

Meas. 1–2. Beginning with right foot, all slide twice toward center of circle. Swing hands upward on each step.

Meas. 3–4. Beginning with left foot, all slide away from center, swinging arms downward on each step.

Meas. 5–6. Count 1, 2. Balance right (step with R. foot to right, point L. toe across right toe). Count 3, pause; repeat balance to left.

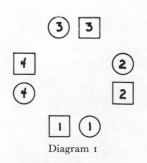

Diagram 1

Meas. 7. Repeat balance to right.

Meas. 8. Count 1, 2. Bring heels together. Count 3, pause.

FIGURE I. SOUSEDSKA

A. Meas. 1. With joined hands raised, beginning with right foot, all balance in a waltz step toward center of circle.

Join in the game we're play-ing, While through the gar-den stray-ing You're teas-ing me.
po ces - tě hu - bič - ku poč - kej po - vím že jsi lou - dil

I'll tell,— I'll tell, How you are teas-ing me, I'll tell,— I'll tell,
poč - kej— po - vím žes na mně lou - di - val poč - kej— po - vím

FURIANT (*presto, ♩.=69*) Figure 2

You're teas-ing me. Se-dlak, se-dlak, se-dlak, Farm-er I'm call-ing you,
že jsi lou - dil Se-dlák se - dlák se-dlák je - ště jed - nou se-dlák

Se-dlak, se-dlak, se-dlak, You're a great man! Proud in your leath-er belt,
se - dlák se - dlák se-dlák je vel - ký pán on má pas na břiše

Meas. 2. With joined hands lowered, beginning with left foot, all balance in a waltz step away from center.

Meas. 3–4. Each girl drops her partner's hand, waltzes 6 steps in a right half turn as boy on her right draws her into the place of his former partner. As the girl turns, she drops boy's left hand, takes his right with her left, and places her right hand in left of boy's at her right, so that all hands are joined again in a large circle. (*See* Diagram 2.)

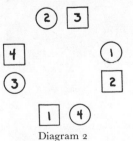

Diagram 2

Meas. 5–12. Repeat Meas. 1–4 twice.
Meas. 13–14. Repeat Meas. 1–2.
Meas. 15–16. With 6 waltz steps girl returns to her

original position but without turning. This brings her with back to center. Boys are facing circle. All join hands.

B. Meas. 17–18. All balance right toward own partners. (*See* balance step in Meas. 5–6 of Introduction.) All balance left away from partners.

Meas. 19–20. Repeat 17–18.

Meas. 21–22. Partners retain right hands held high, and drop left hands. Beginning with right foot, partners take two walking steps in circle, one to each measure.

Meas. 23–24. All take 6 small running steps in a small circle to complete the turn (one to each beat). This brings all to original positions, facing center of circle as in Diagram I.

FIGURE II. FURIANT

POSITION: Girls with hands on hips, boys with arms folded.

Meas. 1–8. Beginning with right foot, girls do 8 peasant waltz steps, turning right about, moving in circle counter-clockwise. Beginning with left foot, boys follow their partners with peasant waltz step without turning. This brings couples to opposite side of square.

Partners take peasant waltz position.

Meas. 9–16. Boy beginning with left foot, girl with right foot, they take 8 peasant waltz steps, turning right about (counter-clockwise in circle) to original positions.

On your great coat of pelt Tu-lips, tu-lips, tu-lips, Spread like a fan.
a na svém ko-ži-še tu-li tu-li tu-li tu tu-li-pán

11 12 13 14 15 16

MARCH (*moderate tempo,* ♩=76) **Figure 3**

Hel-lo, hel-lo, gay mu-si-cians, Play for me a mer-ry tune.
Alou alou za-hra-jte mně hez-kou pí-seň z ve-se-la

1 2 3 4

Then per-haps my dear-est one Will give her an-swer soon.
že mně mo-je nej-mi-lej-ší vy-po-vě-dě-la

5 6 7 8

Anx-ious-ly I ques-tion fate, No one here must guess my state.
z to-ho si nic nedě-lám klo-bou-ček na stra-nu dám

9 10 11 12

FIGURE III. MARCH

POSITION: Partners of Couples 1 and 3 join hands facing center. Couples 2 and 4 face center, partners leave enough space between them to allow one person to pass through.

A. Meas. 1–2. Beginning with right foot, Couples 1 and 3 take 4 walking steps toward each other into center of circle (2 steps to each measure).

Meas. 3–4. Beginning with right foot, Couples 1 and 3 take 4 walking steps backward away from each other.

Meas. 5–8. Beginning with right foot girl preceding the boy, Couple 1 walks 8 steps toward Couple 2, passes between and behind the partners of Couple 2, and takes places beside them. Girl of Couple 1 at right of girl of Couple 2; boy of Couple 1 at left of boy of Couple 2. Simultaneously, Couple 3 does the same with Couple 4. Couples 1 and 3 are now facing Couples 2 and 4. (See Diagram 3.)

Meas. 9–10. Beginning with right foot, all take 4 walking steps toward each other.

Meas. 11–12. Beginning with right foot, all take 4 walking steps backward away from each other.

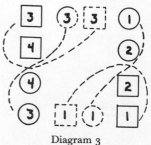

Diagram 3

Couples 1 and 2 join hands; Couples 3 and 4 do like-wise, making two circles.

Meas. 13–15. Each group takes 6 walking steps in a circle clockwise.

Meas. 16. Partners drop hands of other couple. Each couple joins hands crossed, ×. (If correct positions have been kept during previous figure, partners are now facing

I'll ap-pear a dash-ing fel-low Sing-ing as I wait.
pro-to že jsem švar-ný jo-nák so-bě zaz-pi-vám

13   14   15   16

REZANKA (*polka tempo*, ♩=120) Figure 4,

Near the en-trance I'll be wait-ing, You will find me at the grat-ing,
Poč-kej hol-ka za tim roš-tim však já ti to ne-od-pus-tim

1   2   3   4

Near the en-trance I'll be wait-ing With a gift for you. And what? And how? And
poč-kej hol-ka za-tim roš-tim však já ti tam dám a co? a zač? a

5   6   7   8   9   10

why? Not now! You will nev-er, nev-er guess what I shall do.
jak? a nač? dvě hu-bi-čky ne-bo čty-ry tam ti dám.

11   12   13   14   15   16

Fine

each other, girls with backs to center. Boys of Couples 1 and 3 are slightly to right of boys of Couples 2 and 4 to prevent bumping during next figure.) (*See* Diagram 4.)

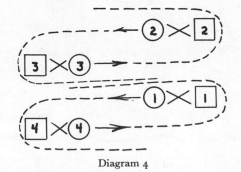

Diagram 4

FIGURE IV. REŽANKA (CHOPPED STRAW)

Meas. 1–4. Shuttle Step. With hands crossed, all couples take 4 polka steps toward the opposite couple, girls dancing backward. Couples pass to right of each other.

Meas. 5–8. All couples return to place taking 4 polka steps back, passing to left of each other, boy dancing backward.

Meas. 9. Count 1. Partners point right toes toward each other. Count 2, pause.

Meas. 10. Repeat with left toes.

Meas. 11–12. Count 1, 2, 1. In quick succession point right, left, right. Count 2, pause.

Partners link right arms.

Meas. 13–16. Beginning with right foot, they turn in place clockwise with 6 springy steps, moving into original position.

Note: Figures III and IV are now repeated with Couples 2 and 4 beginning in the same manner as Couples 1 and 3. In Figure III, Meas. 5–8, Couples 2 and 4 walk toward Couples 3 and 1, respectively. In Figure IV the shuttle moves in the opposite direction.

UNIT VI: TRIPS ABROAD—THE SOUTHERN SLAVS

by STELLA MAREK CUSHING

YUGOSLAVIA

About the sixth century, a branch of the Slav people swept south into the Balkan peninsula. Eventually separated into groups, three of these, the Serbs, Croats, and Slovenes, are now united in the Kingdom of Yugoslavia formed after their struggle for independence during the World War.

Much of the territory occupied by the Southern Slavs was once a part of a powerful kingdom, Serbia, which attained its zenith from the tenth to the fourteenth centuries. But when the Turkish armies moved westward, hoping to conquer Europe, Serbia and her people were subjugated. For five hundred years Turkish rule held sway over all the Balkan countries. The Croats and Slovenes were more strongly influenced by western civilization, having become a part of the kingdoms of Austria and Hungary. In 1878 the central portion of present Yugoslavia (Bosnia and Hercegovina) was added to the Austro-Hungarian Empire until 1918 when the Southern Slavs once again gained their freedom. Though long divided by political, religious, and cultural influences, the Southern Slavs resisted all attempts to denationalize them and maintained their identity as a race.

Most inspiring are the accounts of how wandering bards went from town to town singing of the cherished glories of the past, thus keeping alive old hero tales and legends. These ancient epics and folk lore are among the most treasured heritage of the Southern Slavs. The glorious folk songs cannot be matched for variety and character. The beautiful, flowing melodies of the Slovenian people living in the north differ greatly from the primitive melodies in peculiar rhythm found in the mountains of South Serbia.

The songs from the Dalmatian coast allude to the beauties of the Adriatic Sea, for it was from these ports that some of the best sailors in the world first learned the fascination of the sea.

One finds an echo of the cruel, stark mountains of Montenegro in the cold, limited scale of its songs. But to participate in the gay Kolo, the circle dance, so common with all the Balkan peoples, is a thrilling experience, as perhaps fifty people wind in a broken circle to the marked rhythm and definite accent of this social dance. One cannot count the number of melodies played in the Kolos, but the invariable closing on the syllable *re* and the prevailing $\frac{2}{4}$ meter are constant reminders of their Balkan origin.

The carols of this unit are old Croatian melodies, dating from the fourteenth century. These ancient tunes fit extremely well the simple themes of the poems, which do not emphasize the pageantry and splendor of our modern Christmas festival, but rather tell the simple Christmas story of the Babe of Bethlehem.

TRIPS ABROAD — CENTRAL EUROPE, MAP BY MILDRED KAISER

Kyrie Eleison

Lord Have Mercy

(Recorded)

Translated from the Yugoslav

Yugoslav Carol

The accompaniment of the opening theme is light and dainty, as if little bells were tinkling in the distance. In the refrain the accompaniment should be very *legato* suggesting breadth and dignity. The song is quiet and simple, without pomp and ceremony.

Peace to All

svim na zemlji mir
(Recorded)

Translated from the Croatian　　　　　　　ANCIENT CROATIAN CAROL (14TH CENTURY)

It is the custom in many Yugoslav towns for the people to attend midnight Mass to celebrate the birth of the Christ-child. The choir and people join in the carols with which they have been familiar from childhood. One can also imagine a peasant family singing this lovely old carol around the manger scene at home.

Cheerfully, with rhythmic swing (♩=88)　TWO-PART FORM

Hark the an-gel voic-es sing-ing,— Through the
Ev-'ry one the word is bring-ing,— "Peace, good
svim na zem-lji mir ve-se-lje bu-di

night their songs are wing-ing. Heav'n an-nounc-es— ti-dings of
will," the mes-sage ring-ing. "Peace, good
po-lag do-bre vo-lje to sad ne-bo na-vě-šču-

cheer,— Heav'n con-firms the news that we hear; hear!
je i glas sne-ba pot vr-đu-je je.

The Holy Season

u se vrjeme godišća
(Recorded)

Translated from the Croatian　　　　　　　ANCIENT CROATIAN CAROL (14TH CENTURY)

This carol emphasizes the holy character of the season rather than its festivities. It must not be hurried, but a full, broad tone quality should be maintained throughout. When sung unaccompanied, it is very effective from a distance.

Slowly and peacefully (♩=60)

Ho-ly time— of all— the year;
Chimes ring out— from ev-'ry tow'r,
u se vrje-me go-di-šća
u pol noć se Bog ro-dil

What Light Is That?

kakva je to svetlost

Translated from the Yugoslav

ANCIENT YUGOSLAV CAROL

This is a song of rejoicing as the people leave the church and turn homeward to continue the Christmas rites.

Brightly and happily (♩ = 112) FORM: A, A, B, A, A

What shines on the— moun-tain What light-ens the plain? What
What thou-sands ob- serve it, What mil - lions re- joice, To-
kak - va - je to— svet - lost skom Bet - lem go - ri glas

glis-tens and spar-kles O'er fair Beth-le - hem? It bright-ens the
geth- er all sing-ing With one heart and voice. Still lead-ing, re-
ču - da sve- sel- jem poz- ra- ku le - ti čast Bo - gu vi -

heav-ens, It— gleams through the night, O Je - su, dear Je - su, Thy
veal-ing, We plead once a- gain. O Je - su, dear Je - su, Bring
si - ni mir lju- dem vni - zi - ni o Je - zuš o— Je - zuš pre -

Twelve o'Clock Is Striking

dvanajsta je sad vura

Translated from the Croatian — ANCIENT CROATIAN CAROL (14TH CENTURY)

Imagine yourselves in a church in Yugoslavia on Christmas Eve. As the people are gathering, quiet carols are sung. Just before the midnight hour everything is hushed as they kneel in prayer. Suddenly the great clock in the tower booms the hour of twelve. A star, symbol of a great light that shone in the sky, is illuminated in the nave of the church high over a manger scene. Almost without a signal the people fervently join in this carol.

SERBIAN KOLO (NATIONAL DANCE)

BULGARIA

When wave on wave of nomadic peoples swept over from Asia in the early centuries of the Middle Ages certain tribes, called Bulgars, occupied territory in the Eastern Balkans. They conquered the Slavs and settled among them. Little more is known of the Bulgars, for today not a trace of their language may be found; only the name, Bulgaria, remains.

It is on the Bulgarian plains that the old trade routes meet, coming from Central Europe to Constantinople and the East. Here, at one of the great crossroads of the world, invading forces met and terrific battles were fought. It was in Bulgaria that the Turkish armies gained their first foothold on European soil and pointed the crescent toward the conquest of all Europe. After five hundred years of Turkish rule, the Bulgarians finally regained their freedom in 1878, though still little more than a vassal state to their former rulers. Early in the twentieth century, Bulgaria gained more territory in the Balkan wars, but lost most of this in the World War.

Bulgaria is an agricultural state — eighty percent are peasants. It is famous for its Valley of Roses from which is drawn attar of roses for the world's perfumes.

The music sounds primitive to Western ears, embodying as it does a strange mixture of Eastern and Western scales and intricate and fascinating rhythms. Like the other Eastern Slavs, the music of the orthodox church ritual sung in many parts but not accompanied by instruments has influenced the Bulgarian people to harmonize their simple carols.

He Is Born

На излизане

Translated from the Bulgarian

BULGARIAN CAROL

With broad dignity ($\quad$ = 72)

1. He is born, raise now your voic - es;
2. O - pen wide all hearts and por - tals;
3. Do not wait, go, youth and maid - en.

По - ри - залъ, ми синь, зе - ленъ конь

An - gels chant Glo - ry, Ech - o glad sto - ry!
Man - ger bed low - ly Cra - dles Him ho - ly.
Guard him now sleep - ing Qui - et watch keep - ing.
REFRAIN *Hai - de, bells ring - ing; Hai - de, come sing - ing.*
хей ко - ла - де - ле, мой ко - ла - де - ле

Haide (Hī-dĕ) means "To come" or "Hail"   56

UNIT VII: SINGING THE BASS PART

The bass part is the foundation of the chord, and consequently the essence of harmonic thinking and feeling. To follow, understand, and appreciate the beauties of a musical composition, one should be able to hear the bass part distinctly and to sense the way in which the other chord tones grow out of the fundamental bass. The best way to acquire this feeling for harmony is to sing the bass part of songs harmonized very simply, chiefly with the tonic, dominant or dominant-seventh, and sub-dominant chords.

Such study becomes particularly interesting in the junior high school years, where the voices of some of the boys are changing and they can sing the actual bass tones. But even those students whose voices are unchanged, especially the boys, can profitably sing such simple bass parts an octave higher than written. The feeling for fundamental tones and bass progressions is so important in the development of musicianship that all should have this experience.

The songs of this unit, therefore, are arranged so that you may learn to read from the bass staff and may have the experience of singing the fundamental bass progressions, either in the actual range of the bass part or an octave higher. By studying and analyzing the chords in the accompanying Tone Blending Drills and by observing how the same chords and progressions occur in the songs of the unit, you will soon find your harmonic consciousness awakening and expanding and your capacity for musical enjoyment vastly increasing.

The relationship of the treble and bass staves is shown on the following diagram, in which appears a consecutive series of notes from F below the bass staff to g̅ above the treble staff. Observe also the traditional manner of indicating the relationship of the several octaves by capital and small letters and the addition of one or more lines to designate particular octaves. These octaves are called, "Great Octave," "Small Octave," "One-lined Octave," "Two-lined Octave," etc.

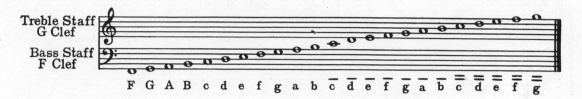

Challenge to Youth

JULIA W. BINGHAM   LUDWIG VAN BEETHOVEN (1770–1827)

This song is set to the theme of Beethoven's celebrated *Concerto for Violin*, in D Major, Opus 61.

1. Hark, a chal-lenge ring-ing, Hear the call re-sound-ing,
2. Trou-bled lives to bright-en, Wrongs and ills a-bat-ing;
3. Have we strength and vi-sion? Let them rule our think-ing,

Life to-day is bring-ing Tasks for us to do.
Bur-dens sore to light-en; Cour-age to re-new.
Guide each keen de-ci-sion, Make our lives ring true.

TONE BLENDING DRILL

I   -   -   -   IV   V   I

57

Daybreak

Paraphrased from the German, by
ALDIS DUNBAR

FRIEDRICH SILCHER (1789–1860)

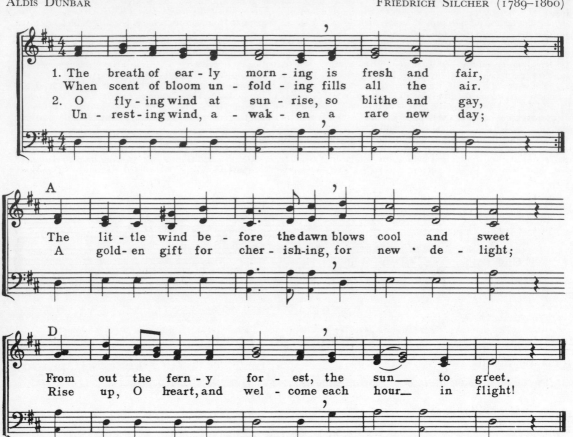

1. The breath of ear-ly morn-ing is fresh and fair,
When scent of bloom un-fold-ing fills all the air.
2. O fly-ing wind at sun-rise, so blithe and gay,
Un-rest-ing wind, a-wak-en a rare new day;

The lit-tle wind be-fore the dawn blows cool and sweet
A gold-en gift for cher-ish-ing, for new de-light;

From out the fern-y for-est, the sun to greet.
Rise up, O heart, and wel-come each hour in flight!

Autumn Song

Words paraphrased by
ALDIS DUNBAR

TUNE, "LE GENTIL HUSARD"

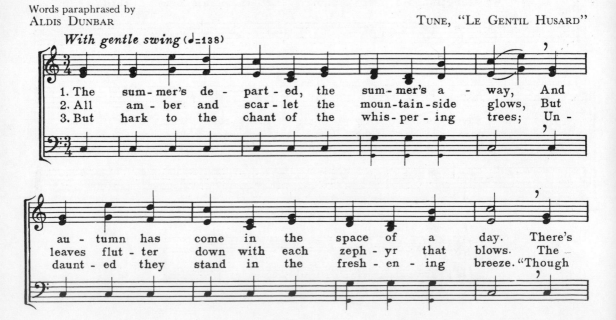

With gentle swing (♩=138)

1. The sum-mer's de-part-ed, the sum-mer's a-way, And
2. All am-ber and scar-let the moun-tain-side glows, But
3. But hark to the chant of the whis-per-ing trees; Un-

au-tumn has come in the space of a day. There's
leaves flut-ter down with each zeph-yr that blows. The
daunt-ed they stand in the fresh-en-ing breeze. "Though

frost in the val - ley, the nights have grown chill, And
wind's from the north, and they fade as they fall, For
win - ter winds blow, and our leaves dis - ap - pear, Yet

col - or makes roy - al each tree on the hill.
win - ter will soon hold the for - est in thrall.
we shall see har - vest through man - y a year!"

Three Rousing Cheers

Hoch

Adapted from the German, by
PHYLLIS McGINLEY

FRANZ ABT (1819–1885)

This song, known by Germans throughout the world as a toast on social occasions, may be adapted to various school needs, such as: "To Junior High, three rousing cheers"; "Now give our team three rousing cheers"; "To Arthur Brown three rousing cheers," etc.

Briskly (♩=144)

Three rous - ing cheers, three rous - ing cheers, Three rous - ing
Er le - be hoch, er le - be hoch, er le - be

cheers, three rous-ing cheers, three rous-ing cheers, Three cheers, three rous-ing cheers, Three
hoch, er le - be hoch, er le - be hoch, ja hoch, er le - be hoch, ja

cheers, three rous - ing cheers, Three rous - ing cheers!
hoch, er le - be hoch, ja drei - mal hoch!

TONE BLENDING DRILLS

a.   b.   c.

I V I   I IV I   I IV I⁶₄ V I

The Bee

Adapted from the German, by
PHYLLIS McGINLEY

CHRISTIAN HEINRICH HOHMANN

Moderately fast (♩=108)

1. Yes - ter-day I met a bee Toil - ing in the mead - ow,
   When I hailed him mer - ri - ly This is what he said - O:
2. "Stop a mo - ment, Bee," said I, "From your bus - y wing - ing."
   But he sharp-ly made re - ply, And his words were sting - ing:
3. Now I shun a toil - ing bee Quick-ly as I can, sir,
   Lest he like-wise ten - der me Sharp and point - ed an - swer.

G

"I've no time to chat or play," Thus I heard him mum - ble,
"Par - don if I give you pain, But you need not grum - ble;
Nev - er do I pause or play Where they buzz and tum - ble;

C

"I - dle fel - low, run a - way! Bum - ble, bum - ble, bum - ble."
Mead - ows are my own do - main. Bum - ble, bum - ble, bum - ble."
Bus - y men must have their way. Bum - ble, bum - ble, bum - ble!

Farewell to the Woods

Traditional

CHRISTIAN HEINRICH HOHMANN

Quietly (♩=80)

1. Ver - dant grove and shad - y dell, Love - ly leaf - y bow'r, —
2. What de - light to lin - ger here, In thy shad - y bow - ers,
3. But the night for - bids my stay; I must leave in sor - row;

C

Hear my song of fond fare-well, 'Tis the part - ing hour; —
By the sil - ver foun-tain clear Cull - ing fra - grant flow - ers;
To your rest, ye birds a - way, Dream-ing of the mor - row.

F

Let the song-bird's tune-ful throng Bear the ech-oes of my song
Would I might, with gar-lands crown'd, Breath-ing o-dors sweet a-round,
Now fare-well, ye shad-y bow'rs, With your bloom-ing, fra-grant flow'rs,

Far o'er hill and val-ley, Far o'er hill and val-ley,
Tar-ry with thee long-er, Tar-ry with thee long-er.
Till an-oth-er meet-ing, Till an-oth-er meet-ing.

Sing to the Seasons!

Paraphrased from the German, by
PHYLLIS McGINLEY

GERMAN FOLK SONG

Calmly ($\quarternote$=72)

1. When the swal-lows Quit the hol-lows And the
2. When the spi-cy Pines are i-cy And the
3. When the wak-ing Buds are break-ing And the

wild goose fol-lows aft-er, Come! in-to the woods we'll has-ten,
North Wind shakes the raft-er, Come, in-to the woods we'll has-ten,
flow-ers blos-som aft-er, Come, in-to the woods we'll has-ten,

Come! in-to the woods we'll has-ten, There to greet the fall with laugh-ter.
Come, in-to the woods we'll has-ten, Wel-come win-ter in with laugh-ter.
Come, in-to the woods we'll has-ten, Bring the spring-time in with laugh-ter.

TONE BLENDING DRILLS (*indicates Suspension)

a.   b.   *

I V I   I V₇ I

Aspiration

SAMUEL LONGFELLOW

JOHN MARTIN

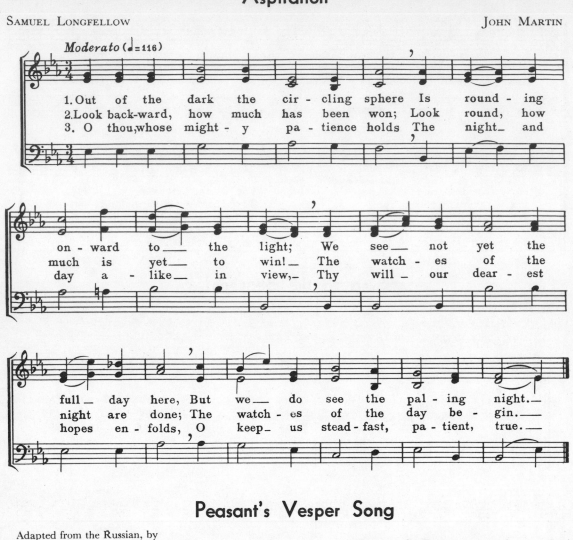

Moderato (♩=116)

1. Out of the dark the cir - cling sphere Is round - ing on - ward to the light; We see not yet the full day here, But we do see the pal - ing night.
2. Look back - ward, how much has been won; Look round, how much is yet to win! The watch - es of the night are done; The watch - es of the day be - gin.
3. O thou, whose might - y pa - tience holds The night and day a - like in view, Thy will our dear - est hopes en - folds, O keep us stead - fast, pa - tient, true.

Peasant's Vesper Song

Adapted from the Russian, by
FLEUR CONKLING

DIMITRI S. BORTNIANSKY (1752–1825)

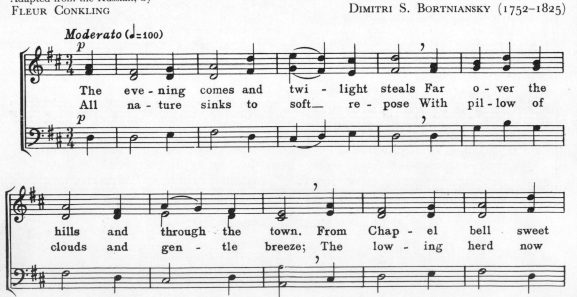

Moderato (♩=100)

The eve - ning comes and twi - light steals Far o - ver the hills and through the town. From Chap - el bell sweet
All na - ture sinks to soft re - pose With pil - low of clouds and gen - tle breeze; The low - ing herd now

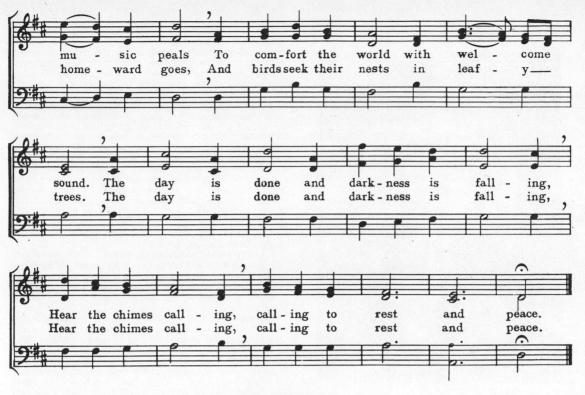

mu - sic peals To com-fort the world with wel - come
home - ward goes, And birds seek their nests in leaf - y —

sound. The day is done and dark - ness is fall - ing,
trees. The day is done and dark - ness is fall - ing,

Hear the chimes call - ing, call - ing to rest and peace.
Hear the chimes call - ing, call - ing to rest and peace.

The Pilgrim

Paraphrased from the German, by
ALDIS DUNBAR

BEURLE

Moderato ($\flat$ = 120)

1. Who fares, a lone - ly pil - grim, in lands a - far from home, Shall
2. The stars, the flow'rs his boy-hood knew, he longs to see once more, From
3. For once a - roused, that long - ing for home, for love and peace Shall

come to know deep yearn - ing, wher - ev - er he may roam. —
king - ly pal - a - ces he turns, to seek a cot - tage door. —
nev - er sleep with - in — him, till Heav - en grants re - lease! —

TONE BLENDING DRILLS

a.   b.

I V V₇ I   I — ii I⁶₄ V I

UNIT VIII: SONGS OF THE CLASSICAL PERIOD

with Appreciation Notes by LILLIAN L. BALDWIN

JOHANN SEBASTIAN BACH

A surprising number of people use the word "classical" to describe the music they happen to dislike or do not understand. "Popular" is their word for favorite pieces or for the song "hits" and dance tunes featured by vaudeville and radio. Indeed, many of us are so accustomed to hearing that exclusive little *or* between these two familiar words that the idea of a piece of music being both classical *and* popular is somewhat surprising!

Yet this very idea that, with a little understanding, classical music may become popular is one of the important reasons why music is taught in our schools today. For popular really means "liked by people generally," and girls and boys everywhere are discovering that there is much to be enjoyed in the great music — the classical music — which has been loved by many generations.

The word "classical" is a bit confusing because it has two meanings. Coming from the Latin *classicus*, classical originally meant "belonging to the first or highest class of society." Our dictionaries still give "first class" as the general meaning of the word.

And now for the particular meaning. For many centuries learning and culture belonged exclusively to the upper classes. Music, art, and literature, except when found in the church, were the ornaments of court life. Orchestras were merely the paid players who made dinner-table music for kings and princes and gave concerts to entertain their guests.

On the surface, life was very polite — but artificial. To be free and natural was considered vulgar, and young people were taught to hide their feelings behind a mask of pretty, conventional manners. When we read the old books, plays, and letters of this period, we smile at the stiff, little speeches and the elegant, formal language and think, "Why, no real people ever talked like that!"

The music of the composers of this period reflects the life of the upper class for which it was written. It, too, is polite and serene and as conventional as the etiquette of an eighteenth-century court. The instrumental music is particularly formal. Those early *suites*, modeled on old dance tunes, and the *sonatas* (which first meant pieces to be "sounded" not sung) are as primly designed as a formal garden.

Haydn was a master pattern maker. He revised the sonata and planned that largest and most elaborate of musical designs, the *symphony*, which is a sonata for orchestra. Mozart added a gracious, singing beauty and Beethoven, who was to be the forerunner of a very different kind of music, filled the symphony with rugged strength and deep human tenderness. With him, form began to give way to feeling.

The time when these great masters lived, the time when the life of the upper class was distinguished by its formality and when perfection of design in architecture, painting, literature, and music was considered the height of artistic beauty, is known in the history of art as the "Classical Period."

Do not think, however, that because these classical composers were formal they lacked feeling or that their music was meant to sound like glorified technical exercises. Far from it. Bach, the most misunderstood of them all, was a lovable man and his music is as gay, as tender, and as noble as music can be. The symphonies of Mozart and Beethoven express all that the heart can hold of love and joy, of sadness and longing. It is simply that these old-time composers did not prepare the listener for the mood of a piece or advertise their feelings by titles which suggested the emotions of their music. True to the fashion of their day, they masked their feelings behind formal labels, such as *fugue*, *sonata*, *concerto*, or a tempo mark such as *allegro*, *andante*, *presto*, though Beethoven dared to use *scherzo*, which means "a joke!"

The songs of the Classical Period are formal, too. Since songs, however, are so much shorter than symphonies and claim part of our attention for their verses, we are not quite so conscious of their conventional design. What we notice most about them is a certain primness of tune, a thinness of accompaniment, and a quaint and formal sentiment. Even the most ardent love songs are stiff with "thee" and "thou" and old-fashioned elegancies. Unfortunately, most of us know these old songs only through translation, which a great artist once said, "withers the flower of expression."

But even a pressed flower may be enjoyed for its delicate outline, soft coloring, and faint fragrance. And so the songs of the Classical Period charm us with the serene and formal beauty of a by-gone age.

And now you know that the word "classical" may be used to describe either a composition belonging to the Classical Period or simply any first-class music, and that often both meanings may apply to the same piece. It is not a word for boasters and posers — one is always suspicious of the person who says, "I just love classical music!" as though music were to be loved in a lump. Nor should anyone expect to enjoy all classical music or any piece of music merely because it is classical. On the other hand, one need not be unfair to a piece because it happens to be in eighteenth-century fashion or because it is rated high class. The intelligent music lover tries to value each piece for its own sake and to understand and enjoy its individual beauty.

O Saviour Sweet

O Jesulein süss

JOHANN SEBASTIAN BACH (1685–1750)

The name of Johann Sebastian Bach is, perhaps, the greatest name in all the history of music, for no other man has made as many important contributions to musical art. Bach was the bridge between the *polyphonic* (many-voiced) music of the early church and the *harmonic* (one melody with accompaniment) music of our own day. His works are a glorious summary of the past and an introduction to the present.

All his life long Bach served the church as organist, choirmaster, and composer. His great chorales, oratorios, and preludes and fugues are still the shining monuments of sacred music. No composer has ever surpassed Bach in beauty of workmanship or reverence of spirit.

Yet this great master was a lovable, unpretentious man. He lived simply and happily with his large family and took as much pleasure in writing a merry dance tune or a little hymn for his children as in the great works for the organ and choir of his famous church.

From Schemelli's Hymn Book, published in 1736, which, as its preface states, contains melodies "partly composed and partly improved in their figured basses by Herr Johann Sebastian Bach of Leipzig," comes "O Jesulein süss." Compared with the elaborate church chorales, this simple song is undoubtedly in the Bach-at-home style. It was probably one of the little hymns intended for "domestic devotions" and may even have been used in Bach's own household. One likes to picture Bach at the clavichord with all the little Bachs led by the mother, Anna Magdalena, lustily singing the new hymn which father had written for their morning prayers.

Verdant Meadows

Verdi prati

From the Opera, "ALCINA"

GEORGE FREDERICK HANDEL (1685–1759)

*The Fire Fugue, Painted by Harry Townsend
Courtesy of Steinway and Sons, New York*

HANDEL AT THE CLAVICHORD

For more than thirty years Handel composed and produced operas — no less than forty-seven — in London. These operas were successful in their day, but since they were all made on the old, artificial Italian model they have long since been laid aside as antiquated. However, many beautiful airs have survived and taken their places on concert programs. Of these airs from forgotten operas, none is more beautiful or more typical of Handel than "Verdant Meadows" from *Alcina*.

Alcina was a Circe-like sorceress who bewitched and bewildered a young knight until he no longer recognized even his betrothed bride. With a magic ring his sweetheart rescued him. Then the lovers broke the urn which held Alcina's power and, as it crashed, the palace of the sorceress fell in ruins and her enchanted garden turned into a dreary wilderness.

"Verdant Meadows" is the song the young knight sings as he watches the enchanted garden disappear. Although he is happy to be free from Alcina's wicked spell, his song has a touch of sadness at the destruction of the beautiful garden. It is the regret which always comes when leaves wither and flowers fade.

There is an amusing incident connected with the first performance of "Verdant Meadows." The tenor, a conceited fellow who was to sing the knight's role, complained that this song was not showy enough and refused to sing it. Handel, in one of his famous rages, drove to the singer's house and burst in upon him crying, "You dog! Don't I know better as yourself vat is good for you to sing? If you do not sing all the songs vat I give you, I vill not pay you ein stiver!" There was no more argument. "Verdant Meadows" was sung in all its beautiful simplicity and the London audiences loved it.

This number, originally a solo, may be sung as such or as a unison song. The varied possibilities for ensemble performance are indicated in the score.

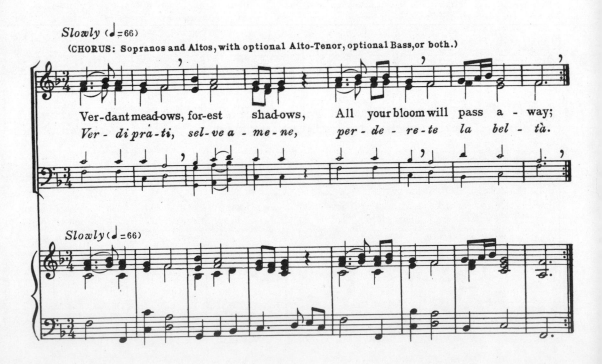

Slowly (♩ =66)

(CHORUS: Sopranos and Altos, with optional Alto-Tenor, optional Bass, or both.)

Ver-dant mead-ows, for-est shad-ows, All your bloom will pass a - way;
Ver - di prà-ti, sel-ve a - me-ne, per - de - re-te la bel - tà.

Slowly (♩ =66)

(SOPRANOS in unison or Soprano Solo)

Purl - ing streams, Flow'rs fresh-ly glow - ing, All your beau - ty,
Va - ghi fior, cor - ren - ti ri - vi, la va - ghez - za,

swift-ly go - ing seem-eth fair — but — for a day.
la bel - lez - za pre sto in voi — si — can - ge - rà.

Ver - dant mead-ows, for-est shad-ows, All — your bloom must pass — a - way;
Ver - di pra - ti, sel - ve a - me - ne, per - de - re - te la — bel - tà.

(ALTOS in unison or Alto Solo)

E - ven thou, O, love - ly maid - en,
E can - già - to il va-go og - get - to

With such charms, such sweet - ness la - den,
all' or - ror del pri - mo a - spet - to

Grow - est old, and pale, and gray,
tut - to in voi ri - tor - ne - rà.

Things of earth re - turn to clay.
tut - to in voi ri - tor - ne - rà.

Glorious Things of Thee Are Spoken

The Austrian National Hymn

JOHN NEWTON

FRANZ JOSEPH HAYDN (1732–1809)

FRANZ JOSEPH HAYDN

In his later years, Haydn's fame as a composer of symphonies brought him to London. He had always been a devoted patriot and when he heard the English singing their "God Save the King" he was seized with a desire to write a similar song for his own country. On his return to Vienna he wrote the now familiar "Austrian Hymn." It was first publicly sung to the words "Gott Erhalte Franz den Kaiser" on the emperor's birthday in 1797 and was at once enthusiastically received and adopted as the national hymn of Austria.

It was the composer's favorite of all his tunes and later he used it as one of the conspicuous themes of his *Emperor Quartet*.

During the last year of Haydn's life the French were bombarding Vienna and the patriotic feeling of the Austrians ran high. The aged master asked to be helped to the piano and with trembling fingers played his national hymn. It was Haydn's last performance. Five days later he was beyond the sound of Napoleon's cannon.

Haydn's hymn is one of the many fine tunes which have been taken over by the church. Although not written as a religious hymn, it is quite at home in any service, for it is the work of a man who looked upon his music as a gift of God and who prefaced even his symphonies with the words *Laus Deo* and signed them *In nomine Domini*. If ever a tune expressed man's courage and high devotion it is this noble hymn.

Our hymnals appropriately call Haydn's tune "Austria," and we know it best sung to Newton's words, "Glorious things of thee are spoken, Zion, city of our God."

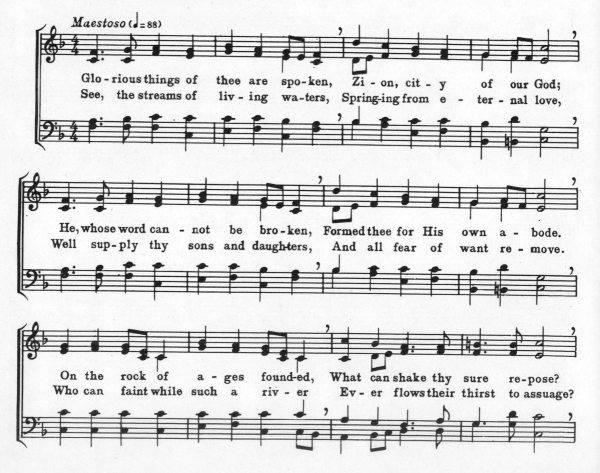

Maestoso (♩ = 88)

Glo-rious things of thee are spo-ken, Zi-on, cit-y of our God;
See, the streams of liv-ing wa-ters, Spring-ing from e-ter-nal love,

He, whose word can-not be bro-ken, Formed thee for His own a-bode.
Well sup-ply thy sons and daugh-ters, And all fear of want re-move.

On the rock of a-ges found-ed, What can shake thy sure re-pose?
Who can faint while such a riv-er Ev-er flows their thirst to assuage?

With sal-va-tion's walls sur-round-ed, Thou mayst smile at __ all thy foes.
Grace, which like the Lord the giv-er, Nev-er fails from age to __ age.

Night and Day

ROBERT LOUIS STEVENSON   FRANZ JOSEPH HAYDN (1732–1809)

Andante (♩ = 84)

1. When the gold-en day is done, Through the clos-ing por-tal
2. In the dark-ness hous-es shine, Par-ents move with can-dles:
3. In the dark-ness shapes of things, Hous-es, trees and hedg-es

Child and gar-den, flow'r and sun, Van-ish all things mor-tal.
Till on all, the night di-vine Turns the bed-room han-dles.
Clear-er grow; and spar-row's wings Beat on win-dow ledg-es.

As the blind-ing shad-ows fall, As the rays di-min-ish __
Then at last the day be-gins In the east a-break-ing, __
Just as it was shut a-way, Toy-like, in the e-ven, __

Un-der eve-ning's cloak, they all Roll a-way and van-ish.
In the hedg-es and the whins Sleep-ing birds a-wak-ing.
Here I see it glow with day Un-der glow-ing heav-en.

TONE BLENDING DRILLS and HARMONIC ANALYSIS

a. *b.*

I V₇ V I   I IV ii I V V₇ I

Sweet Bells

From the Opera, "THE MAGIC FLUTE"   WOLFGANG AMADEUS MOZART (1756–1791)

The story of *The Magic Flute* is little more than a string of fantastic incidents but Mozart's immortal melodies have made this one of the great operas. In the opera the delightful little melody which here appears in the right-hand piano part, is played by Papageno, the birdcatcher, on the chime of magic bells which are his protection in time of trouble. "Had everyone such a chime," says Papageno (and such a tune, say we) "foes would be turned to friends and people would live in the most beautiful harmony!"

If playing bells are available, it is most effective to use them in this accompaniment. The bass part of the song may be sung an octave higher as an alto. The conductor may secure a smoother performance by beating two beats to a measure.

la,   la, la,   la ra la, la,   la,   la ra la!   Our

heart leaps   to   hear you,   our blood beats in time: La ra

la,   la, la,   la ra la, la,   la ra, la!   Our la!

TONE BLENDING DRILLS and HARMONIC ANALYSIS

a.   *b.*

I V₇ V I   I IV ii I⁶₄ V I

Contentment

Der Zufriedene

Adapted from the German, by
PHYLLIS McGINLEY

LUDWIG VAN BEETHOVEN (1770–1827)

Like Haydn, Mozart, and other composers of the Classical Period, Beethoven, the great master of the symphony, gave little attention to song writing. He thought, felt, dreamed in terms of the orchestra, and his genius seemed to need space and larger forms in which to work out its bold patterns. Indeed, he once remarked to a friend, "I do not like to write songs." Nevertheless the songs he did write are characteristic of his style and treatment, especially the accompaniments, which were of great value to later song writers in their artistic suggestions. Such a song is "Der Zufriedene" (literally "the contented one") with its simple, happy melody and twittering accompaniment of sixteenth-note triplets. By extending the opening phrase to five measures, and following it with a six-measure phrase, Beethoven cleverly keeps the contentment from growing commonplace.

meas-ure, a com-rade sworn and true, so true, A com - rade sworn and
trou-ble who has a trust-ed friend, a friend, Who has a trust-ed
geth-er would find it al-ways spring, yes, spring, Would find it al-ways

true.
friend.
spring.

2. Then
3. What

The Scale

Three-Part Canon

LUDWIG VAN BEETHOVEN (1770–1827)

Beethoven had a keen sense of humor and a fondness for practical jokes which were sometimes none too delicate. His humor, quite naturally, found expression in his music. Indeed, it was Beethoven who substituted the *Scherzo* (meaning "a joke") for the more dignified minuet, as the third movement of the sonata. In opening the fourth movement of the *First Symphony*, Beethoven makes humorous use of the ascending major scale. In this canon, also, the scale becomes another one of Beethoven's little jokes.

O tell me, O tell me How can I learn to sing the scale.

do re mi fa so la ti do, do ti la so fa mi re do.

mi fa so la ti do re mi, mi re do ti la so fa mi.

UNIT IX: SONGS THE COWBOY SINGS

Collected and Arranged

by ALICE GIDEON WHITMIRE

What is it in the cowboy's life that so fires our imagination and quickens our sense of romance? Is it not that the very heart of America is found in the spirit of the cowboy? In picturesque outfit, from his big hat to his roweled spurs and boots, his chaps,[1] and a gay-colored handkerchief at his throat, he rides through American history as truly a pioneer as the grim, dauntless men who crossed the Appalachians and settled the plains and valleys of our West. In the days when the West was first being opened up he was one of its most picturesque figures.

Even today the life of the cowboy is colorful in its intense and varied activities. With the spring comes the Spring Roundup. The ranch is fairly astir getting the outfit together. The cowboys come drifting in, the cavy[2] is gathered from the winter ranges, the mess wagon and bed wagon are fitted up ready to lumber forth when the outfit moves. It makes a regular cavalcade as it trails on to spend the next few months on the range. Much gay banter is swapped back and forth, covering up a boyish eagerness and a homesickness for the range which is deep seated in the heart of every cowboy but which he is ever loath to admit. To be riding down a wind-rippled coulee,[3] yelling the cattle out of the draw,[4] facing the dust of the trailing herd, then night and a bed under the friendly open sky, — this is the life on the range.

Each day the cowboys round up the cattle and drive them to the mouth of the creek where the camp is pitched. Then follows the working of the herd, cutting out the cows with calves, and branding the calves. After the herd is worked and the branding finished, most of the day's drive is thrown back up the creek. The work of the spring roundup usually lasts until the first of July, when the outfit pulls into the ranch for supplies and repairs.

A few weeks at the ranch, then the beef roundup begins. With the beef roundup comes real work. In the midst of bawling cattle, dust clouds from milling hoofs, and heat rising from the parched earth, the cowboy works and sweats, weaving in and out of the herd, cutting out the fat ones, riding down bolting steers, alert to be here and there until the working of the roundup is over. Throughout the day, until after supper everyone is moving.

As the sun goes down the peculiar stillness of twilight pervades the camp. A clear bird call, the rustling of small animal life through the grass, the whir of a sage hen's wings, and the distant lowing of the cattle blend with the quiet night.

Not yet has the restless beef herd bedded down for the night. But the cowboy is skilful. With just enough riding 'round the herd to get them huddled, with just enough patient standing and waiting, they become quiet and a few at a time begin lying down. And while he stands guard he, has much time to think and to drink in the beauties of a roofless world. Or in soft tones he drawls a yarn with a comrade or sings a song as they two stand at a vantage point.

But not always does the night slip quietly by. Often in a downpour of rain the first guard finds the riders sliding and slithering in mud, as 'round a rain-huddled herd the men call to each other above the bawling of the cattle and peals of thunder, straining and alert to catch any sudden break which might occur and to check it before the herd should stampede.

Again in late fall, when blasts of winter bring a blinding sleet, or snow squalls sweep over the landscape, the cattle turn their tails to the wind, and the riders with the wind behind them, stand in the storm until the dawn. This is a glimpse of the cowboys' days of toil, danger, and romance.

The dance, too, plays a large part in the cowboy's life for it is the main social or community affair in which he takes part. Many an outfit celebrates the beginning of the spring roundup with an all-night dance to which neighbors within a radius of a hundred miles or more come. Also, as the outfit moves through the country some hospitable owner of a brand will open his home to a night of merrymaking and dancing.

Out of experiences such as these the cowboy songs have come — songs of adventure, songs of the trail. In the olden days when the cattle were trailed from Texas to Wyoming and Montana for grass, or to Kansas to be loaded on cars and shipped to Chicago, the trail which the cattle followed came to be known as the "Old Chisholm Trail." These long drives, no doubt, gave birth to many an adventure and heroic deed which later became the basis for a cowboy ballad. The events and work of the trail itself fell into the rhythmic meter of the cowpony's lope and became those songs commonly known as the "trail songs." All the cowboy's moods are in his songs from carefree daring to quiet solitude of lonely frontiers.

Stories of the West have rooted deep in the American mind the romance of the early cattle country with its wide ranges, its trails and herds, its roundups and cowboys. So the cowboy folk songs, which are a product of that life, crystallize that romance in melody and meter, and are fast finding a fond place in the hearts of all music lovers and all Americans.

---

[1] *Chaps.* A pair of leather leggings (sometimes covered with fur or angora wool) full length, laced together in front and connected at the waistline by a belt. Worn for protection from brush and thorns in thickly wooded country and also for protection against the cold, the rain, and the snow.

[2] *Cavy.* The herd of horses used on the roundup. The cavy is held together in the daytime by a cowboy called the *horse wrangler*, and at night by another usually called the *night hawk*. The cavy includes both the cowponies on which the cowboy does his work, and the work horses used for the mess wagon and bed wagon when moving camp. The word probably comes from the same root as cavalry, cavalier, and cavort. Cavy is a word used in the northwest; the southwestern cowboy uses the Spanish word, *remuda*. The word cavy is thought by some to come from the word "covey," as a "covey of quail or grouse."

[3] *Coulee.* A branch or side prong of a draw; a small draw.

[4] *Draw.* A dry creek bed running from the divide to the main creek (a small stream). The draw carries water only when it rains, and serves as a catch basin for the slopes which it drains. It shelters the cattle from the summer heat and winter cold. In working a country the draws must be thoroughly combed by the riders in order to find all the cattle.

THE BLANKET SIGNAL, BY FREDERIC REMINGTON

The Dying Cowboy

Wyoming Version

COWBOY BALLAD
Figure Notation for the C Harmonica

There seems something very elemental in the melody and mood of this song. It has a decided folk song flavor, typical of so many American ballads with their mournful melodies and stories. There is something eternal in it, as though the cowboy could no more get away from the prairies than could the hills that enfold them.

2.
"O, bury me not on the lone prairie
Where the wild coyotes will howl o'er me,
In a narrow grave just six by three;
O, bury me not on the lone prairie.

3.
"I've always wished to be laid when I died,
In the little church on the green hillside
By my father's grave, there let mine be,
And bury me not on the lone prairie.

4.
"O, bury me not," and his voice failed there,
But we took no heed to his dying prayer.
In a narrow grave, just six by three,
We buried him there on the lone prairie.

5.
Where the dewdrops glow and the butterflies rest,
And the flowers bloom o'er the prairie's crest,
Where the wild coyote and the winds sport free,
On a wet saddle blanket lay a cowboy-ee.

6.
O, we buried him there on the lone prairie
Where the wild rose blooms and the wind blows free,
Oh, his pale young face never more to see,
For we buried him there on the lone prairie.

7.
Yes, we buried him there on the lone prairie
Where the owl all night hoots mournfully,
And the blizzard beats and the winds blow free
O'er his lowly grave on the lone prairie.

8.
"O, bury me not on the lone prairie,
Where the wolves can howl and growl o'er me;
Fling a handful of roses o'er my grave,
With a prayer to Him who my soul will save."

The Trail to Mexico

Traditional

TRAIL SONG
Figure Notation for the C Harmonica

Note: This song may also be played on the G harmonica.

The Zebra Dun

COWBOY BALLAD
Figure Notation for the Chromatic Harmonica

Wyoming Version

This typical cowboy ballad has a strong appeal. It is characteristic both of the cowboy and of the American spirit of judging by "What can you do?" rather than "Who are you?" or "What have you?"

With a swing; but be sure that words are distinct (♩=92)

1. We were camp'd up-on the plains___ at the head of the Ci-mar-ron.___ When a-long came a stran-ger___ and stopp'd to ar-ger some.___ He look'd so ver-y fool-ish___ we be-gan to look a-round,___ We thought he was a green-horn___ that had just es-cap'd from town,___ We

CHORUS

Note: Arrow ⊙→ indicates when lever of Chromatic Harmonica is to be pressed in. This song may al-so be played on the E♭ harmonica.

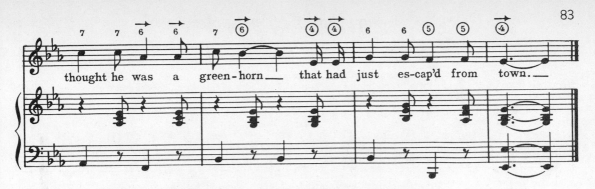

thought he was a green-horn ___ that had just es-cap'd from town. ___

2. We asked if he'd had his breakfast, he hadn't had a sniff,
   So we opened up the chuck box and bade him help hisself.
   He took a cup of coffee, some biscuits, and some beans,
   And then began to talk and tell of foreign kings and queens.

3. About the Spanish wars and fighting on the seas,
   With guns as big as steers and ramrods long as trees,
   About old Paul Jones, a mean fighting son-of-a-gun,
   Who was the grittiest cuss that ever pulled a gun.

4. Such an educated feller, his thoughts just came in herds,
   He astonished all them cowboys with them jawbreakin' words,
   He just kept on a-talkin' till he made the boys all sick,
   And they began to look around just how to play the trick.

5. He said he'd lost his job down on the Santa Fe,
   And had struck across the prairie to find the 7-D;
   He didn't say how came it, some trouble with the boss,
   But said he'd like to borrow a nice fat saddle hoss.

6. Now this tickled the boys all over, they laughed 'way down in their sleeves,
   And said, "We will lend you a horse, sir, just as fresh and fat as you please."
   Then Shorty grabbed the lariat and roped Old Zebra Dun,
   Then turned him over to the stranger and waited to see the fun.

7. Now Old Dunny was an outlaw that had grown so awful wild,
   He could paw the white spots out of the moon for every jump for a mile;
   Old Dunny stood right still, as if he didn't know,
   Until he was saddled and ready for to go.

8. When the stranger hit the saddle, Old Dunny quit the earth,
   He traveled right straight upward for all that he was worth,
   A pitching and a-squealing, and a-having wall-eyed fits,
   His hind feet perpendicular, his front ones in the bits.

9. We could see the tops of the mountains under Dunny every jump
   But the stranger he was growed there just like a camel's hump:
   The stranger sat upon him a-twirling his mustache
   Just like a summer boarder a-waitin' for his hash.

10. He thumped him in the shoulders, and spurred him as he whirled,
    To show them flunky punchers that he was wolf of the world,
    And when the stranger dismounted once more upon the ground,
    We knew he was a thoroughbred, and not a gent from town.

11. The boss was standing 'round a takin' in the show
    Walked right up to the stranger and said, "You needn't go.
    If you can use the lariat like you rode Old Zebra Dun
    You're just the man I've been lookin' for ever since the year of one."

12. Well, he could twirl the lariat and he didn't do it slow,
    He could catch them fore feet nine out of ten for any kind of dough
    And when the herd stampeded, he was always on the spot
    To set them for to millin' like the boiling of a pot.

Conclusion: There's one thing and a sure thing I've learned since I've been born,
Every educated feller ain't a plumb greenhorn.

For the the lines in the final stanza marked "Conclusion," repeat solo and chorus from the place in the music marked ⊕

Little Joe, the Wrangler

COWBOY BALLAD

Traditional

Figure Notation for the Chromatic Harmonica

Having a definite story about a young boy starting out to "paddle his own canoe" and losing his life in the performance of his duty and loyalty to his outfit, this characteristic ballad makes a strong appeal and typifies a fine American ideal. Remuda is the Spanish for cavy; Cocinero, Spanish for cook; Pecos, a river in Texas.

Note: Arrow ⟶◯ indicates when lever of Chromatic Harmonica is to be pressed in. This song may also be played on the D harmonica. From *Songs of the Cowboys* by N. Howard Thorp, by permission of the publishers, Houghton Mifflin Company, Boston.

lit-tle Tex-as po-ny he called, "Chaw," ___ With his bro-gan shoes and o-ver-alls, a

tough-er look-in' kid, You ___ nev-er in your life be-fore had saw. ___

2. His saddle was a Texas "kak" built many years ago,
With an O.K. spur on one foot lightly swung;
His "hot roll" in a cotton sack so loosely tied behind
And his canteen from his saddle-horn was swung.
He said he had to leave his home, his pa had married twice,
And his new ma whipped him every day or two;
So he saddled up old Chaw one night and lit a shuck this way,
And now he's trying to paddle his own canoe.

3. He said, if we would give him work, he'd do the best he could,
Though he didn't know straight up about a cow;
So the boss he cut him out a mount, and kindly put him on,
For he sort-a liked this little kid somehow.
Learned him to wrangle horses and try to know them well,
And get them in at daylight if he could;
To follow the chuck wagon and always hitch the team,
And to help the cocinero rustle wood.

4. We had driven to the Pecos, the weather being fine;
We had camped on the southside in a bend;
When a norther came a-blowin', we had doubled up our guard,
For it had taken all of us to hold them in.
Little Joe, the wrangler, was called out with the rest
Though the kid had scarcely reached the herd,
When the cattle they stampeded, like a hailstorm long they fled,
Then we were all a-ridin' for the lead.

5. Amidst the streaks of lightnin', a horse we could see in the lead,
'Twas little Joe, the wrangler, in the lead,
He was ridin' Old Blue Rocket with a slicker o'er his head,
And a-tryin' to check the cattle in their speed.
At last we got them millin' and kind-a quieted down,
And the extra guard back to the wagon went,
But there was one a-missin', and we knew it at a glance,
'Twas our little Texas stray, poor wrangling Joe.

6. The next mornin' just at daybreak, we found where Rocket fell,
Down in a washout, twenty feet below;
And beneath the horse, mashed to a pulp, his spur had rung his knell,
Was our little Texas stray, poor wrangling Joe.
And now Joe, the wrangler, will wrangle nevermore,
For his wrangling days forever now are o'er;
He has left his spurs and saddle for others here below,
So we bid farewell to little wrangling Joe.

Old Paint

Cowboy Waltz
Figure Notation for the C Harmonica

Wyoming Version

This song expresses the thoughts of the lonely rider as he leaves for a new range. "Old Paint" is the name of his pony. The song, with its characteristic and colorful mood, has a definite and well-marked pony rhythm.

Good - by my lit - tle Ann - ie I'm a - leav - in' Chey-

Piano marks the rhythm of the pony.

enne, And I'm a - rid - in' Old Paint and a - lead - in' Old

Sam And it's good - by lit - tle Ann - ie for Bald - y won't

stand, And I'm leav - in' Chey - enne and I'm off for old Mon-

*Observe that in several chords the Alto-Tenor sings *above* the melody; the stems of the notes will tell you where.

The Old Chisholm Trail

TRAIL SONG

Wyoming Version

Figure Notation for the Chromatic Harmonica

Its gay rollicking rhythm, its carefree mood, its pictures of cowboy life, especially his grief with the cattle on the trail in rain or snowstorm, on day herd or night guard — all serve to make this song a general favorite. It is a true "moving picture" of cowboy life.

Note: Arrow ⟶◯ indicates when lever of Chromatic Harmonica is to be pressed in.   This song may also be played on the G harmonica.

2. I started up the trail October twenty third,
   I started up the trail with the 2 U herd.
      Refrain: Come a-ti-yi-youpy youpy ya youpy ya,
              Come a-ti-yi-youpy youpy ya!

3. On a ten dollar horse and a forty dollar saddle
   I'm goin' to punchin' Texas cattle.
   (Same Refrain as above after each verse)

4. Woke up one morning on the Old Chisholm Trail,
   Rope in my hand and a cow by the tail.

5. I'm up in the mornin' afore daylight
   And 'fore I sleep the moon shines bright.

6. Old Ben Bolt was a blamed good boss
   But he'd go to see the gals on a sore-backed hoss.

7. It's cloudy in the West and a-lookin' like rain
   And my darned old slicker's in the wagon again.

8. Crippled my horse, I don't know how,
   Ropin' the horns of a 2 U cow.

9. No chaps, no slicker, and it's pourin' down rain
   And I swear, by gosh, I'll never night herd again.

10. Last night was on guard and the leader broke the ranks,
    Hit my horse down the shoulders and I spurred him in the flanks.

11. The wind began to blow, and the rain began to fall,
    It looked, by grab, like we was goin' to lose 'em all.

12. I jumped in the saddle and grabbed holt of the horn,
    Best blamed cowboy ever was born.

13. We rounded 'em up and put 'em on the cars,
    And that was the last of the old 2 Bars.

14. Oh! it's bacon and beans 'most every day,
    I'd as soon be a-eatin' prairie hay.

15. I went to the boss to draw my roll,
    He had me figured out nine dollars in the hole.

16. I'll sell my outfit as soon as I can
    And I won't punch cattle for any old man.

17. With my knees in the saddle and my seat in the sky,
    I'll quit punchin' cows in the sweet bye and bye.

Charlie Knapp

Cowboy Waltz
Figure Notation for the C Harmonica

Wyoming Version
HARMONICA or VIOLIN

Leather Breeches

Traditional

COWBOY SQUARE DANCE
Figure Notation for the C Harmonica

We are off on a tour aboard the good ship "U.S.A." Our voyage will take us to many of the principal ports of Latin America. We plan to go ashore from time to time and travel a bit inland to hear some of the folk music sung and played and danced by the people of those lands. In no better way may we come to understand and appreciate our neighbors to the south than through enjoying their music.

A MUSICAL TRAVELOGUE THROUGH LATIN AMERICA

MAP BY MILDRED KAISER

UNIT X: A MUSICAL TRAVELOGUE THROUGH
LATIN AMERICA

by IRMA LABASTILLE

To the average North American, Latin American music generally means a more or less familiar acquaintance with a limited number of Mexican songs, which, for historical and other reasons, have become widespread. It is perhaps natural that our attention should be called first to the musical contributions of our nearest Latin neighbor. To the south of the United States, however, lies that vast territory which extends from Mexico's Rio Grande River to the Straits of Magellan known as Latin America. Rich in unexplored musical material, it offers such widely contrasting sources as songs and dances of the Caribbean countries, of the region of the majestic Andes, the boundless, lonely Pampas, the torrid basin of the Amazon, and the gay coastal cities of the South American continent.

Perhaps because of the Mexican songs we know, we have come to think of all Latin American music as being definitely Spanish. It is true that after the discovery of the New World the original settlers were chiefly Spaniards. It is surprising, however, that the Spanish influence is absent in much of Latin America's music. At the time of the Spanish Conquest, old Indian cultures already existed in the Andean countries. Here music had been developed to an outstanding degree. The influence of native and invader was reciprocal but not always equally so. The Indian is known to retain his customs tenaciously — his music longer than any other phase of his culture. To the countries touching the Caribbean the Spaniard himself brought the African Negro with his astounding rhythmic gift. Thus it is that the Negro has left a deep and important imprint on the music of this region.

Where the music of Spain or Portugal and Africa have intermingled, where noble old Indian melodies have survived or have been deftly touched by the gayer, more dynamic accompaniments of the Conquistadores, where subsequently other nations have conquered or have been conquered, there has arisen a music distinctly original in character. It has an intangible quality which sets it apart from the music of the Hispanic peninsula. It is rich in emotional expression far from primitive, melodically enchanting, haunting, rudimentary in its harmonic content, rhythmically fascinating, and above all peculiarly vital. Singing and dancing are so linked together in Latin America that it is sometimes difficult to classify the music. Both types, the song proper and the song which belongs to a dance, have been included in this collection. Attention is called to the fact that in performing the song accompaniments the interpretation of the left hand is important. Herein is embodied the character of the native instruments — drums, guitar, cajon, maruga, etc.

This unit presents a cross section of the music of Latin America. Each country is represented by a type which is both distinctive and characteristic. It is a music difficult for one of another race faithfully to interpret. Technical mastery is insufficient. It is not until one has been touched by the soul of these people that the beauties of Latin American music can be fully revealed.

Lovely Cuba, 'tis You

Tu

FERNAN SÁNCHEZ   EDUARDO SÁNCHEZ DE FUENTES

The lovely Cuban habañera "Tu" by Eduardo Sánchez de Fuentes, one of Cuba's popular composers, belongs to that large group of songs which embraces certain characteristics peculiar to folk songs without actually being a folk song in the strict sense of the word.

The habañera, which may be either a song or a dance, grew up in Cuba, probably in Havana as its name indicates. Properly performed, its execution should be slow, graceful, languorous, especially when danced. It is a dance of the tropic zone. Contrary to popular belief, the rhythmic foundation of the habañera is not Spanish but of African origin. It may be attributed to the African Negroes imported in large numbers by the Spaniards to Cuba and other islands of the West Indies in the early days of Spanish exploration. Wherever the African has gone he has left his musical traces, and the essential quality of pure Negro music is its unbounded rhythmic variety.

The simplest form of the habañera rhythm is ♪.♪♪♪ We find this rhythm recurring again and again throughout the music of Latin America. "Tu" has all the swing which we expect of a true Cuban habañera and is expressive, as well, of the gaiety of the Cuban disposition.

darkness of night | and the sun's gleaming
yond all compare; | lovely Cuba, 'tis
no-che y la luz | de los rayos del
mo-sa sin par ¡Ay! | por-que Cu-ba e-res

1. ray. / you! / sol. / tú! A flame that's ray. **2.** ray. / you! / sol. / tú.
The cane is you!
Fue-go sa- sol.
Dul-ce es la tú.

Choucoune

Creole Words by
OSWALD DURAND (1840–1906)

HAITIAN FOLK SONG

"Choucoune" is Haiti's most popular melody. Its rhythm is that of the *meringue*, the national dance of Haiti, a complicated habañera rhythm. The Haitians claim that the *meringue* cannot be played adequately by a white man. Certainly it is true that the intricate rhythmic shadings which the Haitian achieves in his performance are impossible to reduce to writing, employing, as we must, the conventional symbols of notation in current use.

"Choucoune" is a girl's pet name. The words of this song were written by Oswald Durand, Haiti's foremost poet. The actual composer of the music is unknown. The text of the song is in creole, the *patois* (a mixture of French and African) spoken by the natives.

Moderato (♩=92)   FORM: Three distinct themes

I first saw my sweet Chou-coune With-in a thick grove of
The eyes of my dear Chou-coune Shine clear as the can-dle

trees;   I   said, "You're as fair as noon!"   She
light;   Her smile, like the sun at noon,   Is

smiled and she seemed quite pleased.   I   said, "You're as fair as
ra - diant, and warm, and bright;   Her smile, like the sun at

noon!"   "I   thank you, sir," said Chou - coune.
noon,   Is   ra - diant; my fair Chou - coune!

Briskly (♩=100)

Lit - tle birds heard all that we had to say;

Lit - tle birds were lis - ten - ing all the day!

Ah, my ten - der one, Dain - ty, slen - der one,

By the stars a - bove I de - clare my love! Ah, my ten - der one,

Dain - ty, slen - der one, Smil - ing, gay Chou - coune! coune!

NOTE: The quintuplets (5) are sung with rhythmic freedom, without attempting exact divisions of the measure.

The Pearl

La Perla

Translated from the Spanish

PUERTO RICAN FOLK SONG

Puerto Rico, which means "rich port," is the smallest of the West Indian island group known as the "Greater Antilles." Although it is at present under the government of the United States of America, Spanish is still the language of the island and many of the Puerto Rican songs reflect the spirit of Spain in their melodic content. The gentle, pensive mood of "La Perla" is typically Puerto Rican. Their dances, however, often display intricate rhythmic patterns which again may be traced to African influence.

Sirup Is So Sweet

Tant Sirop Est Doux

Translated from the Creole

MARTINIQUE FOLK SONG

Martinique is one of the group of islands east of Puerto Rico known as the "Lesser Antilles" and generally spoken of as the French West Indies. It is famed as the birthplace of the charming Empress Josephine, the creole wife of Napoleon. In Latin America, the term "creole" does not signify African ancestry. Originally, and correctly, the word was applied by the French and Spanish colonists to the children of European parents born in the American colonies.

The song, "Tant Sirop Est Doux" is popular through the French West Indies and among the descendants of the early French settlers of Louisiana. Like many songs of this type its words are relatively unimportant, but rhythmically it has retained much that is African and has an irresistible fascination.

Sir - up is so sweet, Ma-de-lei-ne, Sir - up is so
Tant sir-op est doux, Ma-de-lei-ne, Tant sir-op est

sweet. You must not dance so hard, Ma-de-lein', You must not dance so
sweet. You must not sing so loud, Ma-de-lein', You must not sing so
doux. Ne faites pas tant de bruit, Ma-de-lein', Ne faites pas tant de
doux. Ne cri-ez pas si fort, Ma-de-lein', Ne cri-ez pas si

hard, Ma-de-lein', This house is not our_ house, Ma-de-lein', This
loud, Ma-de-lein', This house is not our_ house, Ma-de-lein', This
bruit, Ma-de-lein', La mai - son n'est pas à nous, Ma-de-lein', La
fort, Ma-de-lein', La mai - son n'est pas à nous, Ma-de-lein', La

house is not our_ house.
house is not our_ house.
mai - son n'est pas à nous.
mai - son n'est pas à nous.

D. C.

(ritard. last time)

GATHERING COFFEE BEANS ON A PLANTATION IN BRAZIL

My Pretty Cabocla

Cabocla Bonita

Translated from the Portuguese

BRAZILIAN FOLK SONG

This is a Brazilian *modinha* from the south of Brazil. The *modinha* is one of the best known types of Brazilian song. *Modinha* means "little mood" — the suffix "inha" is the diminutive in the Portuguese language and it was from Portugal that the *modinha* was brought to Brazil. In its mother country, the character of the *modinha* was one of pensive tranquillity, but in the New World this type of song was enriched by the more complicated rhythms of the African Negro. During the early days of colonization, African slaves were brought to Brazil, just as they were to the West Indies, and their influence on the music of Brazil has been marked.

A *cabocla* is a person of mixed blood — white and Indian. There are many Indians in Brazil, but their influence on the music of Brazil has been slight. In Brazil, the music of the Indians and that of the Conquerors has not intermixed, while in Peru, on the other hand, it has.

The song may be sung in unison or in two parts.

When you are danc-ing the sam-ba, my love,____ A hum-ming bird seems a-
Quan-do tu sam-ba no sam-ba ai meu bem,____ Par-re-ce um bei-ja fro-

fly - ing,   When you are danc-ing the sam-ba, my love,____
si - nho!   Quan-do tu sam-ba no sam-ba ai meu bem,____

A hum-ming bird seems a - fly - ing. Seek-ing a place for
Pa-re-ce um bei-ja fro-si-nho! Que vem de gaio em

nest-ing you rove,_____ Ne'er a mo-ment for rest-ing; Ah, pret-ty Ca-
_gaio, ai meu bem!_____ em bus-ca-do seu ninh'ai, Ca-bo-cla bo-_

bo-cla for you I am sigh-ing, Ah, pret-ty Ca-bo-cla for you I am
ni-ta me da um bei-jinh'ai! Ca-bo-cla bo-ni-ta me da um bei-

sigh - ing!
ji - nho!

Adios Te Digo

Translated from the Spanish

NORTHERN ARGENTINE SONG

The Quechua Indians, once members of the great Inca kingdom, have a rich musical heritage in numerous songs and dances composed on the five-tone scale. In the regions they inhabit this music is still to be found. "Adios Te Digo" is a song from Northern Argentina which once was part of Peru, and is of the type known as the *vidala*, which means "a little bit of life." This particular *vidala* shows its primitive origin by the gradual descent in pitch, the last note is the lowest note of the song. Its words are still sung in the Quechua language. Like so many Argentine songs, a note of sadness pervades it. The accompaniment suggests the primitive beat of the drums which the Indians still use.

3. Ay, ay, ay, Ay, ay, ay,
   I am surrounded With anguish and pain.
   Ungrateful one Whom I care for in vain.

4. Ay, ay, ay, Ay, ay, ay,
   All the night long I weep My heart doth yearn
   Farewell I bid thee, I will not return.

3. *Ay, ay, ay, ay, ay, ay,*
   Me estoy muriendo de pena y dolor,
   porque una ingrata no me tiene amor!

4. *Ay, ay, ay, ay, ay, ay,*
   Toda la noche de pena lloré.
   Adiós te digo ya no he de volver!

PERUVIAN MUSICAL INSTRUMENTS

The *quena* is the simple, vertical flute used by the highland shepherds of today and found in Peru hundreds of years ago. It is usually made of bone or cane and is pierced with finger holes. It produces a plaintive-sounding tone which adds to the melancholy of the pastoral melodies. The ancient Peruvian trumpet is made of clay. The other principal melodic instrument in use among the Quechuas is the *antara*, the Pipes of Pan. These instruments were used by the pre-Inca people of the Peruvian coast and the Incas themselves. The figure playing the *antara* is an ancient one.

Palapala

From the Quechua and Spanish   From the Pampas of Argentina

The gaucho has many dances — the *gato*, the *chacarera*, the *zamba*, and others which have been derived from these. The *palapala*, more than any other gaucho dance, has retained its indigenous character in the rustic perfection of its figures, the tinge of cunning in its mimicry, and in its Quechua words. Its theme is essentially descriptive. It is danced in pairs, one couple alone performing at a time, mimicking the animals spoken of in the text, doing as the animal would do.

The *chuña*, spoken of in the first verse of Spanish, is a large bird by that name. The *cajon* is the wooden box on which the rhythm is tapped out in any real gaucho orchestra. The tapping of the feet is that part of the gaucho dance called the *zapateo*, which calls for intricate foot work on the part of the dancer.

Because of the cross rhythms, the selection is arranged so that, when preferred, the accompaniment on the bass staff may be played by both hands, the voices only singing the melody from the treble staff, omitting the small notes. Or, the accompaniment may be played as a duet, a performer playing from each staff. Following the metrical and rhyming plan, the pupils may compose additional stanzas, bringing the various birds and beasts into the jungle band.

Gaucho = cowboy of the pampas.   108

1. Come to the jun-gle fair-o____ All of the world is there-o,____
2. Gai-ly the ja-gu-ar-ro____ Strums on his light gui-tar-ro,____
1. Pa-la-pa-la pul-pe-ro,____ Pa-la-pa-la pul-pe-ro,____

See ev-'ry-one ar-rive on the run The frol-ic and fun to share-o.____
Clear through the air it sounds ev-'ry-where To ban-ish all care and sor-row.____
Pa-la-pa-la pul-pe-ro Chu-ña sol-te-ro, Chu-ña sol-te-ro.____

Nor is a band de-nied them, Bird-ies with beasts be-side them,
Gay lit-tle birds are hum-ming, Mon-keys the ban-jo strum-ming,
Am-pa-tu ca-jo-ne-ro,____ Am-pa-tu ca-jo-ne-ro,____

Sly Mis-ter Fox with tap-ping and knocks Con-ducts from a box to guide them.
Vi-ols and lutes and shrill pi-ping flutes, And wild jun-gle brutes a-drum-ming.
Am-pa-tu ca-jo-ne-ro U-tu gui-tar-re-ro U-tu gui-tar-re-ro.

2. *Ampatu cajonero, Ampatu cajonero,*
   Ampatu cajonero
   Utu guitarrero, Utu guitarrero.

3. *Icaco taconero, Icaco taconero,*
   Icaco taconero
   Hualo flautero, Hualo flautero.

4. *Caraipuca tucumano, Caraipuca tucumano,*
   Caraipuca tucumano
   Huiñi salteño, Huiñi salteño.

THE PATIO OF CASA VELASO IN SANTIAGO, CHILE

This is the oldest house in the city, a careful restoration that shows the typical architecture of early Spanish life in America. On the right wall hang the meat scales; to the left is the old water well. The wrought iron gate leads from the patio to the street. The balconies, barred windows, and stone bench are still characteristic of homes in Latin America.

Buy My Tortillas

El Tortillero

CHILEAN FOLK SONG

Translated from the Spanish

As sung by Señor José Picó of Rancagua, Chile

Chilean folk music, more than any other South American music, has retained characteristics peculiar to Spain. The music of Chile is cheerful, nearly always in the major key, and in either ¾ or ⅝ time.

El Tortillero is a street vendor who sings this song of the popular type called a *tonada*. He is calling his wares known to every Chilean, the crisp, little pancakes, *tortillas*, which are kept hot over glowing coals and sold on the streets. The accompaniment suggests the small harp which is the instrument second only to the guitar in popularity in Chile and accompanies all folk songs and dances.

110

1. In the dark-ness I see noth-ing, By my fee - ble
2. From her win-dow not an an-swer, To my cheer - ful
3. With my bas-ket full of pan-cakes, I have near - ly

p BASS optional; may be sung octave higher by Altos

lan - tern light; I am pass-ing by your
night - ly call, And I won-der if she
passed from sight, Vain-ly wait-ing for a

win-dow With a mer - ry song to - night._____
hears me, For she an - swers not at all._____
mes-sage For your ven-dor boy to - night._____

Loud - - er I'll sing, dear, _____ Mak - -

- ing my call clear; _____ Who'll come and buy crisp-y lit-tle

pan - cakes,— Tor - - ti - llas buen - os.*

* Pronounced
(Tor-teé-yas bwaý-nos)

TONE BLENDING DRILLS

a.   b.

I   V₇   I   I   V₇   I

Yaraví

Translated from the Quechua

FOLK SONG OF THE PERUVIAN ANDES

In Peru we find two types of folk music — that of the coastal area, a joyful music — and that of the highlands, a district 9,000 to 12,000 feet above sea level, sparsely populated with Indians. Here it is that we hear the "Yaraví," the song of love and sorrow, a sad and slow-moving melody based on the old five-tone scale used by the Indian tribes which inhabited the land long before the coming of the Spanish Conquistadores. Just how much the melodies of the Indians of the Andes have been influenced by the folk music of Spain and by the Gregorian chant introduced into the country by the Christian padres is difficult to determine.

1. Why, O white dove, Why, my dove, O tell me, Hast thou taught, Why, why hast thou taught me?

2. Why, O white dove, Hast thou made me drink, dove, Mirk-y draught, Wa-ter of ob- liv - ion?

3. Why, O white dove, Why, my dove, O tell me, Hast thou made, Made me sleep so deep - ly?

Flower of Changunga

Flor de Changunga

ANCIENT INDIAN FOLK SONG OF MEXICO

As sung by Luis Cabrera

From the Tarascan and Spanish

In the Mexican State of Michoacan live a very highly-civilized Indian people, the Tarascos, which even in the ancient days maintained their independence against the Aztecs and still preserve much of their archaic culture.

This very old and lovely Indian dance, known as the *canacuas*, originated in the mountainous region of Michoacan before the Conquest and has been handed down from generation to generation. It is the fiesta of crowns (Canacuas, in Tarasca, the language of the Michoacan Indians, means crowns) a ceremonial of hospitality which originally was part of the marriage festivities. There are no crowns used in the fiesta today but garlands and branches of flowers are used instead. The loveliest Tarascan melodies are used in this festival and for this reason it is the best loved of all Michoacan folk customs. "Flor de Changunga" is sung by one of the *guaris* (unmarried maidens) during the latter part of the ceremony. Her lament is interrupted by the chorus of other *guaris* commenting in a single phrase, "Ah, thou art far away!"

These songs exist today in a jumble of Spanish words mixed with Tarascan, which leads one to believe that the original texts have been lost. The translation is a very free one which merely attempts to preserve the general feeling of the song.

APOLLO INSPIRING THE YOUNG POET, BY NICOLAS POUSSIN

MUSIC AND PAINTING

The arts of music and painting are both expressive of man's inner sense of beauty. Great music is movement always in perfection. Great painting is movement caught in a moment of perfection. The classical composers achieved structural unity through the balance of themes, tonalities, and rhythms. The painter draws the eye to a center of interest through the medium of lines and forms.

The picture, "Apollo Inspiring the Young Poet," by the great French master, Nicolas Poussin (1594–1665), is one of the finest examples of classical painting. Here we find an arrangement of figures solidly built upon the idea of balance and proportion. Possessing beauty of line, it is like melody in music. The interplay of light and shade lends poetic charm. Apollo, the god of music, resting on his lyre, points to the manuscript of the poet, whose upward glance indicates the moment of inspiration. The attendant muse on the left, classically draped, gives balance to the composition. Complete harmony of design is achieved through the two cherubs. And so the melody, harmony, and rhythm of music find their counterpart in this famous picture. (*See* Unit VIII: Songs of the Classical Period, p. 64.)

It is interesting to realize that just as in music the Romantic Period followed the Classical, so likewise in painting the desire to express individual emotion succeeded the emphasis on pure design. On p. 201, "Recollection of a Meadow near Brunoy," is a typical example of the Romantic School of painting by the great French master, Corot (1796–1875). Unlike the classicist, Poussin, Corot never defines objects sharply. A diaphanous mist veils the verdure of nature. A vaporous haze, shot with silver sparks of light so typical of the work of this master, suggests the lyrical charm of the Romantic composers. Corot conveys a feeling of spaciousness through the scale of the figures against the trees. The beautiful distribution of light and shade, together with the accents of rich color, give a feeling of unity. The Romantic painter here seeks to convey emotion and feeling through closer contact with nature. It is a beautiful pattern of rhythm through the re-creation of nature in one of her most joyous moods, with a perfect blending of form, line, tone, and color. (*See* Unit XI: Songs of the Romantic Period, p. 117; also the painting, "The Blind Violinist," by Irolli, p. 188, and Unit XVII: Songs of Modern Composers, p. 189.)

UNIT XI: SONGS OF THE ROMANTIC PERIOD

with Appreciation Notes by LILLIAN L. BALDWIN

At the close of the eighteenth century the long-threatened storm broke over the polite world of court society. Poor folk who had gone cold and hungry to pay for the artificial elegance of court life had reached the limit of their endurance. Thinking men were determined to change conditions under which so many human beings lived miserably. Strangely enough, the first blow for personal liberty was struck in the far-away colonies of America. Soon, people everywhere were demanding the right to "life, liberty, and the pursuit of happiness." Revolution spread throughout Europe and greatly modified the social, political, and economic conditions of all classes of society. For the first time in the world's history, individuals became more important than classes.

Freedom always makes men sing. Now the joy in what seemed to be a new and better world found expression in a great outburst of lyric poetry. Poets no longer sang of gods and goddesses or of pretty make-believe shepherdesses. They sang of real men and women and even of the joys and sorrows of their own hearts.

With this new interest in people came also a new love of country. "Why," said the poets, "should our plays and operas take their stories from Greek mythology when we have beautiful old legends of our own?" And they began to search forgotten books and manuscripts for the hero tales which had delighted their own great-grandfathers.

They found these tales written in the quaint languages of the days of knighthood. Because these medieval languages had grown from Latin or Roman roots they were called "Romance Languages" and the fanciful tales they recorded were known as "Romances." Gradually the word romance widened its meaning until today a romance is not merely a tale of medieval chivalry but any fanciful story of love and adventure. And its adjective, romantic, as any good dictionary will tell you, means picturesque, imaginative, and is used to describe any musical or literary work in which the emphasis is on feeling or emotion rather than the classical emphasis on form.

Romantic is a perfect word for the music of the nineteenth century for it is music in which form gives way to feeling. Composers were no longer content to work out lovely designs in tone and to express general moods. Like the poets, they wanted to express particular and personal feelings and definite pictures. The composer of the Classical Period wrote his quiet piece, called it simply *Andante*, and left the listener to his own imagination. But the Romantic composer wished his hearer to see the particular picture which he had in mind as he wrote and so he called his quiet mood "Evening." Later romanticists even tried to express in tones whole series of pictures of the incidents of a story. They are called "realists."

Often the old formal patterns would not fit these new ideas. For example, the sonata pattern, with its elaborate detail, was too long and too varied for a little single-mood sketch called "Evening." Or perhaps the sonata themes, recurring every so often as they must to complete the design, might not agree with the incidents in a musical story, such as that of "Romeo and Juliet." And since the mood or the story was now considered more important than the manner in which it was told, composers did not hesitate to alter the old forms or to make new ones to suit their purposes.

The poetry and romance of the nineteenth century quite naturally made it the century of song. Composers of the Classical Period had written songs but, true to the fashion of their day, they had cared only for charming,

FRANZ SCHUBERT

smoothly-balanced tunes which suited the general spirit of the poem they were using. Indeed, to them a poem was little more than a peg upon which to hang a tune.

But with Schubert came a completely new kind of song in which the composer followed the poet line by line, suiting his music to the changing moods of the verse. Schubert's "Erlking," [1] in which the melody tells the story as plainly as the words while the accompaniment of galloping hoofs gives all the excitement of that wild ride with Death, marks a turning-point in the history of song writing. Never again would people be satisfied to hear a dramatic poem sung to an uneventful ballad tune, the same for every stanza, and with an insignificant chordal accompaniment.

This new type of song, in which the music follows the verses, reflecting their varying moods, is said to be "through-composed," and is called the *Art Song*. It was the first important musical innovation of the nineteenth century.

But this great wave of poetry and feeling, which marks the nineteenth century as the Romantic Period in the history of music, by no means swept away the work of the masters of the Classical Period. Schubert, the creator of the art song, wrote symphonies, beautiful singing symphonies of perfect pattern; Schumann, the poet of the piano, wrote masterly chamber music; Mendelssohn, the musical landscape painter and composer of *Songs Without Words*, was also a composer of overtures and sonatas; and Brahms, whose songs many people think the most beautiful and romantic of all, wrote four master symphonies that would have made Beethoven shout for joy.

In art, as in life, growth does not mean discarding the past for the present. Where would a tree be if we lopped off last year's branches in our enthusiasm for this year's shoots? And so it is with music. The romantic movement was simply a shifting of emphasis from one phase of music to another, a new branch, we might say, which grew from the old and made the whole tree more symmetrical and beautiful.

[1] A listening lesson on this greatest of all descriptive songs is excellent preparation for studying the songs of this unit.

The Hurdy-Gurdy Man

Der Leiermann

From the German, by
LILLIAN L. BALDWIN

FRANZ SCHUBERT (1797–1828)

With "The Hurdy-Gurdy Man," the *Winter Journey* song cycle reaches a disconsolate end. The picture of the old man standing barefoot in the snow, holding out his empty plate and playing tunes to which no one will listen, is doubly pathetic to those who know the tragic story of Schubert's life.

He, too, had known the bitterness of playing his tunes to unheeding ears. Seldom fell a penny on his little plate, and in his poverty he afterward sold these same wonderful *Winter Journey* songs, whose faded manuscripts are now worth a fortune, for twenty-three cents apiece!

The music of this great little song is a miracle of emptiness. There is only the monotonous melody, telling the story of the old man, and the hurdy-gurdy accompaniment with its drone bass and melancholy little tune ground out by the stiffened fingers.

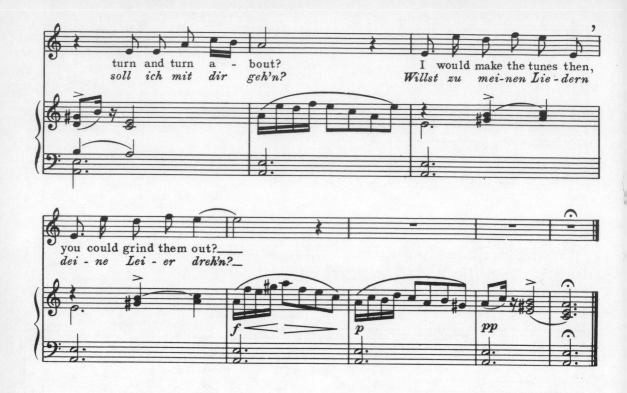

turn and turn a - bout?
soll ich mit dir geh'n?

I would make the tunes then,
Willst zu mei-nen Lie-dern

you could grind them out?___
dei - ne Lei - er dreh'n?__

Serenade

FRANZ SCHUBERT (1797–1828)

Of all the Schubert songs, none is better known or more beloved than the "Serenade." It was the first of his songs to achieve widespread popularity in America and led people to want to know his other great songs and symphonies. Full of the magic of moonlight, of fragrant night winds, and the tenderness of young love, the "Serenade" is typical of the Romantic Period.

SOPRANOS

Through the leaves the night-winds mov-ing Mur - mur low and sweet,
Moon-light on the earth is sleep-ing, Wa - ters whis-per low,

To_thy dream-ing heart,   To_thy dream-ing heart.
Sleep and dream in peace,   Sleep and dream in peace.

D CODA
mf **Animato**

Sad - ly in the for - est mourn - ing   Wails   the whip-poor-

Sad - ly in the for - est mourn - ing

To the Sunshine

An den Sonnenschein

Translated from the German of Reinick

ROBERT SCHUMANN (1810–1856)

Schumann called the year 1840 "my great song year," and a truly great year it was that could produce one hundred and thirty-eight Schumann songs, nearly every one a masterpiece. Up to this time Schumann had devoted himself to piano music, but in this the year of his marriage all the joy of his life overflowed in song. "I could sing myself to death like a nightingale," he wrote to his fiancée. With such a happy background it is small wonder that these songs, so fresh and free, seem almost to have sung themselves.

The piano does much more than accompany the melody in Schumann's songs. It introduces the voice with charming little preludes, makes the final comment after the poem is done, and, like a second voice, answers the singer in alternating phrases.

Schumann had a keen appreciation of poetry and in his songs the music echoes and intensifies every beauty of the verse.

One cannot imagine a more joyous song than "To the Sunshine." The music seems to soar on happy wings and every bright note reflects the poet's lines.

heart of mine, And wak-est with thy ar-dent beams, With-in my breast Love's
Herz hin-ein, weckst drin-nen lau-ter Lie-bes-lust, dass mir so en-ge____

sweet-est dreams.
wird die Brust.

Too nar-row are my room and home,
Und en-ge wird mir Stub' und Haus,

And out of doors when-e'er I roam, Thine eye doth pierce the
und wenn ich lauf' zum Thor hin-aus, da lockst du gar in's

ver-dant shades, And glanc-es on the fair-est maids, And glanc-es on the
fri-sche Grün, die al-ler-schön-sten Mäd-chen hin, die al-ler schön-sten

fair - est maids!
Mäd - chen!

O sun-shine bright, dost
O Son - nen-schein, du

Sun - shine,

think I'll prove, Like thee, in-con - stant in my love, And kiss each fair half-
glau-best wohl, dass ich wie du es ma-chen soll, der je - de schmu-cke

I'll prove,

kiss each

o - pen flow'r That blos-soms in its__ leaf - y bow'r? Hast thou so long kept
Blu - me küsst, die__ e - ben nur sich__ dir er-schliesst. Hast doch so lang die

flow'r__

watch a - bove, And know-est not how true my love? Why
Welt er-blickt, und weiss, dass sich's für mich nicht schickt? Was

trou - ble then this heart of mine? O sun - shine! O sun - shine!
machst du mir denn sol - che Pein? O Son - nen-schein, O Son - nen-schein!

Little Folk Song

Volksliedchen

From the German, by
LORENE HOYT

ROBERT SCHUMANN (1810–1856)

In this delicate "Little Folk Song," so called because of its almost childlike simplicity, we find both Schumann and his poet in whimsical mood. She must have been very naïve, this maiden who confesses that when she goes into the garden in the early morning in her green hat (as though that had anything to do with it!), her first thought is, "What is my sweetheart doing now?" She grows quite dramatic, and so does Schumann, vowing that there is not a star in the sky which she would not give him. Why, she would gladly give him her heart itself — if she could take it out! Then, back again to the green hat and that first thought, "What is he doing now?"

Both the poem and the music imitate the familiar A–B–A pattern appropriate to a folk song. But there is a playful touch, artful in its simplicity, that betrays the hand of a master.

Tone Blending Drills: Use small sections of the song for this purpose.

Harmonic Analysis: Try to determine the key successions in the swiftly changing transitions.

Each star in heav'n I'd give To him, if I could do it. My heart I'd give him, too, If on-ly he but knew it. 'Mong the flow'rs at ear-ly morn, In hat of green so

Am Him-mel steht kein Stern, den ich dem Freund nicht gönn-te, mein Herz gäb' ich ihm gern, wenn ich's her-aus thun konn-te. Wenn ich früh in den Gar-ten geh', in mei-nem grü-nen

gay, In my heart I am think-ing, "What does my Love to-
Hut, ist mein er - ster Ge - dan - ke, was nun mein Lieb - ster

fp

rit.

day?" In my heart I am think - ing, "What does my Love to -
thut, ist mein er - ster Ge - dan - ke, was nun mein Lieb - ster
rit.

rit.

day?"
thut.

In the Woods

Waldfahrt

From the German of F. Körner, by
LORENE HOYT

ROBERT FRANZ, Op. 14, No. 3 (1815–1892)

"Fresh and bright," Franz marks this song and in those two words he gives both directions and description. The lilting melody accompanied by gay ascending triplets seems as fresh and joyous as the woods on a summer morning.

ROBERT FRANZ

cresc.

glad in the joy- -ous gleam Of the clear blue
stirred by the gen- -tle breeze As we lin- -ger
lacht und in's Herz___ hin- ein das___ Him- -mel -
Blu- men ein ko- sen- der Wind, und ich wieg' und

cresc.

sky and the sun's bright beam, In wood - lands,
un- der the spread- -ing trees, In wood - lands,
blau und der Son- -nen- schein im Wald', im
küs- se dich, herz'- -ges Kind, im Wald', im

shad - y wood- -lands. The
shad - y wood- -lands. When
küh- len Wal- -de. Im
küh- len Wal- -de. Glüht

red through the branch-es the sun-set ray Sends
roth durch die Zwei-ge der A- bend-schein, und

twi- -light shad-ows at close of day,
däm- -mert lei - se die Nacht her - ein;

Home- ward we stroll— and seek —— our rest,——
dann zieh'n wir heim,— dann klingt—— und blüht——

Filled with the peace of the wood - lands blest— The
Wald - lust, Wald - rau - schen noch durch's Ge - müth vom

wood - lands, shad - y wood - lands.
Wald', vom küh - len Wal - de.

Evening Song

Abends

From the German of Eichendorff

ROBERT FRANZ, Op. 16, No. 4 (1815–1892)

In this lovely evening song Franz proves himself a true Romanticist, a creator of moods. It is a nature picture done in softest pastel shades. The melody, smooth and subdued as the graying light, moves to a rhythm gentle as the swaying of treetops in the night wind. It rises to a climax as delicate as the first glimpse of the evening star, then sinks·back into silence. More expressive than any words, lines, or colors is this music, for as we sing or listen we actually feel the quiet and the wistfulness of twilight.

air.
Wald.

All the world now seeks re-pose;
Al - les geht zu sei - ner Ruh',

On - ly in the gloam - ing
Wald und Welt ver - sau - sen,

On the wea - ry wan - d'rer goes
schau - ernd hört der Wan - drer zu,

Through the for - est roam - ing;
sehnt sich wohl nach Hau - se;

But while herds are slow - ly hom - ing,
hier in Wal - des grü - ner Klau - se,

Thou, my heart, shall find re - pose.
Herz, geh' end - lich du auch zu Ruh'.

Come Soon

Komm Bald

From the German of Klaus Groth, by
LORENE HOYT

JOHANNES BRAHMS, Op. 97, No. 5 (1833–1897)

Brahms was a philosopher. He was also a shy and rather unsocial bachelor. He took life and music seriously and in his instrumental works, the great symphonies and concertos, he is sometimes accused of being austere and self-contained. But there is nothing heavy or overserious in the Brahms of the songs. Here we meet a man with heart as warm as his head is cool, and we marvel at the variety of his moods and the lightness of his fancy.

Simplicity is one of the hall-marks of true greatness. This little song is as typical of Brahms and as much a test of his genius as one of the elaborate symphonies. Unpretentious as a folk song, warmly human, and as intimate as a personal message, every note shows the touch of the master hand.

JOHANNES BRAHMS

see;
Traum.

But of them
Und von den

all most ten-der and true,
Lie - ben, die mir ge - treu,

To me most
und mir ge -

love - ly, my own, 'tis you;
blie - ben, wärst du da - bei,

'Tis
wärst

you, my own,— 'tis you!
du, wärst du da - bei!

May Night

Die Mainacht

From the German of Ludwig Hölty, by
PHYLLIS McGINLEY

JOHANNES BRAHMS, Op. 43, No. 2 (1833–1897)

Quietly following the steps of the diatonic chord, as was Brahms' habit, the lovely "May Night" creates the mood of the lover's longing. There is something strangely appealing in that held high note (in the German it always comes on the word, "tears"), which lingers for a moment like slow tears, then, brimming over, falls in a gentle sub-dominant chord. But the real magic of the "May Night" lies in the breath-taking harmonies of the last four measures. This is the great Brahms speaking in a language which no words can ever translate.

UNIT XII: HERE COMES THE BAND

At "pep" rallies, on the athletic field, in local celebrations, the marching band is always a center of interest in school events. Scarcely a junior or senior high school in the country but has its well-organized band, of which the student body is justly proud and to which it is an honor to belong. Neat and striking uniforms, well-drilled formations under a dashing drum major, and, especially, richly sonorous and rhythmic performance are the essentials of an effective marching band.

The fundamental difference between an orchestra and a band is the presence or absence of stringed instruments. The strings — violins, violas, 'cellos, double basses — are the tonal basis of the orchestra, with woodwinds, brasses, and instruments of percussion adding contrast, color, and climax. The band, on the other hand, consists wholly of woodwinds, brasses, and percussion. In the finer bands these choirs are enriched by the inclusion of a wider variety of each type of instrument than is required for the orchestra. The swing and sonority of the band are especially appealing, and the readiness with which the early steps of instruction can be covered makes the formation of school bands relatively simple and highly practicable. The band has always been a popular form of musical expression, and today junior and senior high schools throughout the country have developed a large number of splendid bands both for marching and concert, fully equipped in every detail and playing the best music in thoroughly artistic performance.

Make a list of instruments used in the band of your own school and check it with the list of instruments in the score on p. 146.

THE MARCHING BAND
John Adams High School, Cleveland, Ohio
Amos G. Wesler, Director

EDWIN FRANKO GOLDMAN AND HIS BAND

Everybody thrills to the strains of a band. The feet are lifted and the pulse beats quicker. The whole world marches to the music of the band. But the modern band not only leads the procession, it also presents concerts of fine symphonic music.

A famous pioneer in the movement to refine and elevate band music is Edwin Franko Goldman, widely known as the founder of the symphony band. His summer evening concerts on the spacious mall of Central Park in New York City have set new standards for band performance. Dr. Goldman is also a composer of distinguished attainment in the field of the band. He has written a large number of works, mostly marches, among which his "On the Mall" ranks with the most popular marches ever composed.

By training, experience, and interest, Dr. Goldman is eminently qualified as the ranking American band leader. He was born in Louisville, Kentucky, of a family of internationally famous musicians, which moved to New York while he was still a boy. There he studied composition with Antonín Dvořák and cornet with the celebrated Jules Levy. For ten years he was a member of the Metropolitan Opera Orchestra, joining the organization at the age of seventeen — the youngest musician ever to hold so responsible a position with that orchestra. During this time he played under the world renowned conductors, Damrosch, Hertz, Mottl, Toscanini, and others — an invaluable experience. He left the orchestra to devote his time to teaching and conducting, and ten years later to establish the now famous band which bears his name.

Dr. Goldman has always taken a deep interest in improving and elevating band music and band performances and in utilizing the band as an agency for spreading an interest in good music. To his imagination and initiative is due the foundation of the American Bandmasters' Association, of which he was the first President, and is now Honorary Life President. In recent years, Dr. Goldman has been widely in demand as guest conductor and has given unstintingly of his time and effort in the cause of band music. Especially is this true of the great army of school bands throughout the country to whom Dr. Goldman generously contributes his services constantly, encouraging and inspiring the young musicians to worthwhile endeavor.

On the Mall

MARCH

ADELAIDE MAIBRUNN

EDWIN FRANKO GOLDMAN

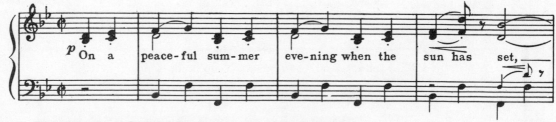

On a peace-ful sum-mer eve-ning when the sun has set,

By permission of Carl Fischer, Inc., owners of the copyright.

On the Mall

MARCH

Theme from the Trio, Band Score

Edwin Franko Goldman

THE CONCERT BAND
The Goldman Band, Edwin Franko Goldman, Conductor

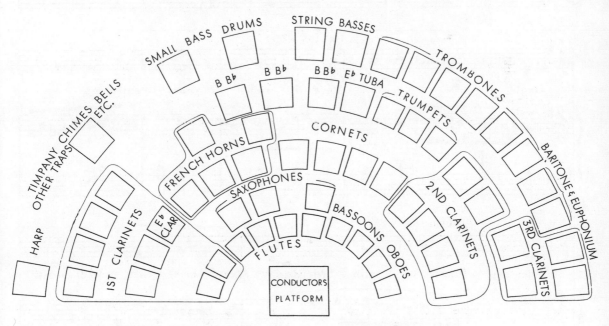

SEATING PLAN OF THE GOLDMAN BAND

The Goldman Band, it will be noted, follows the general seating plan of the orchestra in that the clarinets, like the violins of the orchestra, are seated across the front of the platform. Basses are in the rear-center, horns and percussion to the left, and brasses to the right of the audience. This plan provides for both delicacy and sonority, and for well-marked contrasts of the different instrumental colors. Many bands follow the plan of massing the clarinets to the left of the conductor and the cornets to his right. Some bands place percussion in rear-center and basses across both sides of the rear of the stage.

147

UNIT XIII: A LITTLE NONSENSE NOW AND THEN

Is relished by the wisest men.

Anonymous

The Kitchen Kalendar

Hugh Lofting

Mark Andrews

Brightly (♩ = 132)

Zum Zum   Zum Zum   *(hum or whistle)*

rit.   Pas - try and Bun day

Ought to be Mon-day. Then I - rish Stew's day   Falls on a

Tues-day. Dine - out - with - friends day,   Let's make that Wednes-day.

SOPRANOS and ALTOS

Next, Ap-ple - pie day Should al-ways be Fri - day.

Sau - sage - in - bat-ter day, Put that down
Sau - sage - in - bat-ter day, Sat-ur-day. But

what a - bout Sun-day? Oh, take a rest

one day, (hum or whistle) Take a rest — one day.

slow   fast
slow   fast

There Is a Tavern in the Town

Traditional

AMERICAN COLLEGE SONG

going to leave you, Going to leave you now.

may the world go well with thee.

may the world go well with thee.

Jingle Medley

OLD SONGS

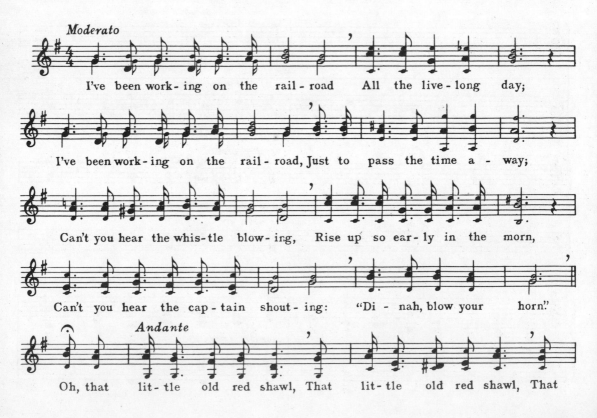

Moderato

I've been work-ing on the rail-road All the live-long day;

I've been work-ing on the rail-road, Just to pass the time a-way;

Can't you hear the whis-tle blow-ing, Rise up so ear-ly in the morn,

Can't you hear the cap-tain shout-ing: "Di-nah, blow your horn."

Andante

Oh, that lit-tle old red shawl, That lit-tle old red shawl, That

This Is the House That Jack Built

Traditional

OLD ENGLISH CATCH

UNIT XIV: ANGLO-SAXON FOLK TUNES IN AMERICA

by JOHN POWELL

Folk music is the natural expression in melody of the characteristic moods, emotions, tastes, and aspirations of a people. It is the result of a process of tradition — passing tunes from person to person and from generation to generation. As the tunes were not written down and standardized manifold changes and variations occurred in them. These changes might result from faulty memory of the singer or from conscious or unconscious impulse on his part to improve the tunes. And so, with the passage of time, these tunes would become ever a more perfect expression of the feelings and tastes of the bearers of the tradition. Music is as much a language as speech: it is not the language of the mind, but of the heart. And so folk music is the supreme expression of the soul of a people.

In order to appreciate the full flavor of folk music, those peculiarities which distinguish it from art music must constantly be borne in mind. Chief of these is the fact that its message is given exclusively in terms of melody, independent of any harmonic basis or background.

Harmony made its appearance in music in relatively recent times. It brought enormous color and variety to music. But it brought serious disadvantages, too, chiefly the limitation and cramping of melody to conform to harmonic convenience. Folk music, however, did not suffer from this disadvantage, for these melodies come to us from a time when harmony was non-existent. Their persistence through the centuries in the mouths and hearts of the folk show that they possess the special excellencies of the pre-harmonic period, namely, vigor, poignancy, and finely-knit organization. The folk music of the English-speaking peoples is large and varied and in no respect inferior to that of any other people. On the contrary, it has a wider range of emotional expression, more subtle gradations of mood: it may have tragedy without melodrama, tenderness without sentimentality, sadness without bathos, gaiety without frivolity, unrestrained high spirits without banality, rakish humor without vulgarity.

Some of the characteristics of Anglo-Saxon folk music are: contrast produced by varying length of phrases; contrast produced by varying length of measures; frequent occurrence of melodies in five or seven time; frequent occurrence of wide intervals; wider melodic compass than is usual in composed tunes; freedom from conventional modulation, actual or implied, to the dominant at the midway cadence; prevalence of modal tunes.

Most fascinating in this folk music is the use of the ancient modes, for three hundred years virtually forgotten in art music, relegated to obscurity by the conveniences of harmony. The modes are scales of the same general type as our familiar major scale. The most usual can be formed on the piano by using only the white keys: The Ionian Mode, from C to C, is identical in its successive steps with the major scale; from D to D is the Dorian Mode; the Phrygian is from E to E; the Lydian from F to F; from G to G, the Mixolydian; from A to A, the Aeolian, identical in steps with our natural minor scale. It is immediately evident that the half-tone steps which come between the third and fourth and the seventh and eighth degrees of the major scale, vary in position in each of these modes; also that only the Ionian and Lydian have a leading tone; all the others have a minor seventh. The resulting unexpectedness of the intervals and emphasis on unusual degrees of the scale, give these modal tunes their unparalleled charm and originality.

In the songs selected for our present purpose, three are Ionian: "Pretty Sally," "The Deaf Woman's Courtship," and "The Frog Went Co'tin'"; "The Two Brothers" is Dorian, and "At the Foot of Yonders Mountain" is Hexatonic, that is, uses only six tones of the scale. As the missing tone is the seventh degree of the scale, it is possible to harmonize this tune either as Ionian or Mixolydian.

In general it may be said of Anglo-Saxon folk tunes that they are remarkable not only for their charm of color, their ear-taking melodiousness, their compelling rhythm, all of which are irresistibly captivating to all hearers whether musically versed or not, but even more on account of aesthetic qualities which only the highly-trained musician can fully appreciate. A critical analysis of these tunes, judged by the most stringent standards, would show that they are well nigh flawless, and have seldom been excelled even by composers of surpassing genius.

Consequently, my purpose in supplying harmonic settings was not to cover flaws or lack of interest in the melodies but rather to interpret them to ears unaccustomed to listening to tunes as sheer melody. I have added nothing extraneous, but have confined myself to emphasis on those qualities inherent in the melodies themselves. I have avoided modulation, altered intervals, and dissonances in order that the accompaniments may be in keeping with the matter and style of the originals, with strict adherence to the respective modes. While trying to keep them as simple as possible, I have not "written down to children." Recollections of my own childhood make me keenly aware that boys and girls even as young as twelve are as sensitive as their elders to emotional appeal and appropriate texture in music. For this reason I have not doubled the melody in unison in the accompaniment. Possibly younger children may need this support, but by the age of twelve young folks should be set free from such leading-strings.

If the rhythm at times seems complicated, let it be remembered that young people have become familiar with far more involved rhythmic patterns through their radio contact with recent popular music.

If the range of some of the tunes seems wide for youthful voices, let it be remembered that for generations young people have been singing these melodies with pleasure and profit, and that, too, without benefit of instruction from private teachers or in the schools. As a matter of fact, these tunes present little difficulty when sung in the proper and natural way, without self-consciousness, with due concentration upon the meaning and enunciation of the words, with no straining after sonority. We must not forget that these are folk songs and not operatic arias.

157

Pretty Sally

Ionian Mode

Recorded by John Powell from the singing of
Mrs. Nancy Baldwin of White Top, Virginia.

Traditional

Arranged by JOHN POWELL

This ballad, less ancient than the others in this unit, is widely extant in America and is a great favorite. Of particular interest is the survival of a very ancient folk custom, namely, the ritual dancing at the grave of a deceased loved-one as an expression of grief and respect (*see* stanza 8).

The melody is one of the most charming that I have found in Virginia and is obviously older than the words. It has quite a marked Scandinavian flavor. I have left the turns and grace notes in the first measure of the tune, as they are very characteristic of the style of the folk singer. If this should prove too difficult, they may be omitted.

mf 1. There was a rich la - dy from Lon-don she came, She
was a poor doc - tor was liv - ing hard by, Who
Sal - ly, dear Sal-ly, Pret - ty Sal - ly," said he, "Can you

called her - self Sal - ly, Pret - ty Sal - ly by name, Her
on this fair dam - sel in — love cast his eye. He
tell me the rea - son our — love can't a - gree? Your

wealth it was more than the — king — he pos-sessed, Her
court - ed her night - ly, a — year — and a day, But
cru - el un - kind - ness my — ru - in will prove Un -

Stanzas 1-8

beau-ty was more than her wealth at the best.
still she re-fused him and ev-er said, nay.
less all your ha-tred will turn in-to love."

2. *p* There
3. *f* "O

Stanza 9

now you must leave me in sor-row and pain."

4. *p* "No hatred I bear you, nor no other man;
But truly to fancy you I never can.
Give over your courting, I pray you be still;
For you I'll ne'er marry of my own free will."

5. *m* 'Twas soon after this, ere a year had passed by,
Pretty Sally grew sick and she feared she would die.
She tangled was in love and herself she accused,
So sent for the doctor she once had refused.

6. *f* "O am I the doctor whose skill you would try,
Or am I the young man you once did deny?"
p "Yes, you are the doctor can kill or can cure;
Unless you will help me, I'm dying, 'tis sure."

7. *f* "O Sally, Pretty Sally, O Sally," said he,
"O don't you remember how you slighted me?
You treated me lightly, my love you did scorn,
So now you must suffer for things past and gone."

8. *p* "If they are past and gone, love, forget and forgive,
And suffer me longer in this world to live."
"I ne'er can forgive you until my dying day;
But on your grave I'll dance when you're laid in cold clay."

9. *m* She pulled from her fingers, then diamond rings three,
p Saying, "Take these and wear them while dancing on me;
I freely forgive you, though me you disdain.
So now you must leave me in sorrow and pain."

At the Foot of Yonders Mountain

Hexatonic melody, harmonized in the Ionian Mode

Recorded by Annabel Morris Buchanan from the
singing of Mrs. Lillie Williams of Marion, Virginia.

Traditional

Arranged by JOHN POWELL

This folk song is one of the most widespread in the Virginia oral tradition. Certain of its features have been incorporated into other songs. Despite its purely lyrical character, it has profound and mysterious connections with the pre-Christian era, being derived from an ancient religious song in Cornwall, which in medieval times evolved into a Latin hymn to the Virgin. The tune as here given has rhythmic movement and lyric fluency, and several structural pauses make the melody one of exquisite tenderness and beauty and set forth the deeper vigor and charm of the basic pattern. The text shows the high degree of lyric tenderness and finish to which folk poetry may attain.

proper, and her ways they are feat; I _____ ask no bet-ter
tain her on __ sil-ver and gold, And _____ as man-y oth-er
wa-ters just__ for to let her know I _____ think of pret-ty
win-dow all__ night long and cry That_____ for love of pret-ty

1.2.3.

pas-time than to be__with my sweet.
fine things as my love's house can hold.
Ma-ry wher-ev-er I go.
Ma-ry I__ glad-ly would

4.

die.

rall. *a tempo*

espress.

Ped. *Ped.*

The Frog Went Co'tin'

Ionian Mode

Recorded by John Powell from the singing
of Mrs. John Hunter of Richmond, Virginia.

Arranged by JOHN POWELL

Traditional

"The Frog Went Co'tin'" comes of a large and very ancient family of folk ballads which has had an enormously wide dispersal. It is found all over the United States, in England, Ireland, Scotland, and Wales, and is even said to have existed in ancient Greece. As an example of the attributing of human qualities to animals, it obviously derives from the most primitive folk lore. It at once suggests Aesop, Reynard, Kipling's Mowgli stories, Uncle Remus, and innumerable other folk tales.

Like many such rhymes in our tradition, it has often been parodied and made the vehicle of biting political irony. A notable example is "The Frog He Would a-Wooing Go, Whether His Mother Would Let Him or No," which is said to have been aimed at Henry the Eighth's courtship of Anne Boleyn, despite the disapproval of Mother Church. In America there are countless variants which in a general way can be divided into five classes in accordance with their different refrains, namely, "Hm-hmm," "Sing-song Kitty, Can't You Kimeo," "Roly-poly, Gammon and Spinach," "Kitty Alone," and "Toora-loora-lay." To this last group belongs our present version.

Too - ra, loo - ra - lay.____ The Frog went co'-tin' and
Too - ra, loo - ra - lay.____ He rode up to____ Miss

he did ride, His sword and pis - tol by____ his side, Sing
Mous - e's hall, He gave a loud knock and then a loud call, Sing

too - ra - loo, too - ra - loo, Too - ra, loo - ra -
too - ra - loo, too - ra - loo, Too - ra, loo - ra -

Ending for stanzas 1 through 15

lay.____ *p* 2. He

Ending for stanza 16

lay.

3

mf "O Mistress Mouse, are you within?
With your long nose and narrow chin?"

4

p Said Mistress Mouse,"I am within,
O yes, kind Sir, I sit and spin."

5

mf "O Mistress Mouse, will you marry me?
And if you do, a queen you'll be."

6

p "Oh! I cannot consent to that,
Until I ask my Uncle Rat."

7

mf Then Uncle Rat came riding home.
Said,"Who's been here since I've been gone?"

8

p "There has been here a gentleman,
Who says he'll wed me if he can."

9

mf Then Uncle Rat went back to town,
To buy Miss Mouse her wedding gown.

10

p "What shall the wedding supper be?
A crust of bread and a cup of tea."

11

mf "Where shall the wedding supper be?
Up in the crotch of th'old peach tree."

12

p Then first came in the Bumble bee,
Who played the bagpipe on his knee.

13

mf And next came in a Hoppergrass,
Who danced the hornpipe first and last.

14

p The next to come was Mistress Cat,
Who danced a jig with Uncle Rat.

15

mf Then Mistress Mouse was put to bed,
And Mistress Cat slept at the head.

16

p Then Mistress Cat did eat Miss Mouse,
And that was the end of that old House.

The Two Brothers

Dorian Mode

Recorded by John Powell from the singing of
Mrs. Mary E. Hicks of Albemarle County, Virginia

Arranged by JOHN POWELL

Traditional

This very old ballad, probably extinct in the oral tradition in England and Scotland, is very frequent in America, having been recorded from oral tradition in North Carolina, Virginia, Massachusetts, New York, West Virginia, Mississippi, Nebraska, Indiana, Kentucky, and Missouri.

The striking and powerful Dorian melody is one of the most unusual and beautiful in my collection, especially in its rhythmic structure. Note the cumulative expansion of phrase in the first three measures: the first containing 4 eighths; the second, 5; and the third, 6 (¾); followed by a return to the regular ⁴⁄₄ time, as inexorable as the hammer strokes of fate.

bur - ied in cold clay"

cresc.

ff dramaticamente

rall.

a tempo

dim.   *mf*   *f*

Ⓟed.   ✻

3

mp "I'll neither play at tossing stones
   Nor neither will play at ball;
   But I'll go up to yon green hill
   And there we'll wrestle a fall."

4

p They wrestled up, they wrestled down,
   The younger fell to the ground;
   A penknife in his brother's pouch
   Gave him a deathly wound.

5

mf "O brother, take my holland shirt
   And split it from gore to gore,
   And bind it 'round my bleeding wound
   That it may bleed no more."

6

mp He's taken off the holland shirt
   And split it from gore to gore,
   He's bound it 'round the bleeding wound,
   But still it bled the more.

7

pp "O Brother, bear me in your arms
   To yonder church-yard so green;
   There hide my corpse beneath the turf,
   That it may ne'er be seen.

8

pp "My Bible bury at my head,
   My Psalter close by my feet;
   My bow and arrow at my side
   To make my rest more sweet."

9

mf "What tidings shall our father have
   When asking for his dear son?"
p "You'll say I'm to the greenwoods gone
   To teach young hounds to run."

10

mf "What tidings shall our mother hear
   When calling for her last born?"
p "You'll say that I am at the chase
   Learning to wind my horn."

11

m "O Brother, if your own true love
   Should ask me where do you stay?"
pp "You'll tell her sooth that I am dead,
   And buried in cold clay."

The Deaf Woman's Courtship

Ionian Mode

Recorded by Winston Wilkinson from the singing
of Miss Margaret Purcell of Greenwood, Virginia.

Traditional

Arranged by JOHN POWELL

This folk song is widespread in different versions in Virginia and the neighboring states. It is unexcelled in sly humor and effective comedy. The melody is closely related to that of the old Scotch song, "Maggie Lauder," which is derived from an earlier Anglo-Scottish song, "Moggy Lawther on a day."

The Virginia variants show the folk genius for adaptation. Our present version is remarkable for its melodic elocution and even more for its characterization of the two participants in the dialogue. I know of nothing in the whole realm of music more realistic than the way the old woman's voice sinks into her boots only to crack into a shrill falsetto. Note in the setting how the wooer speaks more and more softly and the old woman with ever increasing volume.

The range of the melody is very wide and there might seem to be a problem as to how to make it practicable for singing. The solution of the problem is not to treat the song as a lyric, but as a dramatic dialogue. The words should not so much be sung as spoken and the tune will take care of itself as the natural inflection evoked by the situation and the characterization.

Italy is the land of flowers, sunshine, laughter, and song. Music is heard everywhere. The boatmen sing as they guide the gondolas through the canals of Venice or ply their oars on the blue waters of the sea. The carnivals are alive with happy song — snatches of popular melodies from the familiar operas and melodies especially composed for the occasion. "Funiculi Funicula," for instance, was written by Luigi Denza in honor of the opening of the "funicular," or inclined railway up the slopes of Mt. Vesuvius. It became a universal favorite and now is accepted as typical of the Italian spirit of revelry. The songs of this unit are representative of the music of several provinces in Italy.

The Grasshopper and the Ant

Oh, come la va mai bin!

Translated from the Italian

ITALIAN FOLK SONG

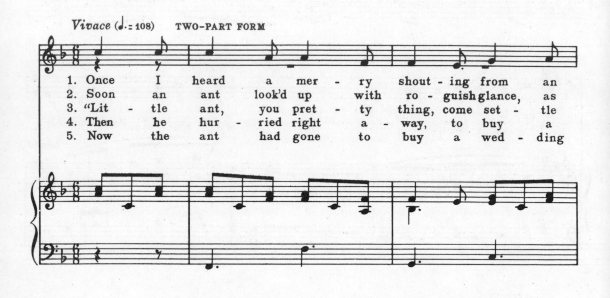

Melody from *Canzoniere Popolare Dell' Italia Settentrionale* collected by Elisabetta Oddone, published by G. Ricordi and Company.

say - ing, but he sang it lust - i - ly, O,
face, his heart was pal - pi - tat - ing fast. O,
plied, "to - day, to - night, which shall it be?" O,
slen - der lit - tle reed and broke a wing. O,
bought for mourn - ing one as black as night. O,

grass-hop-per, are you mad? O, grass-hop-per are you glad? O,
grass-hop-per, are you mad? O, grass-hop-per are you glad? O,
grass-hop-per, are you mad? O, grass-hop-per are you glad? O,
grass-hop-per, are you mad? O, grass-hop-per are you glad? O,
grass-hop-per, are you mad? O, grass-hop-per are you glad? O,

grass-hop-per, what a noise you make 'tis ver - y, ver - y bad.
grass-hop-per, have a care, it may be just a pass - ing fad.
grass-hop-per, think a - gain, you are a ver - y hast - y lad.
grass-hop-per, you will need to rest up - on a down - y pad.
grass-hop-per, such a bit - ter end - ing must be ver - y sad.

The Scissors Grinder

Il povera arrotino

Translated from the Italian

ITALIAN FOLK SONG

Moderato (♩ = 76) FORM: A, B, A, B¹; (four measure phrases)

1. Poor   scis - sors grind - er,
2. Look,   scis - sors grind - er,
3. Good   scis - sors grind - er,
4. Gay   scis - sors grind - er,
   S'è   am - ma - la - to

poor_____ scis-sors grind - er; Slow-ly you wan-der a - long the dull street,
look,_____ scis-sors grind - er; Some-one is call-ing, now work you have found,
good_____ scis-sors grind - er; Now you have mon-ey, no   more must you roam,
gay_____ scis-sors grind - er; Ar - ti-chokes, ap-ples, ba - na-nas so sweet,
l'ar - - ro - ti - no. Ti - ra - lo, ti - ra - lo, ti - ra - lo su,

1,2,3,   *4.*

Look-ing for work, that your chil - dren may eat.
Scis-sors and ra - zors and knives to be ground.
Buy what you wish for your loved ones at home.
Ti - ra - lo, ti - ra - lo, ti - ra - lo su.   All that they want to   eat!
                                                         Ti - ra - lo ca - ro biel!

Melody from *Canzoniere Popolare Dell' Italia Settentrionale* collected by Elisabetta Oddone, published by G. Ricordi and Company.

FESTA CAMPESTRE (COUNTRY FESTIVAL), BY VINCENZO IROLLI

THE MODERN SPIRIT IN ART AND MUSIC

Vivacity and light-hearted gaiety, so characteristic of folk music in Italy, are likewise to be found in its art. One of the great living Italian masters of modern painting, little known in America but acclaimed in Europe today, Vincenzo Irolli (born in Naples in 1860), gives us in this sparkling picture a glimpse into the colorful life of a rural district during the grape harvest festival. The villagers are enjoying a well-earned holiday. The guitar player leads a procession of dancing couples through arbors heavy with ripened fruit. Richness of vegetation and a profusion of flowers are suggested by the lavish use of color which pleases with its splendor without destroying the balance and harmony of the scene.

Unlike the picture by Poussin, p. 116, in which design and proportion exemplify classical art, or that by Corot, p. 201, in which a romanticist idealizes a commonplace meadow with placid charm, "Festa Campestre" represents one aspect of modern art — its vivid realism. Irolli is calling attention to the daily life of a rural community which he wants you also to know. It is characteristic of him that he looks with imaginative curiosity at objects and people, studying their unceasing motion which he reproduces in his painting with animated fervor. Because he records his impressions sanely and vigorously, we feel the everyday humanity of his pictures, a quality that gives them universal appeal and lasting success.

In contrast to the gaiety of this festival, another aspect of Irolli's power to portray everyday scenes is shown in his water color, "The Blind Violinist," reproduced on p. 188. The central figure is the aged violinist who is pathetically and courageously trying to lilt a gay tune with his fumbling fingers. About him are effectively grouped several children listening attentively to his music. As we watch them and feel as though we were actually a part of the scene depicted (one of the tests of great art), our emotions are strongly divided. First we feel a deep sympathy at the plight of the old musician, but then rejoice at the obvious enjoyment which his music is giving. Notice how differently the children respond. The older ones are absorbed but a little shy and hesitate to come too near to the player. Only the youngest is completely self-forgetful and stands close beside him, fascinated by the melody.

In this great picture Irolli not only catches and beautifully portrays for us a touching incident of everyday life, but also perfectly demonstrates how modern art combines the outstanding qualities of previous eras — the charm of design from the classical period and the appeal to emotion and sentiment from the romantic period.

The same tendency to combine the characteristics of previous eras is found in the work of the great modern composers. In Unit XVII (beginning on p. 189), you will find that all the songs are distinguished by harmonic richness, which we call "musical color." Yet, Grieg's "In the Boat" is as simple and unaffected as a folk song in strophic form, whereas we are profoundly moved by the romantic appeal of Tschaikowsky's "Only the Lonely Heart." The treatment of a beautiful melody in the classically severe form of the canon is the unique feature of "Panis Angelicus." Hugo Wolf recalls the great romanticists in "The Gardener." Perhaps Rimsky-Korsakov's song is the most obviously modern in spirit with its suggestion of the shepherd's pipe in the opening measures, for besides harmonic richness, the modern composer frequently imitates in his music the sights and sounds of the world about him.

The inclusion of the two paintings by Irolli shows graphically how pictures, like music, are universal in their appeal. Music and art are not the property of any one people or country. They are universal, reaching beyond the barriers of frontier, race, and speech to unite the hearts of men in admiration of what the ancient Greeks called, "the good, the beautiful, and the true."

Maddalena

Canzone Scherzo

Translated from the Italian

ITALIAN FOLK SONG

Harmonic Analysis: Observe that the accompaniment to Part I consists of two chords only, I and V₇.
Melody from *Canzoniere Popolare Dell' Italia Settentrionale* collected by Elisabetta Oddone, published by G. Ricordi and Company.

My Bambino

Ninna Nanna

From the Italian

ITALIAN FOLK SONG (*FLORENCE*)

1. Lull-a-by, ba - by, to sleep gen - tly
2. Rock-a-by, dear one, on branch - es of
3. Hush-a-by, pig - eon, to-geth - er we'll
   Fa - te la nan - na co-sci - ne di

go - ing, Moth-er with nee - dle and thread will be
wil - low, Scent-ed with vio - lets, your bed is a
trav - el Far to the land where our fan - cies un-
pol - lo. La vos-tra mam - ma v'ha fat - to il gon-

sew - ing, Mak-ing a col - lar, trimm'd with dain - ty
pil - low. Soft is the cov - er o - ver you I'm
rav - el. Dream-ing to-geth - er while our hearts are
nel - lo. E ve l'ha fat - to con lo smer - lo

stitch - es, Fin-er than gar - ment of silk, bought with rich - es.
plac - ing, Light as a feath - er or down is the cas - ing.
sing - ing, Mak-ing be-lieve on a cloud we are wing - ing.
inton - do Fa - te la nan - na co-sci - ne di pol - lo.

From *Le piu' belle canzoni italiane* by Benelli and Sammartino, Italian Publishers, 135 Bleeker Street, New York City.

Più lento
pp

Nin-na nan-na, nin-na nan-na, My bam-bi-no, sleep for
Nin-na nan-na nin-na nan-na il bam-bi-no e'del-la

mam-ma, Slum-ber boat is rid-ing high, My bam-bi-no, O, do not cry.
mam-ma Del-la mam-ma e di Ge-su' il bam-bi-no non pian-ge piu.

Tic-tì Tic-tà

Adapted from the Italian

GAETANO LAMA

Allegretto moderato (♩=56)

Sun - shine is smil-ing o-ver hill, o-ver dale, O-ver
Doves on the wing are float-ing down from on high Gen-tly
Bel - la mi neghi un ba-cio tu ma per-chè ma per
Pu rei co-lom-bi fan co-si van di quà van di

vine-yards and or-chards to-day;_____ Boun-te-ous har-vest, ev-'ry
coo-ing, they light here and there,_____ Bring-ing the az-ure from the
chè un ba-ciet-to neghi a me._____ Fur-ba tu di-ci sem-pre
là_____ poi si ba-cian là per là._____ Dol-ce'e ba-ciar con-vo-lut-

The Nightingale

La rumagnola

Adapted from the Italian

Melody from *Canti Popolari Emiliani*, collected by Enzo Masetti, published by G. Ricordi and Company.

plain - ing._____ 2. Ves - per
sing - ing._____ 3. In the lay - ing._____

Songs of Hellas (Greece)

Appreciation Notes by Andronike Mekelatos

The people of Greece refer to themselves as Hellenes (hĕl'-lēnz), and to their lovely country as Hellas (hĕl'ás). The ancient Hellenic culture has left its indelible impression on the world, and the high point in their civilization has always been known as the "Age of Pericles."

Modern Greece is the southernmost of the Balkan States. Surrounded by the sea on all sides except the north, there has always been great maritime activity. The country includes dozens of islands, chief of which are Corfu and Crete. The land is a series of mountain ridges and basins with flat lands of considerable fertility, traversed by small rivers and dotted with towns and villages. Athens, Salonika, Patras, and Piraeus are some of its beautiful cities. Tobacco, olives, oranges and lemons, wine and currants constitute the chief products and exports. Only one-fifth of the total area is cultivatable, yet the country is primarily agricultural.

Ancient Hellenic history is almost entirely a matter of speculation such as we get from the picture of Hellenic life described by Homer. The Trojan War is regarded as a fact. The four centuries following the Trojan War, although of the greatest importance in the formation of Hellenic society, are clothed in obscurity.

Beginning in the eighth century, B.C., and continuing into the sixth century, the Hellenes sent successive waves of colonization beyond their Aegean homeland. Wherever the Hellenes went they carried with them their distinguishing political institution, the city state. Each colony became a new self-governing nation. The colonists clung tenaciously to their language, religion, and social customs.

As early as the seventh and sixth centuries, B.C., Hellenic art began to break away from Oriental influence and to assume the characteristics of native genius. It was in this period that the Hellenic culture threw off the first sparks destined to illumine for centuries the lands touching the Mediterranean, and to affect profoundly all subsequent civilizations.

Beyond any question much of the folk music sung and danced in modern Greece is of very great antiquity, some of it coming down from the days when the greatest glory of the world was found in ancient Hellas. It is natural, too, that much of this music still shows the influence of the Orient. For many years the country was under the

Pastoral

domination of Turkey. To the war for independence, 1821, the people owe their great mass of popular ballads. They are known as *Kleftika*, because they tell stories about the *klĕftĕs*, or mountaineer bandits of Turkish times.

Hellenic music has also been influenced greatly by the ancient Byzantine forms used in the ritual of the Orthodox Church.

Up until recent years the bards, or minstrels wandered throughout Hellas singing the old epic poems of the past glories of their country. They accompanied themselves on rude hand harps or lyres. A favorite instrument of the folk is the flute, or pipe, which is similar to our oboe and is played by being blown at the end. In many pastoral songs after each verse a curious refrain is played on this pipe as though the singer were engaging in a few dance steps by way of interlude. The lute, the santouri, the violin, and the pipe, or aulos, are the instruments in general use today.

Unkle Johnnie

Μπάρμπα Γιάννης

Adapted from the Hellenic, by
ANDRONIKE MEKELATOS

HELLENIC FOLK SONG
Transcribed and Arranged by
ANDRONIKE MEKELATOS

"Unkle Johnnie" illustrates several features characteristic of folk life in modern Greece. In the first place, it is filled with the spirit of fun and revelry, as the humorous stanzas are tossed back and forth from solo singer to the group. Then, also, it suggests the ancient manner of singing such songs. The Hellenes have always had a gift for improvization and on many of their festival occasions it is a favorite pastime of the folk to sing innumerable original verses set to traditional airs. Perhaps you will enjoy following this custom by composing personal and topical verses to this spirited ancient tune.

(Friends) 1. Un - kle

John, con - grat - u - la - tions!_____
cept con - grat - u - la - tions!_____
John, on this oc - ca - sion,_____

To the Home of My Beloved

Φωτὰ Τὸ Φεγγαράκι Μου

From the traditional Hellenic, by
ANDRONIKE MEKELATOS

HELLENIC FOLK SONG
Transcribed and Arranged by
ANDRONIKE MEKELATOS

Most of the oldest Hellenic folk music, such as the following song, is found in the obscure villages of the mountains. Little has ever been written down; it has been sung by father to son through countless generations. The use of $\frac{7}{8}$, $\frac{5}{8}$, and $\frac{5}{4}$ rhythms is a noticeable feature of many of the folk dance tunes and songs of Greece today. The native dances are of two kinds, those danced in circle formation and those danced by two persons in Turkish style. In "To the Home of My Beloved" the accompaniment suggests the chords as played on the lute. After the song has become familiar, the gently swaying rhythm will be found to possess a haunting charm.

UNIT XVI: TRIPS ABROAD — JAPAN

by STELLA MAREK CUSHING

Courtesy of the Boston Museum of Fine Arts

LADIES IN A SUMMER VILLA

Nippon, meaning "the land of the rising sun," is the beautiful name the Japanese people call their homeland. Whenever we describe the dainty Japanese women, their charm and courtesy, or the delicately embroidered silks, finely wrought bronze, lovely pottery, lacquer ware, and all other Japanese art, we can use only expressions which mean beautiful or picturesque. If we visit Japan and gaze upon the ancient temples, or wander in the gardens at cherry blossom time, or are fortunate enough to know the people well enough to visit in their homes, our expressions are of awe, wonder, and delight at the beauty of it all. It is the same whether it be a woodblock print showing the sacred mountain, Fujiyama, or the loose-flowing costumes of this soft-spoken race, whose manners and customs come from ages eternal, and who have based their home life, religion, and culture upon beauty and art.

Since 1854, when our Commodore Perry opened Japan to world trade, we have been learning that Japan is not a "quaint box of curios." This small country, originally made up of farmers, fishermen, and the great landowners, has gradually accepted western ideas until it is now an industrial nation like its western neighbors. Along with this development, the Japanese have kept their beautiful ancient customs so that the visitor today sees a fascinating combination of medieval beauty and modern utility.

The old folk songs of Japan are very interesting, but the manner in which they are sung and the lack of harmony in accompaniment and voice parts make them often sound peculiar to western ears. The principal instruments are the *samisen*, a three-stringed instrument that is plucked like a guitar, the older thirteen-stringed *koto*, which to them takes the place of our piano, the bamboo flute, and several kinds of drums.

The Japanese songs in this unit have been chosen because they are old songs which are still popular as well as appealing and varied, and because the texts were adaptable to translation. They create for us something of the atmosphere of this fairyland of beauty, and help us to understand and appreciate the distinctive culture of the Japanese people.

Lullaby

Translated from a Japanese Fairy Tale

JAPANESE FOLK SONG

This lullaby is centuries old. Mothers were singing their babes to sleep with this song in very ancient times and they are still using it today. The words are a general introduction for many household folk tales.

1. Lit-tle ba - by, Hear me sing - ing,
2. Once an old man And his good wife,
3. On the moun-tain He toiled dai - ly,

1. *Shi - ba no o - ri - do no*
2. *O - ki - na wa ya - ma ni*

Lull-a - by of old;
Liv-ing all a - lone;
Gath'ring fag - ots dry;
shi - zu - ga - ya ni,
shi - ba - ka - ri ni,

Hours of slum-ber
La-bored ev- er,
Like all wom-en
O - ki - na to
O - u - ba wa

With-out num-ber,
Com-plained nev- er,
She washed lin- en
O - u - ba ga
ka - wa ni

1.
Till my tale is told.
Se-rene was their home.
In the brook near - by.
Su - ma - i ke - r̂i.
ki - nu su - su - gi.

2.

Cherry Bloom

Sakura

From the Japanese, by
LORENE HOYT

JAPANESE FOLK SONG

"Sakura" was written sometime during the era between 1600 and 1868, known as the *Tokugawa* period. Played with koto accompaniment this song is still a favorite, both on the concert stage and in tea houses. It is also sung out under the trees by the people when they go to view the cherry blooms.

Andante ($\quad$ = 76)

Sa-ku - ra,
Sa-ku - ra,
Sa-ku - ra,

INTERIOR OF A HOUSE IN THE ANCIENT CAPITAL CITY, NARA

Song to Oshima

Oshima Bushi

JAPANESE FOLK SONG
Arranged by YUJI ITOW

Translated from the Japanese

"Oshima Bushi" is a stirring, primitive folk song full of rhythm and symbolism. Oshima is an island straight out to sea from Yokohama, in the center of which is the great smoking volcano, Mihara, long celebrated as the shrine where patriotic Japanese have sacrificed themselves to their ancestors and country. The natives on the island are said to be descendants of the primitive people who inhabited the empire before the Japanese race migrated from the South Seas and the mainland of Asia. The song is traditionally sung to drum accompaniment which suggests its primitive origin. In the piano transcription the rhythm of the drum is heard in the left-hand part.

1. From _____ the is-land O-shi-ma I came,
2. Come _____ and see the la-va gush-ing free,
3. Go _____ to O-shi-ma and to him cry,
E _____ wa ta sha O-shi-ma no yo,

There a god dwells— in great_____ vol - ca — no fires, —
An-gered now Mi - ha - ra_____ sends smok - y clouds; —
"Hear, O Mi-ha - ra, life_____ is more— than death!"
Go ji ka — wa so — — o da — chi yo.—

So my heart—— is ev - er burn - ing____ Con-sumed with
Sad my soul,—— my spir-it dark - ened,—— Your face I
Then my heart—— will lead me glow - ing____ To climb the
Mi ne ni____ ke - mu-ri ga_____ Ta ye ya

ar - dent flame. ____
can - not see. ____
moun - tain high. ____
se nu yo. ____

THE BLIND VIOLINIST, BY VINCENZO IROLLI

UNIT XVII: SONGS OF MODERN COMPOSERS

with Appreciation Notes by Lillian L. Baldwin

After the Romantic Period, what then? Why, the Modern, says many a music history — Classical, Romantic, Modern — that is the line of march. A logical line it seems at first glance, but sooner or later that word "modern" is apt to prove an unruly elephant bringing up the rear of the procession.

Modern has always been a provocative word. If we are to believe the dictionary, modern means "of the present." When applied to music, however, the word tells us nothing of the characteristics of that music. Every piece of music has been modern in its own day. We know that Mozart, Beethoven, and most of the other great composers were criticized by their contemporaries as being too advanced, too modern. If we think of modern as meaning new and startling, we still have an indefinite and unsatisfactory adjective. Who can say what is new in music? Every composer stands on the shoulders of those who have gone before him. In every piece of worth-while music there is so much of the past and so much of the future that the present is often difficult to distinguish! And as for startling effects, they are by no means the invention of the would-be-originals of our day. There are passages of Bach which, even after all these years, startle and thrill us. So you see, the term "modern music" sounds well and means little. Composers living in the Classical and the Romantic Periods wrote music which still sounds "modern," while "modern" composers of our own time often write in the classical forms and in the romantic spirit.

Music is constantly growing and changing, but there is no definite point at which one period begins and another ends. There are, however, as we have seen, certain characteristics which mark the music of a period. Looking backward, we can sum these up and make such labels as Classical and Romantic, which at least give a clue as to what to expect in the music.

Since the Romantic Period, the most important musical explorations and discoveries have been in the field of harmony. Wagner, using the chromatic scale in new and beautiful ways, Debussy, venturing beyond the horizon into an unknown realm of overtones, the Russians, bringing their bizarre national harmonies, all have enriched music's color-box by hundreds of lovely tints and shades.

Today we have even more daring harmonic experimenters. There are those who, not content with keeping their music in one key at a time, want two or more keys or tonalities going on at once. And there are those who want no key centers at all! Much of this experimental music batters the ears and befuddles the brain of the average listener. Only time will tell whether it will some day be as much enjoyed as the "modern" music of Mozart or be merely kept in museums as a musical curiosity.

We have called the nineteenth century a century of song. It is too soon to characterize the twentieth, but judging from its music thus far, one would scarcely predict that it would ever be called a singing century. The elaborate, many-toned harmonies and the instrumental coloring of much of our recent music demand all the resources of a great modern orchestra. Fortunately, however, the singing spirit of the nineteenth century has not been wholly eclipsed by the modern demand for noise and magnitude, but has carried over into our own time, gathering up the new harmonic beauties and the newer poetry, and has given us hundreds of delightfully singable songs.

The outstanding characteristic of the Art Song, as you will remember, was the close relationship between the music and the verse. Later composers, Hugo Wolf in particular, have carried this relationship even further. Wolf had a keener appreciation of poetry and therefore chose better verses than Schubert. And where Schubert

Edvard Grieg

followed his poet line by line, Wolf followed his word by word, never missing an accent or poetic detail. So perfectly are his melodies molded over the verses that the songs are almost impossible to translate. Putting English words to his music is like trying to fit a body into a skin that was not made for it!

The expression of nationalism has also grown amazingly since the early days of the Romantic Period, when composers turned to the folk music of their own countries for inspiration and suggestion. Grieg and the Russians not only used the language and legends of their own countries but even the musical dialect — all the curious scales and intervals and folk traits which give their music an unmistakable Norwegian or Russian flavor.

Then there is the matter of accompaniment which has become more and more important since Schubert revolutionized it with his suggestion of rippling brooks, galloping horses, spinning wheels, and hurdy-gurdies. Schumann and Brahms enriched their songs with lovely countermelodies for the piano. Debussy, with little rhythmic figures and delicate harmonies, created a perfect background for his song pictures. And today many of the more pretentious songs are really duets for voice and piano. The accompanist is, at last, one who "goes with" the singer, sharing his responsibilities and his triumphs. He no longer merely supports the voice by strumming chords and arpeggios. The accompaniments of today require piano technique and appreciation on the part of both player and listener, for they are a definite part of the composer's plan and every note has an artistic purpose.

And so you will find in the songs of these modern composers not much that is new and startling, but rather a rich development, a fine flowering of the seeds sown in the Romantic Period, which was the century of song.

In the Boat

Im Kahne

From the German of Vilhelm Krag by
LORENE HOYT

EDVARD GRIEG, OP. 60, No. 3 (1843–1907)

This charming little boat song reminds one of Carl Larsen's colorful sketches of village life — seagulls flashing their snowy wings in the sunshine, "ducks proudly strutting in yellow stockings, trim and fine," a rowboat rocking on the wavelets of a little lake and in it a country lad whispering to his sweetheart — and through it all, the whippoorwill calling as insistently as if what he had to say really mattered!

Allegretto grazioso (♩=80)   FORM: I, II, III, Codetta

1. Sea-gulls flock-ing, On bil-lows rock-ing In bright sun-shine;
2. Loos-en, loos-en, My dear one, loos-en, Thy tress-es light;
3. Rid-ing, rid-ing, Our boat is glid-ing On rip-ples clear;

Ducks proud-ly strut in yel-low stock-ings trim and fine.
Then let us dance all thro' the warm mid-sum-mer night.
Like a ga-zelle so tall and slen-der is my dear!

pp

Only the Lonely Heart

Nur wer die Sehnsucht kennt

From the German of
JOHANN WOLFGANG VON GOETHE
by Lorene Hoyt

PETER ILYITCH TSCHAIKOWSKY (1840–1893)

PETER ILYITCH TSCHAIKOWSKY

Goethe's famous poem, "Only the lonely heart," has had many musical settings but none so exquisite as this. Tschaikowsky's mood of pathos was never more effective than in this song of homesickness. His music is more than a beautiful expression of the poem's mood. It is a shining example of a composer's complete mastery of his materials or, one might say, his use of his musical tools.

The downward line in art, music, or in real life suggests the droop of weariness or sadness, just as the upward line gives a feeling of vitality and joy. Looking at the score of this song, or better still, humming its melody, one feels the heaviness, the drag of its continual drooping phrases. And, as if he would sound the very depths of dejection, Tschaikowsky builds the song on the widest and most discordant interval possible, the drop from the sixth scale step to the seventh below. The harshness and the pull of that seventh gives the music a restless feeling. Then, beneath the smooth down-flowing melody the composer writes a syncopated accompaniment, persistently dislocating the accents and destroying our rhythmic peace until the restlessness becomes almost unbearable. And it is not a happen-so that the music reaches its emotional climax on the word *allein*, or that with no retard the last word *leide* sinks down exhausted on two soft short quarter notes as the piano draws the curtain on the scene.

A famous critic once said of this song that in intensity of feeling it is a summary of the whole Romantic movement.

Andante non tanto (♩=80)

p espressivo

SOPRANOS and MEZZO-SOPRANOS
p espressivo

On - ly the lone - ly heart
Nur wer die Sehn-sucht kennt,

Can feel the yearn - ing
weiss, was ich lei - de!

Panis Angelicus

Manna of Life from Heav'n

Ancient Latin Hymn

CÉSAR FRANCK (1822–1890)

CÉSAR FRANCK

For more than thirty years César Franck was organist and choirmaster at the church of Sainte Clothilde in Paris. Hard working and untouched by worldly ambition, he was content to devote his life to his church, his music, and his students. The dim organ loft of Sainte Clothilde became for Franck a little world of his own. There, suspended between heaven and earth, this gentle, scholarly man found the peace and power which flows through his music.

Franck's place in modern music is firmly established by his great and well-known *Symphony in D Minor*. His *Sonata for Violin and Piano* is in the repertoire of every artist, and the last movement contains one of the finest examples of canon in all music literature. His oratorio, *The Beatitudes*, ranks with the greatest masterpieces of this musical form.

"Panis Angelicus" is an ancient Latin hymn for the feast of Corpus Christi and commemorates the miracle of the manna when the bread of angels did in truth become the bread of men. Franck inserts the "Panis Angelicus" between the "Sanctus" and the "Agnus Dei" of his Mass in A.

The simple heart-felt melody comes drifting down as gently as the heavenly gift itself. In the second stanza there is a little canon — a repetition of the theme at a distance of one measure — which seems to suggest the continuous fall of the manna as symbolic of God's never-ending mercy to man.

Pa - nis an - ge - li - cus   Fit   pa - nis   ho - mi - num,
Man - na of life from heav'n   To   need - y   man is giv'n,

RECOLLECTION OF A MEADOW NEAR BRUNOY, BY COROT

The Gardener

Der Gärtner

EDUARD MORIKE (1804–1875)
Translated by Lorene Hoyt

HUGO WOLF (1860–1903)

Hugo Wolf's success as a song writer lies in his keen appreciation of poetry and his skill in expressing its every detail of character and delicate shade of feeling without sacrificing musical beauty, that is, beauty of tone and tonal design. This charming little song is really the song of the princess who comes "riding a steed white as snow." The melody devotes itself to her dainty grace, and the accompaniment prances to the hoof beats of her milk-white steed. The gardener, overcome by her beauty and ready to give her every blossom he has, is merely a bystander through whose eyes we see the lovely little princess.

201

glis - tens   like gold.   O
blin - ket   wie Gold.   *Du*

mf   *pp*

plumes   gay   and   ros -   y   That   dance   up   and
ro - sen - farbs   Hüt - lein,   wohl   auf   und   wohl

down,   Pray waft   me   a   feath - er   To keep   as mine
ab,   o   wirf   ei - ne Fe - der ver - stoh - len   her-

own.   And   wouldst   thou   ac - cept   them   Here are
ab!   Und   willst   du   da - ge - gen   ei - ne

NICOLAI RIMSKY-KORSAKOV

Song of the Shepherd Lehl*

Translated by
FLEUR CONKLING

NICOLAI RIMSKY-KORSAKOV (1844–1908)
FROM THE OPERA, "SNÉGOUROTCHKA"*

Rimsky-Korsakov, like most of the famous Russian composers, was devoted to the folk and fairy lore of his native land. The quaint old tunes and fantastic tales were the inspiration of his colorful music. One of his most charming operas is *Snégourotchka*, "The Snow Maiden," based on an old Russian fairy story. The Snow Maiden, daughter of King Frost and the Spring Fairy, has been brought up in the wintry woods safe from her father's old enemy, the Sun God. From afar, little Snégourotchka has heard the happy songs of a mortal, Lehl, the shepherd boy, and has fallen in love with him. But Lehl is quite indifferent, for he loves a peasant girl. The poor little Snow Maiden calls on her mother, Spring, to comfort her and, as if in answer to her cry, the Sun God kisses her and she melts away.

"Song of the Shepherd Lehl" is one of the loveliest bits of the opera — no wonder the Snow Maiden lost her heart to the singer!

UNIT XVIII: TRIPS ABROAD—CHINA

by STELLA MAREK CUSHING

Courtesy of the Boston Museum of Fine Arts

SILK BEATERS, SCROLL OF THE SUNG DYNASTY, EARLY TWELFTH CENTURY

The people of China call their nation Chung-Hua. Their country flourished as a highly-civilized people long before the days of ancient Greece. But for the outside world China was shrouded in mystery until in more modern times the doors were opened by Western traders and explorers. Now we know China as a land of 500,000,000 people living in coastal cities, inland towns and villages, on terraced mountainside, in the fertile valleys of the two great rivers, Yangtze-Kiang and Hwang-ho, and even in houseboats, or *sampans*, on rivers and sea.

Primarily an agricultural nation, the farmers are able to grow rice, tea, mulberry, bamboo, cotton, tobacco, sugar cane, indigo, soy bean, and other products of immense commercial value. Every available lowland space and even the hillsides are under cultivation, as are also the fertile but dangerous valleys where spring floods frequently bring destruction and famine.

The Chinese people by nature are patient, industrious, and tolerant. Indeed, patience and industry as well as artistry are needed to fashion with such skill the finely-embroidered silks, gold and silver filigree, lacquer ware, and carvings in wood and ivory which delight our eyes.

The melodies of Chinese music are based on a five-tone scale not unlike the Scotch pentatonic scale. They have a quality which we often fail to perceive because of the manner in which they are played and because of the unusual melodic progressions and the absence of harmonies and form to which we are accustomed in our own music. When written in our notation we can readily see the real character and charm of these old tunes.

The songs of this unit are popular in various sections of China. Chinese folk songs cover a variety of themes and reveal that the Chinese people not only love the quiet beauty of nature but also have a sense of humor which we as Americans can easily understand because it is quite like our own.

The Street Vendors

Fong Yong
(Recorded)

CHINESE FOLK SONG
As sung by Li Jenkung

Translation based on Chinese text in *Songs of Cathay*, by T. Z. Koo

Dr. T. Z. Koo, who is well known to American audiences as lecturer and author, calls attention to the fact that this typical rollicking song is popular with boys and girls in China and refutes the notion that all Chinese music is melancholy in character. The chorus imitates the sound of cymbals, drums, and clappers, and it is suggested that when this song is sung characteristic motions be used in imitation of these instruments.

The Chinese words are given as spelled by Li Jenkung. For correct pronunciation, listen to the recording of the song on Victor Record, № 25380.

Strike the gong! Ven-dors are we who up-on the street be-
You may buy. Pa-per of gold shin-ing, bam-boo smooth and
That I do. Keen-ness and skill to my in-stru-ments be-
Good fore-tell. Come try your luck, for the sticks are nev-er
Li Chong Gê, Bieh Dih Gê Er O Yea Boo Hwai

long; Call-ing our wares to the Fong Yong song.
strong, Call-ing my clear ring-ing Toy-man's song.
long, Call-ing my clear ring-ing Bar-ber's song.
wrong; Call-ing my clear ring-ing For-tune-tell-er's song.
Chong, Dan Li Chong Gê Fong Yong Gê.

Fong Shi Fong Yong Gê Ai Ye Yahr Ai Drr Long Dong Biah Yih Biah

Drr Long Dong Biah Drr Biah Biah Ye Drr Biah Biah Ye Drr Biah Yih Biah.

Kites Are Flying

(Recorded)

CHINESE FOLK SONG
As sung by Li Jenkung

Adapted from the Chinese

This is a popular song in many provinces of China. It should be sung lightly, suggestive of kites floating in the air. One of the chief sports of a Chinese boy is to make his own kite and then take it to the fields to fly. The kite is small and made of plain paper on which is painted a dragon, fish, or other animal in bright colors.

Lanterns Glowing

(Recorded)

Translation based on Chinese text in *Songs of Cathay*, by T. Z. Koo

CHINESE FOLK SONG
As sung by Li Jenkung

This song is very popular during the Chinese spring festival, which is similar to our Arbor Day. At many of the festivals in China it is the custom for all the members of the family to carry large, round, red lanterns in their processions as they visit the ancestral graves or go to the temple. The song should be sung with a quiet swing to suggest the lanterns nodding up and down to the rhythm of the music.

1. Lan-terns in the ear-ly eve-ning glow - - ing,
2. Twi-light shad-ows now are slow-ly fall - - ing,
3. Droop-ing wil-low branch-es low-ly bend - - ing,

Light up-on the home-ward path is show - - ing.
Low the friend-ly lark to slum-ber call - - ing.
Catch the yel-low gleam the lamps are send - - ing.

Gen-tly nod, high-er, low-er, Soft-en gloom of night.
Lan-terns swing, high-er, low-er, Shine with col-ors bright.
Shad-ows dance, high-er, low-er, In the lan-tern light.

I Couldn't Hear Nobody Pray

Traditional

NEGRO SPIRITUAL

Arranged by John Wesley Work, one of the original
Fisk Jubilee Singers, and used by permission of his son, John W. Work.

This is one of the most beautiful and pathetic of all Negro spirituals. It illustrates two characteristic ways in which the singers gave expression to their emotions: first, interjections during the singing of the refrain, and second, solemn and quiet chant-like responses to exclamatory passages sung by the leader.

* The interjections used here are not the only ones which can be used, but may be changed according to the emotions of the leader.

† Let this stanza be exceedingly slow, about half as fast as the others, and the chorus very soft; but go into the refrain *a tempo*.

D.C.

And my Sav - iour!_ O Lord!
In - to Ca - naan!_
With my Je - sus!_

D.C.

could-n't hear no-bod-y pray; A could-n't hear no-bod-y pray.

Carol

Ballade de Jesus-Christ

From the French

ANCIENT FRENCH CAROL

Andante con moto (♩=72)

Gen - tle Lord, in gar - ment_ low - ly, Grant to me Thy
La - dy from the win - dow_ glow - ing, Grant to me Thy
Jé - sus-Christ s'ha - bille en - pau - vre: Fai - tes-moi la

Grant

char - i - ty!_ Gen - tle Lord, in gar - ment_
char - i - ty!_ La - dy from the win - dow_
cha - ri - té! Jé - sus-Christ s'ha - bille en -

low - ly, Grant to me Thy char - i - ty! Of the crumbs that
glow - ing, Grant to me Thy char - i - ty! Ah, come up, come
pau - vre: Fai - tes-moi la cha - ri - té! Des miet - tes de

Grant

*(Crumbs)
(Come)

leave Thy ta - ble I shall dine most joy - ful - ly.
up, poor fel - low, Find a sup-per rich and_ free.
vo - tre ta - ble. Je fe - rai bien mon dî - ner.

*(Dine)
(Sup)

* Text for Second Sopranos.

Prayer for Peace

Chorale: Herr Christ, der einig' Gottes-Sohn

Paraphrased from Elisabeth Creutziger (1524), by
FLEUR CONKLING

JOHANN SEBASTIAN BACH (1685–1750)

The *chorale*, which originated in Germany during the Reformation, is really a sacred folk song, introduced into the service so that all of the people may join in the singing. Bach's harmonizations of these hymn tunes are unsurpassed.

O King on high who leads us, We pray Thee bring us peace; Dark
O King on high who leads us, Let trou-bling dark-ness cease.
Spread wide the wings of mer - cy And bear us through the night; On
Spread wide the wings of mer - cy And guard us with Thy might.
Er - tödt' uns durch dein' Gü - te, er - weck' uns durch dein' Gnad'; wohl
den al - ten Men-schen krän - ke, dass der neu' le - ben mag,

storm clouds now have filled our skies, O, bear a - way our sor - rows: Yea, let our sor-rows cease.
earth di - rect our hearts, we pray, Di-rect us through the dark-ness And lead us to Thy light.
hie auf die-ser Er - den den Sinn und all Be - ger - den und G'danken hab zu dir.

Branch of the Sweet and Early Rose

From the Original Irish, by
DR. DRENNAN

IRISH MELODY

Grazioso (♩ = 88)

Branch of the sweet and ear - ly rose, That in the
Who, in the dew - y eve - ning walk, Shall pluck thee

pur - est beau - ty blows, So pass - ing sweet to
from the ten - der stalk? Whose tem - ples blush - ing

smell and sight, On whom shall those be - stow de - light?
shall thou twine, And who in - hale thy breath di - vine?

The Little Red Lark

Traditional

IRISH FOLK SONG

SOLO VOICE
Allegretto (♪= 144)

O swan of slen-der-ness, Dove of ten-der-ness, Jew-el of joys, A-
The dawn is dark to me, Hark, oh hark to me, Pulse of my heart, I

CHORUS

(Humming, individuals breathing at different times so that the accompaning tone will flow
without interruption, following the solo voice.)

rise.___ The lit-tle red lark, Like a soar-ing spark of Song, to his sun-burst
pray,___ And out of thy hid-ing, with blush-es glid-ing, Daz-zle me with thy

flies.___ But till thou'rt ris - en Earth is a pris - on full of my lone-some
day.___ Ah, then once more to thee Fly-ing I'll pour to thee pas-sion so sweet and

One solo voice with words

sighs.__ Then a-wake and dis-cov-er To thy fond lov-er The morn of thy match-less eyes. __
gay;___ The__ lark shall lis-ten, And dew-drops glis-ten 'Laugh-ing on ev - 'ry spray.__

CHORUS

(Humming)

Logie O'Buchan

GEORGE HALKET

ANCIENT SCOTTISH SONG

1. O___ Log - ie O' Bu - chan, O Log - ie, the Laird, They hae ta'en a - wa' Jam - ie that delv'd in the yard; Wha___ play'd on the pipe and the vi - ol sae sma'; They hae ta'en a - wa' Jam - ie, the flow'r o' them a'.

2. Though Sand - y has ous - en, has gear, and has kye, A___ house and a had - din and sill - er for - by; Yet I'd take my ain lad wi' his staff in his hand, Be - fore I'd hae him with his hous - es and land.

3. My___ dad - dy looks sulk - y, my min - ny looks sour, They___ frown up - on Jam - ie, be - cause he is poor; Though I lo'e them as well as a daugh - ter should do, They're___ nae half sae dear to me, Jam - ie, as you. He said, "Think nae lang, Lass - ie, though

4. I___ sit on my creep - ie and spin at my wheel, And___ think on the lad - die that lo'es me sae weel; He___ had but ae sax - pence, he brak it in twa, And he gied me the ha'f o't, when he gaed a - wa'.

5. Then___ haste ye back, Jam - ie, and bide na a - wa', Then___ haste ye back, Jam - ie, and bide na a - wa', The___ sim - mer is com - ing, cauld win - ter's a - wa', And___ ye'll come and see me in spite o' them a'.

I gang a - wa'; For___ I'll come and see thee in spite o' them a'."

America, the Beautiful

KATHARINE LEE BATES   SAMUEL A. WARD

"It was thirty-five years ago, in the year of the World's Fair, that I made my first journey to the far West. My first great thrill was at Chicago. I saw America in the making, and this lovely city turned all men into poets, realizing that against the smoke-stained, sin-stained city of the day there lay the possibility of some spiritual invention that should give us cities that were all beautiful.

"We went out and crossed the prairies and the farm lands and the richness of the farm lands and the great wheat fields impressed the memory of those poets, Pilgrims from East to West who were building at such cost the material prosperity of our country, and we came at last to the Rocky Mountains in all their majesty, and climbed at last the mystic height of Pike's Peak. It was during our brief stay there that summer, looking out over that great expanse, that the opening stanza was promoted in my mind. Coming down to Colorado Springs where a band of eastern educators were working for a few weeks in a summer school, I remember writing the opening stanzas in a notebook that was traveling with me, a notebook that I did not open again for two years. It was not until the summer of 1899 that I came upon that notebook and copied out this song and sent it to a Boston concern which very kindly published it. To my great surprise, people began immediately that very year to write music for it. It has been sung to many tunes."

From an address by Katharine Lee Bates, National Education Association, Boston, 1928.

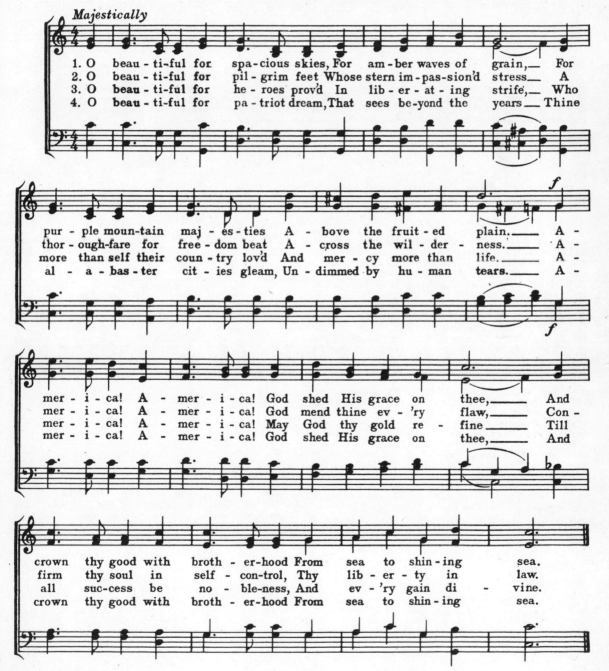

1. O beau-ti-ful for spa-cious skies, For am-ber waves of grain,— For pur-ple moun-tain maj-es-ties A-bove the fruit-ed plain.— A-mer-i-ca! A-mer-i-ca! God shed His grace on thee,— And crown thy good with broth-er-hood From sea to shin-ing sea.

2. O beau-ti-ful for pil-grim feet Whose stern im-pas-sion'd stress— A thor-ough-fare for free-dom beat A-cross the wil-der-ness.— A-mer-i-ca! A-mer-i-ca! God mend thine ev-'ry flaw,— Con-firm thy soul in self-con-trol, Thy lib-er-ty in law.

3. O beau-ti-ful for he-roes prov'd In lib-er-at-ing strife,— Who more than self their coun-try lov'd And mer-cy more than life.— A-mer-i-ca! A-mer-i-ca! May God thy gold re-fine— Till all suc-cess be no-ble-ness, And ev-'ry gain di-vine.

4. O beau-ti-ful for pa-triot dream, That sees be-yond the years— Thine al-a-bas-ter cit-ies gleam, Un-dimmed by hu-man tears.— A-mer-i-ca! A-mer-i-ca! God shed His grace on thee,— And crown thy good with broth-er-hood From sea to shin-ing sea.

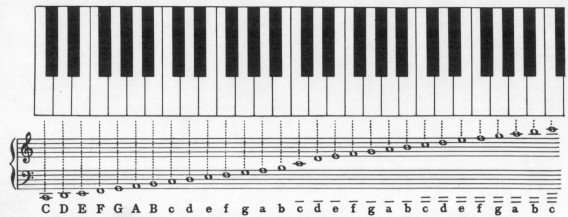

C D E F G A B c d e f g a b c d e f g a b c d e f g a b c

The material of this unit serves three particular purposes: 1. To provide training in basic musicianship; 2. To review and consolidate the technical studies of the earlier grades; and 3. To provide a brief course for students whose previous studies did not include this phase of musical development. It is recommended only for classes of average and above average ability. The songs in the book offer material for the suggested studies.

I. NOTATION

A. Pitch

THE PIANO KEYBOARD gives a graphic picture of pitch relationships.

Pitches are named by the first seven letters of the alphabet, which are repeated to name higher and lower octaves, as shown above. (*See* also p. 57.) The white keys on the piano keyboard sound these pitches; between certain of them are intermediate pitches, sounded by the black keys. The pitches sounded by the black keys are named from their neighboring white keys. They are called *sharp* (♯) if reckoned as above a white key, and *flat* (♭) if reckoned as below a white key.

STAFF: In written music, pitches are represented by lines and spaces of the staff. We usually see staves of five lines, as that seems the largest number of lines the eye can grasp readily. One such staff, however, would not be sufficient to indicate all the high and low pitches, so two staves are ordinarily employed, the *treble staff* for high pitches and the *bass staff* for low pitches, as shown above. Even these do not cover every need, so added lines (*leger lines*) and the spaces between them are used in writing pitches above or below the range of the staves. (Sometimes other staves are used, as shown in MUSIC OF MANY LANDS AND PEOPLES, p. 39.) Also, when especially high or low notes are required, the sign, 8va, followed by a dotted line, above or below the notes, indicates sections to be played an octave higher or lower than written. The ending of the dotted line, or the word *loco*, indicates the end of such passage. (*See* pp. 51, 29, etc.)

CLEF: A *clef* is placed at the beginning of each staff to show which staff is intended; the *G clef* for the treble staff and the *F clef* for the bass staff. (*See* p. 57.)

NATURAL: A line or space on which a sharp or flat has been written is restored to the original pitch (white key) by the use of a *natural*. This is true whether the signs occur in the *key signature* or as an *accidental*.

B. Time

NOTES: Various kinds of *notes* and *rests* are used to represent different durations of time. Above are shown *whole, half, quarter, eighth,* and *sixteenth* notes and *rests* in a chart which pictures their relative values.

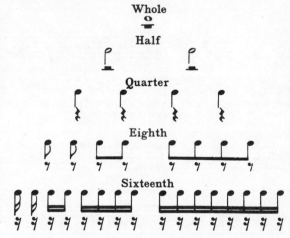

Whole

Half

Quarter

Eighth

Sixteenth

Comparative Values of Notes and Rests

TIME, RHYTHM, TEMPO: These words are often confused. *Time* means the duration, or length, of the tones of a piece of music. *Rhythm* is the flow of the music, as determined by the grouping of sounds by accents. *Tempo* is the speed at which a composition moves.

BEAT: The *beat*, or *pulse*, is the basic unit of time.

MEASURE: Beats are grouped into twos or threes to form *simple measures*. When in fours, sixes, or other groupings, they form *compound measures*.

BARS AND DOUBLE BARS: Measures are indicated by *bars* across the staff. The close of a composition or a movement is shown by a *double bar*.

TIME SIGNATURE: The kind of measure (meter) in which a composition is written is indicated by two figures, one above the other as in fractions, placed at the beginning of the piece or wherever the meter changes. The upper figure shows the number of beats in the measure; the lower figure shows the kind of note used to represent each beat.

There are certain conventional exceptions to this rule, as in the case of *six-eight measure* ($\frac{6}{8}$), which may mean either six beats in the measure, each represented by an eighth note (*see* p. 63), or two beats in the measure, each represented by a dotted-quarter note (*see* p. 172). The signatures, $\frac{9}{8}$ and $\frac{12}{8}$ may likewise have this dual meaning.

Occasionally the sign, C, appears, meaning four-four measure (*see* p. 15). When a vertical line crosses the sign, the time is said to be *alla breve*, meaning that a half note receives a beat, usually as two-half measure, sometimes as four-half measure (*see* pp. 42, 144).

TIE AND SLUR: When two notes of the same pitch are connected by a curved line (*tie*), one tone is sounded for their combined values. This must not be confused with the *slur*, which groups sounds of different pitches.

FLAGS: Eighth notes and notes of smaller values may be indicated by *flags* or may be joined by *cross-bars* (*balkins*), depending on whether each is to be sung to a separate word or syllable, or several notes sung to the same word.

ABBREVIATIONS: The following devices save space when certain portions of a composition are exactly alike:

Repeat signs (||: :||). The portion enclosed between the dots is to be performed twice (*see* pp. 9, 21). On p. 9, observe that the repeat mark indicates a return to the beginning of the song. If the final measure or measures are unlike, this difference is indicated by a *first and second ending* (*see* pp. 11, 81).

Da Capo (D.C.), meaning "to the head," that is, return to the very beginning of the music (*see* p. 30).

Dal Segno (D.S.), meaning "to the sign," that is, return to the sign $\text{\%}$ (*see* pp. 35, 74).

'*Fine* (fee'-nay), "the end," indicating the place to close after repeating a portion of the composition (*see* p. 38).

II. THEORY

A. Scales and Key Signatures

STEPS AND HALF-STEPS: A simple way to reckon the relationship of pitches is to refer to the keyboard at the beginning of this unit. From any key to its nearest neighboring key, black or white, up or down, is a *half-step*. Two half-steps make a *step*. Three half-steps make a *step-and-a-half*.

DIATONIC SCALES: A *diatonic scale* consists of eight tones built upon successive lines and spaces of the staff (no letter name is repeated or omitted).

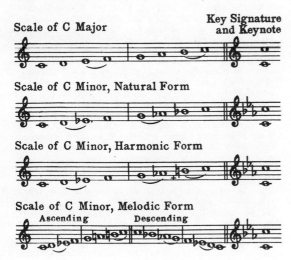

Scale of C Major — Key Signature and Keynote

Scale of C Minor, Natural Form

Scale of C Minor, Harmonic Form

Scale of C Minor, Melodic Form — Ascending — Descending

MAJOR AND MINOR SCALES: Variations in diatonic scale patterns are effected by different arrangements of steps and half-steps. The most familiar diatonic scales are the *major scale* and the three forms of the *minor scale*, *natural* or *normal*, *harmonic*, and *melodic*. There are many other scales, a few of which are discussed under the word *mode* (*see* pp. 27, 157). See p. 75 for an interesting and amusing use which Beethoven has made of the major scale. The first tone (1) of the scale is called the *tonic*, or *keynote*, and the other tones are named in ascending order: (2) *supertonic*, (3) *mediant*, (4) *sub-dominant*, (5) *dominant*, (6) *sub-mediant*, (7) *leading tone*. In the foregoing examples all successive tones are a step apart except where a slur indicates a half-step and a plus sign indicates a step-and-a-half. By referring to the keyboard, the necessity for sharps and flats to secure the proper scale patterns will be clear. The foregoing scales are built by *tetrachords*, that is, by half scales of four tones each. Observe that the lower tetrachords are alike in the three forms of the minor scale, the upper tetrachords being different. Study the scales to see what other likenesses and differences occur in the tetrachords (*see* pp. 8, 9).

KEY SIGNATURE: The sharps or flats essential to the construction of a scale are assembled as a *key signature* at the beginning of the staff and are in effect all through the composition or until the key signature is changed. The conventional groupings of sharps and flats in the various keys will be found in the songs of this book.

TONIC AND RELATIVE MAJOR AND MINOR: The foregoing examples illustrate the relationship of the major key with its *tonic minor* in that the same pitch serves as *keynote* (or *tonic*) in both major and minor.

Another relationship, called the *relative major and minor*, occurs when both major and minor keys have the same number of sharps or flats in the key signature. The keynote of the relative minor key is a *minor third* (step-and-a-half) below the keynote of the relative major key (*see* p. 12, "Neptune," which begins in C major, continues for a time in the relative minor key, A minor, and then returns to C major).

SCALE BUILDING: The following procedure will be helpful in building major and minor scales:

1. Place keynote for major or minor scale on the staff at assigned pitch.

2. Complete the group of eight notes on successive lines and spaces of the staff.

3. Indicate whole and half-steps (step-and-a-half in harmonic minor), and through reference to keyboard put in necessary sharps and flats.

4. Extract the key signature, placing correct number of sharps or flats in their conventional order upon the staff.

CHROMATIC SCALE: A scale built of twelve tones in successive half-steps is called a *chromatic scale*. *Ascending chromatic scales* utilize sharps largely, and *descending chromatic scales* employ flats chiefly in their construction. Naturals occur when made necessary by the key signature. Chromatic passages will be found in many songs throughout the book (*see* p. 4).

B. Intervals

The pitch relationship between two tones is called an *interval*, whether sounded simultaneously or successively. Intervals have two designations; first, the *numerical name*, determined by the relationship of the two notes upon the staff, and second, the *specific name*, determined by the actual number of steps and half-steps between the two tones.

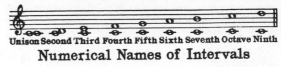

Unison Second Third Fourth Fifth Sixth Seventh Octave Ninth

Numerical Names of Intervals

NUMERICAL NAMES: In finding the numerical name, begin with the degree of the staff upon which the lower note occurs and count the lines and spaces to the upper note, including both notes.

Specific Names of Intervals

SPECIFIC NAMES: In determining the specific name, the lower note may be considered as the first tone of a major scale. If the upper tone is in the scale pattern, the interval is either *major* or *perfect*. Any variation in the span of the interval will change its specific name but not its numerical name.

INTERVAL STUDY: Our ears have become accustomed to enjoying progressions of thirds and sixths, as you will notice in many of the songs in this book. Mere successions of these two intervals soon lose their interest, however, and modern music is increasingly using a wide variety of other intervals. Study a number of the songs in this book and observe the effects of the various intervals (*see* pp. 26, 28, 31, 40, 101, etc.).

The tones of a melody follow each other as intervals, some of which are more difficult to sing than others. Singing "in tune" is dependent largely on a perfect knowledge of interval relations, and a student is amply repaid for giving careful attention to this field of study.

CONSONANCE AND DISSONANCE: All perfect, major, and minor intervals (excepting seconds and sevenths) are *consonant*, which means that taken by themselves they are more or less satisfying to the ear.

Seconds, sevenths, and all augmented and diminished intervals are *dissonant* and demand a progression to a consonant interval to be musically satisfying. (Compare the consonant and dissonant intervals between soprano and alto parts on pp. 13, 101., etc.)

augmented fifth; *augmented triad* (III+) (*see* p. 38). By building triads on each degree of the minor scales you will discover that the relationship of thirds and fifths differs from that of the major scale, consequently the specific names of triads will vary.

DOMINANT SEVENTH CHORD: The seventh chord most frequently used is on five of the scale, the *dominant seventh chord* (V7) (*see* pp. 21, 43, etc.). Another seventh chord, the *diminished seventh chord*, is not uncommon, and its dissonant character lends tang to the harmony (*see* pp. 15, 38, 45).

INVERSIONS: When another tone than the root of the chord appears as lowest tone, the chord is said to be *inverted*. The only inversion that we need observe particularly at this time is when the fifth of the tonic triad appears as bass. This chord (I$\frac{6}{4}$) is most important in bringing many compositions to a satisfactory ending (*final cadence*) (*see* pp. 19, 35, etc.). Experience in harmonic analysis may be gained by reducing chords in the part songs of the book to their fundamental series of thirds and naming them (*see* p. 41, etc., etc.).

TONE BLENDING DRILLS: The Tone Blending Drills throughout the book will train the ear to distinguish the simpler chords which are used in the part songs. Special emphasis is placed on the *primary triads* (I, IV, V) and the dominant seventh chord (V7) as they appear in simple *cadences* (endings). These chords should be familiar to every musical ear. The drills should be sung slowly and with the greatest attention to purity of intonation. Ability to distinguish clearly the harmony of a composition opens up rich possibilities for musical enjoyment.

C. Harmony

CHORD: A *chord* is a combination of three or more notes which can be reduced to a series of thirds, one above the other. Chords of three tones are called *triads;* chords of four tones are called *seventh chords*. Modern music employs still more complex chords, *ninth chords, eleventh chords*, etc.

When the chord is arranged in its succession of thirds, the lowest tone is called the *root*, and gives the chord its name according to the degree of the scale on which the root occurs.

SPECIFIC NAMES OF TRIADS: By measuring the intervals in the triads in the following illustration, you will find that some consist of a major third and a perfect fifth; these are called *major triads* (I, IV, V). These three triads, known as the *principal triads* of a key, appear in numerous Tone Blending Drills throughout the book. (*See* pp. 2, 16, 24, 57.) Some triads consist of a minor third and perfect fifth; *minor triads* (ii, iii, vi). They are the *secondary triads* (see ii, pp. 3, 35, 73, etc.; iii, p. 29; vi, p. 51). The triad on seven of the scale (vii°) consists of a minor third and diminished fifth; *diminished triad* (see "Daybreak," p. 58). A still different triad is found on the third tone of the harmonic minor scale — it consists of a major third and

D. Modulation and Transposition

MODULATION: In order to vary key feeling (tonality), composers frequently shift from one key to another in the course of a composition. This is called *modulation*. Unless performers and listeners are conscious of these key changes they miss one of the chief beauties of the music. Moreover, music reading is immeasurably simplified if one follows the changes of key. The material in this book is marked to indicate modulations. Where the key changes you will find a capital letter for major keys and a small letter for minor keys. When singing by syllables, change *do* at the point of modulation (see p. 5).

TRANSPOSITION: *Transposition* is the shifting of the whole composition to a higher or lower key. This is sometimes desirable to fit the voice range of certain groups.

E. Form

FORM: Music, like every other art, has well-designed principles of structural arrangement. Otherwise it would not be intelligible. Good form consists of artistically-

I	ii	iii	IV	V	vi	vii°
Tonic	Supertonic	Mediant	Sub-dominant	Dominant	Sub-mediant	Leading tone

Table of Triads

balanced *repetition* and *contrast*, thereby achieving *unity* and *variety*. Unity is essential for clarity, variety to avoid monotony. This is true of the simplest song as well as the most elaborate symphony.

PHRASE: The *phrase* is the structural unit of the song. A phrase in song is the equivalent of a line of poetry. Phrases usually appear in pairs, *antecedent* and *consequent*, much as though they were *question* and *answer*. In analyzing a song, call the first phrase A. Any repetition of this phrase is likewise called A. When the phrase is repeated in a modified form it is called A *prime* (A¹). Other phrases are called B, C, etc., as they occur. (*See* pp. 8, 15, 26, etc., etc., for songs in which the phrases have been analyzed. Make your own analysis of other simple short songs, such as those in Unit VII, etc.) As a rule, especially in folk songs, phrases appear in perfect balance. Occasionally, however, charming effects are produced by means of phrases of irregular length (*see* pp. 28, 74, 165).

PART: Longer songs frequently consist of two or more such short songs in contrasting moods. It is in this manner that the shorter instrumental forms are built. Each of the short songs in such a longer song may be designated as a *Part* and indicated by a Roman numeral. "Neptune," p. 12, for example, is in Three-part Form. Part I consists of a four-phrase song, A,B,A,B. Part II, in A Minor, consists of two phrases, C,D. Part III is a repetition of the opening song, two phrases, A,B. Other illustrations are: Two-part Form, pp. 28, 31, 32; Three-part Form, pp. 37, 39, etc.

Sometimes these forms are extended by *Introductions* and *Codas* (*see* pp. 46 and 53).

Observe carefully the form of the songs that you sing; such study will richly repay you in added interest and pleasure in your growing appreciation of artistic design. Observe also these same principles of structure in the instrumental music that you hear and as they are exemplified in the list of correlated recorded selections (*see* p. 246).

Many of the songs in this book illustrate various Dance Forms (*see* pp. 12, 34, 37, 42, 46, 89, 91, 93, etc.). Instrumental Forms are illustrated in the correlated recorded selections, p. 246. Vocal Forms are represented by the many types of songs and by the notes and selections on pp. 50, 64, 66, 70, 75, 78, 116, 154, 156, 158, 196, 205, etc., etc.

III. A REVIEW OF MUSIC READING

The following review of music reading offers a series of music problems, progressing from simple to more difficult, with references to songs in the book which illustrate them. The successive problems are explained in this unit and may be applied by reading the listed songs. The songs are indicated merely by page number; where more than one song occurs on a page, the first is designated as a, the second as b. It is suggested that they be studied in the listed order. After reading the songs listed under a topic, additional reading experience may be had with other songs in the book or elsewhere in which the problem occurs. Unless otherwise indicated, the reference in part songs is to the soprano part.

A. Tone Relations in the Diatonic Major Scale; the Quarter-note Beat: pp. 2, 58b, 52b, 39.
B. The Quarter-note Beat, Eighth Notes: pp. 160, 174, 36, 57, 54, 52a, 59.
C. Sharp Chromatics: 71, 70, 28, 124.
D. The Quarter-note Beat, Dotted-Quarter-and-Eighth Notes: 65, 12, 62b, 1.
E. Flat Chromatics: 62a, 2 (2nd part), 5 (3rd part), 15 (2nd part).
F. The Minor Mode: (Natural) 27, 107, 26, 56; (Harmonic) 56 (2nd and 3rd parts), 26 (2nd part); (Melodic) 8 (2nd part), 9 (2nd part).
G. The Dotted-Quarter-note Beat: 172, 162, 170, 84, 41.
H. Sixteenth Notes: 34, 60a, 61, 3, 32, 22, 10, 31.
I. Half-note Beat and Eighth-note Beat: 51, 144, 75, 74, 63, 134, 182.

J. Modulation: 5, 58a, 60a, 32, 12.
K. Syncopation: 20, 42, 47 (Furiant), 112.
L. Triplets: 100, 97, 120.
M. Comparative Rhythms: 156.

IV. EAR TRAINING

Ear training is the foundation of listening to music and is an important factor in good singing and playing. A program of ear training should be a part of the music period, not as a separate activity, but integrated with singing and listening. It fits closely into the Review of Music Reading. There are three phases in the development of listening:

a) Training the ear to hear distinctly and accurately.

b) Developing comprehension, that is, through hearing music to recognize the melodic, rhythmic, and harmonic relationship of sounds.

c) Training the power of retention so that increasingly larger portions of a musical composition may be held clearly in mind at one time.

1. RECOGNITION OF PITCH: The first step is to establish a definite and sure recognition of the keynote, the basis of tonality. With this firmly in mind, it is then possible to develop recognition of pitch relationships.

a) Listen to a song or a series of chords; discover and sing the keynote. Sing the tonic chord or the diatonic scale to establish tonality. Repeat frequently in every music period.

b) Listen to melodies which modulate; recognize and sing keynote at each change of key.

c) Listen to given keynote and then name by number any tone sounded in the scale of that key. Gradually develop power to give letter name of pitch sounded after keynote is named.

d) Name intervals with first tone sounded as keynote, first with numerical name only, then with specific name, major, minor, etc. Follow this with intervals whose first pitch is other than the keynote. Ability to recognize intervals develops slowly, and requires frequent, brief drill.

e) A valuable addition to this training is practice in indicating the note changed when a short melody is played or sung twice with one of the notes altered the second time.

2. RECOGNITION OF RHYTHM: The majority of difficulties in music reading and in performance can be traced to weakness of rhythmic ability. Frequent, brief drills will strengthen this phase of musicianship. Use songs in this book.

a) Recognition of basic forms of duple and triple measure patterns: $\frac{2}{4}$, $\frac{2}{2}$, $\frac{3}{4}$, etc.

b) Recognition of compound measure patterns: $\frac{4}{4}$, $\frac{6}{8}$, etc.

c) Recognition of the nature of the beat as divisible by twos or by threes, *i.e.*, $\frac{2}{4}$ versus $\frac{6}{8}$ measure.

d) Various rhythmic measure patterns (divided beats, etc.).

e) Larger patterns (the song phrase).

f) Reproduce rhythmic patterns by stepping, tapping, writing, etc.

3. MELODIC DICTATION: Give the key and time signature before dictating. Later the key may be named and recognition of the time signature made a part of the exercise.

a) Discover keynote of a brief melody (key having been named), and locate it on the staff.

b) Teacher plays or sings and pupils write simple melodic figures based upon (1) the tonic chord; (2) the diatonic scale; (3) tones of the tonic chord alternating with neighboring tones; (4) the dominant and sub-dominant chords; (5) the dominant seventh chord; (6) the secondary triads, etc.

c) Write from dictation phrases of familiar songs studied in this book.

d) Write from dictation phrases of unfamiliar songs (songs in the book not yet used for study).

4. HARMONIC DICTATION: Only the simplest of harmonic problems are suitable for this grade. There should be very little written dictation but considerable emphasis upon the following items:

a) Recognition of major and minor triads, with the addition of diminished and augmented triads for classes of advanced ability.

b) Recognition of degree of the scale upon which a chord is built. Advanced classes may write the chords upon the staff.

c) After establishing tonality by singing keynote, pupils write the two notes for various intervals sounded harmonically.

d) Advanced groups will enjoy using familiar Tone Blending Drills for chord recognition, both oral and written response.

5. RECOGNITION OF SIMPLE FORMS: Name orally or in writing:

a) The phrase relationship of short songs, using the A,B,A,C plan as outlined under FORM, p. 220.

b) Distinguish between two-part and three-part forms in songs.

c) Distinguish between such dance forms as march, minuet, waltz, gavotte, etc.

V. MELODY WRITING

Under THEORY, p. 220, appears a discussion of Form. It was there shown that a song is a balanced organization of phrases related through repetition and contrast. The following plan of instruction in melody writing is based on those studies in song structure. Before attempting to compose his own melodies, the student should study the song analyses as given with a number of songs in this book. Observe how the phrases fall into groups of "Question and Answer" effects (*see* p. 221). Then analyze other simple songs, indicating the form by the A,B,A,C plan.

1. As a first step in composing a song, select a simple poem which appeals to you. A four-line poem may be chosen for brevity and simplicity. Read the poem carefully to determine the structural plan of the melody to which it best lends itself, as A,B,A,C, or A,A¹,B,A¹, etc., etc.

2. Read the words of the poem until a general rhythmic pattern is established, and the meter is determined as $\frac{2}{4}$, $\frac{3}{4}$, $\frac{4}{4}$, $\frac{6}{8}$, or whatever seems most appropriate.

3. Repeat the words of the first line of the poem, following the metrical swing as determined, until a melody is suggested. Write this melody.

4. Having composed the first phrase, its repetitions will occur as determined by your structural plan. Therefore, the nature of the contrasting phrase is now to be decided. Here again, saying the words over and over will probably suggest a contrasting melody, especially with the melody of the first phrase serving as a *question* to be *answered*.

5. Study now the endings of each of the phrases. These phrase endings are called *cadences*, and are like the rhymes in a poetic stanza or like punctuation marks. The final cadence must make a satisfactory close to your song, and the other cadences must be relatively strong or weak according to your structural plan, but never as conclusive as the closing cadence.

By composing a number of short melodies to four-line poems and then comparing your little songs with similar brief songs in this and other books, you will acquire skill both in the invention of melodies and in organizing them into well-planned song forms. Then you will be ready to undertake longer compositions based on models of well-constructed songs found in this book and in other books. Observe how little contrasting melodies may be organized into two-part and three-part forms and analyzed as I, II, or I, II, III, etc. (*see* Form, p. 220). By composing melodies of your own you will find increased enjoyment in studying fine folk songs and the art songs by the great composers.

VI. INTERPRETATION

In musical performance, the singer or player aims to present the music so that its meaning is delivered with the greatest clarity, effectiveness, and beauty. The composer indicates his melodies and harmonies by means of music notation. The spirit of the composition, its movement, forcefulness, and mood are suggested by terms and signs. These help the performer to understand the intentions of the composer and to *interpret* them to the listeners.

A. Technical

Certain of the composer's indications may be called "technical," because they are definite and specific. Such are the *tempo* markings and *dynamic* signs.

1. TEMPO: The general rate of speed with which a composition moves is called its *tempo*. The composer has four means for indicating tempo: (*a*) metronome marks; (*b*) conventional, widely accepted terms for relatively faster and slower movements; (*c*) when the composition is a dance, or in the nature of a dance, the dance title will indicate the rate of speed; and (*d*) often a fanciful title suggests the general movement.

a) *Metronome marks.* The metronome is a clock-like instrument which clicks at whatever speed it is set. The composer gives the metronome marking at the beginning of the piece, as MM ♩ = 60, which means that the speed is sixty quarter notes per minute. The performer thereby knows just how rapidly to play or sing that particular number. (*See* the metronome markings throughout this book.)

b) *Conventional tempo terms*

1. Indicating a steady rate of speed

Grave Largo	} very slow
Adagio Larghetto Adagietto	} slow
Andante Andantino	} somewhat slow
Moderato	} moderate movement
Allegretto Allegro	} fast
Presto Prestissimo	} very fast

2. Indicating a hastening of speed

Accelerando (*accel.*), gradually accelerating
Stringendo (*string.*), pressing ahead, usually with a *cresc.*
Più mosso, faster than before

3. Indicating a slackening of speed

Rallentando (*rall.*) } gradually growing slower
Ritardando (*rit.*)
Ritenuto (*riten.*) } dropping immediately to a slower
Meno mosso } rate of speed
Morendo } slower and softer
Smorzando

Most of these terms occur in the songs in this book.
Quiet movements usually close with a slight *ritardando*. Occasionally the *ritard* occurs in the phrase before the final one, in which case the last phrase closes in steady *tempo*. After a temporary change of tempo, the term, *a tempo*, indicates a resumption of the original speed.

c) *Dance movements.* (*See* Dance Forms under FORM, p. 220 of this unit.)

d) *Descriptive titles.* (For a discussion of descriptive titles, *see* B. Imaginative.)

2. DYNAMICS.

The conventional *dynamic marks* are as follows:

Fortissimo (*ff*), very loud
Forte (*f*), loud
Mezzo forte (*mf*), half loud
Mezzo (*m*), medium
Mezzo piano (*mp*), half soft
Piano (*p*), soft
Pianissimo (*pp*), very soft
Crescendo (*cresc.* ◁), growing louder
Decrescendo (*decresc.* ▷), decreasing in loudness
Diminuendo (*dim.* ▷), diminishing in loudness
Swell (◁ ▷), a *crescendo* and *diminuendo*
Sforzando (*sfz, sf, fz*), with special stress
Accent (>), with emphasis

Under the heading, *dynamics*, the subject of accentuation may also be considered. Every measure has its own accent. These are well marked in dance movements, while in lyric melodies they are less pronounced. Dramatic emphasis also involves accentuation.

As a general rule, ascending passages are likely to increase in tone volume and descending passages to grow softer.

Every musical work has its principal climax, usually approached by a series of lesser climaxes. The artistic relationship of secondary climaxes to the principal climax is one of the performer's chief means for reaching and inspiring his audience.

B. Imaginative

In addition to the technical indications of tempo and dynamics, the performer has numerous appeals to his imagination as guides to his interpretation.

1. DESCRIPTIVE TITLE. The title of a work often suggests the mood or spirit: as Barcarolle, Lullaby, Serenade, Evening Song, Soldiers' March, etc., etc.
2. SUGGESTIVE TERMS. Such as: *Brightly, Espressivo, Maestoso, Semplice, Tenderly, Vivace*, etc. Foreign terms are explained in the Vocabulary.
3. POETIC TEXT. In all good songs, the poetic text will serve as a guide both to the general spirit of the music and to the successive details of mood, thought, and expressive emphasis.

VII. VOCALIZATION

Effective vocalization may be developed through use of the song material in this book or by means of special exercises found in text books about the voice. In either case the following factors must be given careful attention:

a) Development of pure vowel tone and equalization of *quality* and *power* of each vowel and diphthong. Note that the diphthong "I" is pronounced as "ah" with just an instant of "ee" at the very last moment. Similarly in all diphthongs, one of the two vowel sounds receives major stress and the tone should be sustained upon it.

b) Enunciation, or ability to speak or sing with clear and distinct articulation. The consonants must not obstruct the tone of the vowels.

c) Pronunciation, or skill in speaking and singing with correct sound and accent.

d) Flexibility of lips and tongue, open throat, and general relaxation of the muscles concerned in tone production.

e) Natural intake of breath with easy expansion of waist and ribs; comfortable, upright posture without stiffness. An even, steady support of tone. Inhale quietly without overloading the lungs; exhale without breathiness.

f) Carry the head tone downward, retaining a free, pleasant quality. Ascending with the chest register causes the tone to become tight and raucous.

g) Development of tone color through dramatic expression of the text is far better than through artificial technical drill. In general, a live, bright, and fairly full tone is desirable. Avoid a thin, hushed tone.

h) Intervals are sung out of tune when a clear conception of tonal relationship is lacking. Establish tonality and train the ear to hear the two tones accurately in relation to each other and to the key itself. The third and seventh of the scale are the worst offenders, often being flat unless constantly corrected.

i) Improvement in intonation, tone quality, and balance of parts will follow intelligent use of the Tone Blending Drills. In all part singing aim for the velvety smoothness of chords perfectly in tune.

VIII. VOCABULARY OF MUSICAL TERMS

(In words derived from the Italian every vowel is sounded separately, and is pronounced: a-ah, e-ā, i-ē, o-ō, u-ōō)

Absolute Music. Instrumental music which attempts to tell no story but is concerned solely with beauty of structure and loveliness of tone.

A cappella. Without accompaniment, referring chiefly to sacred choral music.

Ad libitum (ad lib.). 1. A passage so marked may be performed with freedom of interpretation. 2. Optional.

Alto. 1. The voice part between soprano and tenor parts. 2. The voice which sings the alto part, either of women or boys.

Animato. With animation.

Appoggiatura. An ornamental tone, sometimes written as a grace note, which borrows its time from the following note (*see* pp. 45, 104).

Arpeggio. A chord played as though on the harp, that is, with the tones in quick succession instead of simultaneously (*see* pp. 110, 130, 133).

Art Song. A composed song (as distinguished from folk song) especially when written by a master (*see* pp. 1, 116). (*See, Popular Song, Familiar Song, Strophic Song, Through-Composed Song.*)

Assai. Very, or very much.

Baritone. A voice or voice part between bass and tenor.

Bass. 1. The lowest man's voice. 2. The lowest part in the harmony (*see* p. 57).

Burden. (*See* p. 114.)

Cadence. The ending of a phrase or other section of a composition; the effect of complete or partial close, similar to punctuation in language (*see* p. 222).

Cantabile. In a singing style.

Capriccio. Free and vivacious style.

Chamber Music. Music for a small group of performers.

Choir. 1. A company of singers. 2. A section of the orchestra or band.

Classical. (*See* pp. 64, 116, 189.)

Coda. (*See* p. 53.)

Con. With.

Con moto. With motion.

Contralto. The lowest female voice.

Counterpoint. The art of combining simultaneously two or more melodies.

Color. Character of tonal quality.

Coloratura. Decorative, ornamental music, or the voice equipped to perform it.

Cross Rhythm. (*See* p. 109.)

Deciso. Decisively (*see* p. 1).

Degree. Lines and spaces of the staff.

Descant. An optional counter melody (*see* p. 150).

Descriptive Music. Music suggesting a definite picture or story.

Dolce. Sweetly (*see* p. 196).

Drone Bass. (*See* p. 118.)

Duet. For two voices or instruments.

Embellishment. Ornamental tones: trill, turn, appoggiatura, etc.

Embouchure. Adjustment of lips in playing a wind instrument.

Encore. Again; repeated by request.

Enharmonic. Different notation for the same pitch, *i.e.*, C♯ and D♭.

Ensemble. Combination of performers.

Espressivo. Expressively (*see* p. 192).

Familiar Song. A simple song, long in favor.

Folk Song. (*See* pp. 3, 16, 157, and Nationality in Classified Index.)

Fermata. The hold (⌒).

Form. (*See* Unit XX, Theory, E.)

Fugue. An orderly contrapuntal treatment of a theme for three or more parts (*see* p. 64).

Giocoso. Jovially (*see* p. 168).

Glee. A vocal composition in three or more parts treated harmonically rather than contrapuntally.

Grace Note. A very short ornamental tone written as a small note with a dash through the flag.

Grazia, Grazioso. Gracefully (*see* pp. 131, 190, 201).

Harmony. Chords and their relationship.

Hymn Tune. A simple strophic setting of a religious poem.

Instrumentation. The art of arranging music for combinations of instruments.

Intonation. Exactness in pitch.

Legato. Smooth and sustained (*see* p. 152).

Leggiero. Brisk, sprightly (*see* p. 201).

Maestoso. Majestically (*see* pp. 1, 206).

Ma non troppo. But not too much.

Medley. A succession of miscellaneous melodies.

Meno mosso. A passage so marked becomes instantly slower.

Modern Music. (*See* pp. 64, 116, 189.)

Modulation. (*See* Unit XX, Theory, D.)

Molto. Much.

Morendo. Dying away.

Non troppo. Not too much (*see* p. 162).

Obbligato. A secondary melody essential for the complete musical effect.

Opus. Work. Many composers indicated the order of their works by opus number (*see* pp. 30, 57, 190).

Part Singing. The association of two or more voices singing parts in harmonic or contrapuntal relationship.

Phrase. The portion of a melody equivalent to a line of poetry (*see* p. 221).

Phrasing. The grouping of tones in a musical idea so as clearly to express its aesthetic intention.

Più. More.

Poco a poco. A bit (*see* pp. 196, 206).

Polyphony. Many voiced; the artistic combination of several melodies: *round, canon, fugue,* etc.

Popular Song. The usual term for light music of the day. Sometimes such songs are retained in favor, and then they may be called Familiar Songs (*see* p. 64).

Postlude. 1 The instrumental conclusion of a song. 2. A musical number closing a program or church service.

Prelude. 1. The instrumental introduction of a song or an instrumental suite. 2. A musical number preceding a program, service, act of a play or opera, etc.

Program Music. Music which tells a definite story or paints a specific picture.

Quartet. A group of four performers.

Quintet. A group of five performers.

Quintuplet. (*See* p. 99.)

Recital. A program presented by an individual or a small group of performers.

Refrain. The closing section of a song repeated after each stanza, sometimes called Chorus (*see* pp. 16, 18).

Repeat. (*See* Abbreviation, p. 219.)

Resolution. In harmony, passing from a dissonance to a consonance.

Rhythm. The flow of musical tones as grouped by accents, (*see* p. 218).

Romantic. (*See* pp. 64, 116.)

Rondo. An instrumental composition in which the principal theme occurs several times with intervening contrasting themes. (Basic form: I–II–I–III–I.)

Rubato. Rhythmic freedom within the measure for expressive purposes (*see* pp. 41, 45).

Scale. (*See* pp. 219, 75.)

Scherzo. A joke, hence a piece of music of playful or humorous character (*see* pp. 64, 75).

Score. Printed or written music in which the different parts are arranged one above another on several staves (*see* p. 146).

Section. A main division of a musical composition.

Semplice. Simply (*see* p. 128).

Sempre. Always (*see* p. 201).

Septet. A group of seven performers.

Sequence. A symmetrical succession of harmonic or melodic progressions (*see* p. 65).

Sextet. A group of six performers.

Signs. Characters of notation for guidance in performance, such as: 1. phrase marks or breath marks; 2. repeat marks; 3. *segno* 𝄋 ; head ⊕ ; swell ◁ ▷; turn ∾ ; etc.

Solo. To be presented by a single voice or instrument.

Sonata. An instrumental composition, usually in four movements, in related keys and contrasting rhythms, in which the first movement follows the elaborate design called "Sonata Form" (*see* pp. 64, 116).

Soprano. The highest female voice and unchanged voice of the boy.

Sostenuto. Sustained.

Staccàto. Detached, disconnected, often indicated by dots above or below the notes (*see* pp. 152, 201).

Stanza. In poetry, a group of lines organized into a unit through rhythm and rhyme, often called a *verse.*

Strophic Song. A song in which each stanza has the same musical setting.

Suite. 1. A set of instrumental dances, usually all in the same key. 2. A series of brief instrumental tone pictures, sometimes selected from a large work.

Suspension. A non-harmonic tone continued from a previous chord after the harmony has changed, and later resolving into its place in the new chord (*see* p. 61).

Symphony. A sonata for orchestra (*see* p. 64).

Syncopation. A displacement of accent, either strong beats coming where weak ones are expected, or accents occurring off the beat (*see* pp. 20, 42, 112).

Tanto. Too much (*see* p. 192).

Tempo. (*See* p. 218.)

Tenor. The highest adult male voice.

Tenuto (ten.). Sustained (*see* p. 7).

Tetrachord. A diatonic tone series within the interval of a fourth. Diatonic scales consist of two tetrachords, lower and upper, with similarities and differences which determine the character of the scale (*see* p. 219).

Theme. A brief melodic idea out of which a musical work or section of a composition is developed.

Through-Composed Song. A song in which there is a different melody for each verse, following the changing mood of the poem (*see* pp. 1, 117).

Time. The durational element in music as distinguished from tone, *i.e.,* pitch (*see* p. 218).

Tonality. Key feeling.

Tone. Sound of definite pitch, as distinguished from noise, wherein pitch is not definite. *Tone* is what is heard; *note* means the written symbol.

Tone Color. 1. Tone quality, as distinguishing voices from instruments, or one voice or instrument from another. 2. The effect produced by using a tone quality suitable to the mood or spirit of a composition.

Treble. Soprano.

Triad. A chord of three tones: root, third, and fifth (*see* p. 220).

Trio. 1. A group of three performers. 2. The third section of a March or Minuet.

Triplet. (*See* pp. 97, 100, etc.)

Turn. Embellishment of a tone by alternating with it the tone above and the tone below it (*see, Signs*).

Tutti. A direction for all performers to take part (as opposed to *solo*); or the passage so performed.

Unison. Two tones are in unison when they are identical in pitch.

Verse. A line of poetry; sometimes used to designate a stanza of poetry.

Vivace. Vivaciously (*see* p. 170).

PLAYS, PAGEANTS, AND FESTIVALS

Built around the songs of the Units, "Trips Abroad"

by STELLA MAREK CUSHING

To the Boys and Girls Using This Book

What kinds of people live in other parts of the world? How do they live? In what ways are they like us and how do they differ from us? Do you ever ask these questions? I do, and they have interested me so deeply that I read about these people, study their ways, and go to visit them in their homelands. There I mingle with them, observe their customs, and learn their songs and native dances. I have found friends everywhere, among all nationalities. They have taught me that we are more alike than unlike, even though our language and looks may be different.

The following festivals and plays have been written because I want to share with you my experiences and to give you a glimpse into the life and customs of these other races and nationalities. You have sung their songs in the units "Trips Abroad," have studied their geography and history, and probably have read stories about them. I hope that by combining their songs, dances, and customs in these folk plays you will come to understand more fully the true spirit and character of these peoples.

Our civilization in America has been enriched by the culture of the whole world. If we realize this we become more appreciative of the contributions that have been made by all peoples. If you were born of American parents, taking part in these plays will be a good way for you to know your neighbors who were born abroad and to understand peoples living in other parts of the world. If you or your parents were born in other lands, you may take new pride in your own rich heritage.

The characters in these plays have been drawn chiefly from peasant life. These country people are proud, strong, and hospitable. We are drawn to them by their simplicity of character, their lusty sense of humor, and their zest for living. Their songs are full of rhythm, feeling, and spirit. Folk dances originated with peasants. They must be danced with vigor, marked accent, and rhythmic stamp of heavy boot. Boys and girls in America dancing these gay figures together will find them to be most fascinating.

Perhaps a day will come when you too will travel to other lands. Who knows but that these glimpses of the people of those lands may enable you to meet them with a feeling of fellowship and understanding.

Suggestions for Production

The following plays may be given in simple form as classroom projects; they may be used as assembly programs; they are appropriate for parent-teacher meetings; or they may become a part of an elaborate community project, using foreign-born or widely-traveled parents and national groups living in the community. Some of the plays form suitable material for out-of-door festivals. All of them have been produced in the various types of projects suggested.

In producing these plays their festival character should be kept in mind. The participants should enter into the spirit of the plays with enthusiasm, the scenes should be gay and spontaneous, and the characters natural. The songs and dances should be well rehearsed so that the musical director need not be conspicuous. Often the direction may come from the wings, or the director and assistants may wear costumes and circulate among the participants. For the festival scenes it has been found extremely effective to accompany the voices with violins only or a combination of strings with clarinet and popular instruments like the guitar and accordion. It seldom is desirable to use the piano for out-of-door scenes as it detracts from the festival atmosphere.

STELLA MAREK CUSHING

The usual stage terms are used, such as "upstage," which is away from audience; "downstage," toward audience; "stage right" and "stage left" as participants face audience, abbreviated throughout text as R. and L.

COSTUMES

The pictures throughout this book show authentic costumes of the different peoples represented. In addition, authentic costumes and suggestions for scenery are to be found in various issues of *The National Geographic Magazine*. Cross references to the most useful pages are noted in connection with the individual plays.

As a further aid to teachers and students in designing and making costumes for festivals and plays, the following books may be secured at the F. W. Woolworth store in Montclair, New Jersey: *Peasant Costumes of Europe* — Paper Doll Cut-Outs by Rachel Taft Dixon, copyright, 1934, by Whitman Publishing Company, Racine, Wisconsin. Authentic costumes of the following countries are represented: France, Bulgaria, Germany, Holland, Poland, Czechoslovakia, Hungary, Roumania, Greece, Austria, Spain, Portugal, Italy, Denmark, Sweden, and Norway. In *Around the World*, No. 2106 — Paper Dolls, designed by Dorothy Hoover Downs and published by The Saalfield Publishing Company, Akron, Ohio, costumes of twenty-one nationalities are represented: Holland, Switzerland, Sweden, France, Scotland, Ireland, England, Russia, Italy, Spain, Hungary, Turkey, Mexico, Argentine, United States, American Indian, Eskimo, Hawaii, China, Japan, and India.

Peasant Costume in Europe, by Kathleen Mann, published by The Macmillan Company, is an excellent reference book for general costumes.

Midsummer Magic

by STELLA MAREK CUSHING

PLACE and TIME: Leksand, Sweden, on the shores of Lake Siljan, in the province of Dalecarlia, mid-afternoon, June twenty three.

SCENE: The "green" in front of the Bostrom home, running down to the lake front. Downstage R. a part of the house shows, red with white trimmings. It has a small porch with white posts. (*See, The National Geographic Magazine*, October, 1928, plates X and XVI.) Upstage at the back is a low white fence with an arched opening in the center. The back drop shows blue sky, a lake, and low green hills. There are a few benches on the stage and a small rocking chair without arms.

CHARACTERS:

FADER and MODER BOSTROM, called Far (For) and Mor (Moor)
Their children — GUSTAV (Goos-tav), HILDA, EBBA
MORMOR (Moor-moor), mother's mother
FARFAR (Fọr-for), father's father
TANT, Aunt
FARBROR, Uncle
LISA (Lee-sa), the Saeter girl (Say'-ter)
RANGHILD (Rahng-heeld)
MÄRTA (Mare-ta)
SVEA (Svay-a)
CARL
OSKAR
Procession of girls, boys, men, women, and children of the village.

(Unless otherwise marked, "a" is pronounced as in father.)

GENERAL SUGGESTIONS: The following play begins with solemnity, but the rest of the scene is festive. (*See, The National Geographic Magazine* article — July, 1934, for description of midsummer's eve celebration.) Violins only should be used for accompaniment, as this is the popular instrument in Sweden. A Saeter girl is one who spends all summer in the hills. There she lives in a small house, tends the cows, milks them, and makes cheese. The young people are very respectful of Mormor and Farfar. This play is also suitable for production out-of-doors, in which case the dialogue should be somewhat shortened. Trees and shrubs may form entrances and a screen may serve as an entrance into the house. The fence and archway may be omitted, except that they provide a place to decorate with garlands.

Properties: long table, white tablecloth, benches, cups, plates, coffee pot, dishes of sandwiches, glasses, candles, eggs, bowls, sheets, handkerchiefs, and Maypole.

MUSIC: (*See* Unit II: Trips Abroad — Sweden, p. 8.)

COSTUMES: (*See, The National Geographic Magazine*, Oct. 1928, plates I–XVI; also pp. 470 and 473; July, 1934, plates 3, 5, 7, 8 and pp. 4, 9, 19, 20, 47, 54, 56.)

INTRODUCTION (*To be printed on program or spoken as a prologue before the curtains open*): Midsummer's Day is celebrated in many parts of the world but in the Scandinavian countries it is of especial significance. In this northern territory, called the "Land of the Midnight Sun," midnight is like midday and is a happy occasion for rejoicing.

No one knows how the festival originated for it began in pagan times, and many of the customs have been merged with Christian ceremonies in the use of symbols, such as the birch tree, sign of victory, and the festooned Maypole, symbol of renewed fertility of Mother Earth.

We go now to Sweden and join with the people in their festival. We shall enjoy the songs and dances, the spirit of fun, and the magic that always is revived on Midsummer's Eve.

[*At rise of curtain, singing is heard off stage, soft as from a distance.*]

Song, My Homeland, p. 9

[FADER *and* GUSTAV *enter through arch, bringing a long table. They place it at extreme L. running upstage to downstage.* MODER *stands nearby with a tablecloth in her hand;* HILDA *and* EBBA *are in the doorway. As table is placed* HILDA *comes to help her mother lay the cloth. They fuss over it to be sure that not a wrinkle shows.* FADER *and* GUSTAV *bring benches, place them near table, then move about the stage assisting as they can. The song is ended.*]

MODER. The procession is forming in the village. That means that soon the people will be coming from the square and we must be ready. Ebba, bring the cups for coffee, glasses for milk, and the food. [EBBA *exits R.*] Help her, Hilda. Call Mormor and Farfar. They will want to watch us.

EBBA [*enters R. with cups and saucers*]. We shall need more cups and glasses for many people will come to visit us.

MODER. Yes, we must be sure to have enough for all. [HILDA *enters R. with* MORMOR *and* FARFAR, *who sit near house, downstage R.*]

HILDA. I am so excited, Mor, I can hardly wait for the festival to begin.

MODER [*sternly*]. Save your excitement until your work is done. For now, keep your head; there is much to do.

MORMOR. Ack, Anna, have you forgotten when you were young? I remember before Midsummer's Festival your cheeks were red as roses and your eyes like the flower *blå-klint* (blow-klint).

MODER. Ack, that was a long time ago.

HILDA. What was Mor like, Mormor?

MORMOR. Like? Like you, Hilda, only her eyes were blue and her hair more golden.

EBBA. And was she gay?

MORMOR. Of course she was gay. She was always the leader in all the customs.

FARFAR. Your Fader was more quiet, I remember, Anna; your mother was always his partner. [*Reflecting*] Did you not plight your troth on Midsummer's Day?

[FADER *and* MODER *have been listening.*]

FADER. Ack, yes!

MODER [*sighing*]. Ack, yes! [*All sigh;* MODER *is startled from her dreams.*]

MODER. Come, come, there is work to do. Our dreams must wait. [*All but* MORMOR *and* FARFAR *move about.*]

[EBBA *and* HILDA *continue to bring food from the house.* FADER *and* GUSTAV *come to the table; all make exclamations about food, etc.*]

MODER. Ack, we shall have a good *Smörgåsbord* * (Smer'-gos-boord) tonight. Put the sandwiches here.

FADER. Ack, the goat's cheese and the crackerbread.

GUSTAV. Mm, the honey and the cakes.

FADER. Gustav, have you finished your work in the barns?

GUSTAV. Yes, Far, long ago. The goats are fed and locked in the barn; the chickens are fast asleep. I put fresh clover for our mother cow, and the new calf has a warm bed of hay.

FADER. It is a nice gift our cow has given us today.

[*Enter, stage center,* FARBROR, TANT (*with a basket on her arm*), *their son,* CARL, *and their daughter,* LISA. *The families greet each other warmly saying,* "God Dag" (Gŏŏd Dog).]

---

* Open sandwiches, cold cuts, etc.

EBBA. Lisa, I thought that you were in the saeter watching the cows.

LISA. Far sent Jan up to watch the cows for me.

FADER. Farbror, we have a new calf born today. Come to the barn and see it.

GUSTAV. Shall we go, too? [GUSTAV and CARL follow. They exit, L.]

TANT [to EBBA and HILDA]. Are you prepared for midsummer magic tonight?

EBBA [suddenly remembering]. Ack, yes, the flowers. [Runs into house.]

HILDA. Ebba and I picked the flowers as you said. [EBBA returns with flowers, half of which she gives to HILDA.] Now what do we do?

TANT. Did you cross nine stiles?

EBBA. Yes, and at each stile we picked a different flower.

TANT. Without saying a word?

GIRLS. Yes.

HILDA. Then we found an empty building and walked around it nine times.

TANT. Without speaking?

EBBA. Yes, now what do we do?

TANT. You must each weave a wreath of flowers, then put it under your pillow to dream upon.

HILDA. And will our dreams come true?

TANT. Of course, if you believe in midsummer magic. [Girls begin to make wreaths. They sing one verse of "My Homeland" as they work. LISA joins them.]

EBBA. Mine is finished, Hilda.

HILDA. And mine. I wonder what we shall dream? [They giggle and enter house. In the distance singing is heard.]

Song, Spring, p. 8

MODER [calls]. Far, Gustav. The procession is coming. The people will soon be here.

[The men and boys enter L. HILDA and EBBA return from house. All look off stage R., or toward audience, whichever entrance is chosen for procession. First to enter are boys and girls carrying garlands of flowers which they festoon around posts, over fences, archway, and table, while singing continues. They are followed by older people, some of whom bring baskets of food. There are greetings of "God Dag." Refreshments are passed. There is general conversation. Singing ends. All the girls surround TANT.]

SVEA. Tant, tell us some magic.

TANT. Who is going to the crossroads with the water?

SVEA. I am, and Lisa goes with me.

TANT. Then fill your glasses with water. Wrap a napkin around so that not a drop spills, or the spell will be broken. [Girls do so at table, then return to TANT.] Not a word must be spoken, no matter who speaks to you. Go to the crossroads and wait for things to happen.

LISA. What will happen, Tant?

TANT. Perhaps someone in a white cloak and mask will come to drink the water, then quickly run away.

LISA. How shall we know who it is?

TANT. Ack, you must run after him and catch him. [LISA and SVEA exit center, turn R. as boys and girls tease them, trying to make them spill the water. GUSTAV and CARL near house whisper together; then go to MODER who is near table with her guests.]

GUSTAV. Mor, we must have two white cloaks.

CARL. Two great white cloaks and masks.

MODER. But I have no white cloaks. Will sheets do?

GUSTAV. Yes, but we must waste no time. [Boys tie handkerchiefs over their faces. MODER hurries into house, returns at once bringing out two sheets which she wraps around the boys. They tiptoe out, following girls. Young people laugh.]

HILDA. What other magic shall we have, Tant? [EBBA does so. Real eggs should be used.] We shall see what fortunes the eggs bring. Three of you must each fill a glass with water. [EBBA, HILDA, and RANGHILD do as she tells them.] Drop the white of an egg into each glass.

EBBA. What shall we do with the yolks?

TANT. Put them into a bowl, nothing must be wasted.

"Saving is a womanly grace." They will go into the cake tomorrow.

RANGHILD. Tell me my fortune.

TANT. Not yet, put them away. Wait for the magic to work. [Girls put glasses on table. Someone starts humming.]

[The fiddlers or pianist begin to play introduction of "Neptune." After first verse some swing into a peasant waltz.* Others join, even the older people who seem to be gayer than the young ones.]

Song, Neptune, p. 12

[By this time participants are in festive mood. As song ends, GUSTAV and CARL come running down one of the aisles of the auditorium with SVEA and LISA chasing them. As the boys reach steps both trip over each other and fall. Girls catch them amid great laughter. Several boys exit L.]

HILDA. Now, may we have our fortunes told?

TANT. Bring the glasses. I must see if the magic has worked. [She takes RANGHILD's glass.] Let me see. [All girls crowd around her.] Ack, I see books and a professor. I see more books and a large building. You will go to the university. Here is a room with desks. You will be a teacher; here are boys and girls, and the number seven. You will teach for seven years. Now, Ebba, what is your fortune? [Looks into glass.] There are many people; it is like a procession. There is a church at the beginning. It must be a wedding, yes, there are wedding bells, but not yet, not for a long time. And Hilda, what is in your glass? [Looks into glass.] Oh my, I see a ship, a big ship. You are going on a long journey. I see autos and tall buildings, many people, and streets paved with gold. You are going to America where you will make new friends and be very happy. There you will find many people who have gone from Sweden to the new land of promise. I am told that they have settled in the great cities and out upon the farmlands.

CARL. When I am grown I shall go to America; I have an uncle in Minnesota. Will you come with me, Gustav?

GUSTAV. No, I am the eldest son. I shall remain here.

[Offstage L. there is a great commotion, with shouting and cheering. All on stage look off stage L.]

CARL. The boys are bringing the Maypole.

GUSTAV. Now the festival really begins.

ALL. The Maypole! We'll dance the whole night through!

[Everyone is excited as boys enter L. with a large Maypole, decorated at the top with a wreath from which hang blue and gold streamers. It appears heavy and difficult to handle. Everyone talks as orders are shouted. At the last efforts to raise it, there is a moment's silence, then, as it is placed, all cheer. The fiddlers or pianist begin to play "Buxom Lassies."]

Song, Buxom Lassies, p. 10

[Everyone sings. Some boys and girls form circle around Maypole and dance. See directions, p. 10. Others gather around table, near fence, or in doorway. Some are eating or drinking coffee as dancing continues. After "Buxom Lassies," the song with dance "Neptune" may be repeated, indicating that the festivities are only beginning, and will continue the whole night through. In the midst of gayety curtains close.]

CURTAIN

---

* Directions for Peasant Waltz

Position: Partners face each other. Boy places both hands on girl's hips; girl places both hands on boy's shoulders.

Count 1. Boy steps forward with left foot; girl steps backward with right foot.

Count 2. Boy brings right foot to left; girl brings left foot to right.

Count 3. Boy steps forward again with left foot; girl steps backward with right foot. (Repeat same with other foot.) When danced to a fast tempo, as in the Beseda, p. 46, there is a slight leap on the first beat and a decided springiness in each step as partners turn alone or together.

A Playground in Kiev

by STELLA MAREK CUSHING

PLACE and TIME: A park in Kiev, Ukraine, on a holiday. (The idea for the following play was suggested by the author's visits to several parks where she watched and mingled with the young people.)

SCENE: The scene is in the beautiful park in Kiev overlooking the Dnieper River. There are trees, a glimpse of the river and hills beyond. Upstage there is a long table on which are tin cups, dark bread, and a few plates of crackers. There are a few long rustic benches or stones on which to sit.

CHARACTERS:

BABUSHKA (Baa-bush'-kaa), an old woman
Katsi (Kaht'-see), a young woman
NIKOLAI (Ni-ko-lie), the leader
Boys
    ANTON (An'-ton)
    MYHASH (MI'-hash)
    VASILI (Va-sI'-lee)
Girls
    MARINA (Ma-ree'-na)
    ELSA (El'-sa)
    ROSANDA (Ro-san'-da)
DIDO and BIDO (Dee'-do, Bee'-do), two clowns who are recreation leaders
Boys and Girls
ANNA, the lost girl
MOTHER, of Anna
IVAN (Ee-van') and ROSA, the dancers
(More Ukrainians may be added.)
(Pronounce "a" as in father.)

GENERAL SUGGESTIONS: When produced, the scene should be natural and spontaneous. It will be seen that the humor of the play centers around Dido and Bido, who are boisterous clowns, popular with the children. Their actions in dialogue and song should be stylized and very vigorous. In assembling the play, some practice will be necessary in having the children march in pairs to the count of raz-, dva-, raz, dva, tri-(one-, two-, one, two, three). This play may be produced out-of-doors, in which case the dialogue should be somewhat shortened.

MUSIC: (See Unit IV: Trips Abroad — Russia and Ukraine, p. 25.)

COSTUMES: All the characters may be in simple dresses and suits similar to those worn in this country, as peasant costumes have largely been discarded. Cotton dresses of plain color or print may be worn by the girls, and plain suits and shirts by the boys. Nikolai and some of the boys may wear Russian blouses, but the Ukrainian dancers should be in costume. (See, The National Geographic Magazine, November, 1914.)

INTRODUCTION (To be printed on program or spoken as a prologue before the curtains open): Russia is a long distance from our country and few of us can travel there except in imagination. Today we shall make such a journey and imagine ourselves to be actually there. In many cities there are parks with special areas set aside for children, very much like the playgrounds in our own country. Some are elaborately equipped with a theater, hall, kino (moving picture house), swings, slides, etc.

Let us imagine that we are in a park in Kiev, Ukraine, where we go to watch and mingle with the boys and girls who have come there for a holiday.

[As curtains open, KATSI and BABUSHKA are discovered at the long table preparing the food for the lunch period. Band or orchestra music can be heard at back of hall or backstage, if boys and girls enter that way. Use a part of school orchestra or a phonograph record. Victor Record No. 1681B or 6514B are suggested for this use.]

[As music ends, girls and boys may be heard applauding.]

KATSI [looking in direction of applause]. The concert is over, the boys and girls soon will be coming this way for their lunch.

BABUSHKA. And very hungry, too. Do you think there is enough food?

KATSI. It will be plenty. I shall bring the milk; here is bread and sausage — surely enough for all.

BABUSHKA. Here in the country air they will welcome the food. But it is not yet time to eat.

KATSI. No, they will play a few games first, for Nikolai is with them.

BABUSHKA. All the boys and girls like Nikolai. Every rest-day he comes here to play with the children instead of going for his own pleasure.

KATSI. This is his pleasure [looks off toward back of hall, or whichever way group is coming]. How gaily he leads the children.

BABUSHKA. It is because he is young with them.

[From back of hall or off stage may be heard the voices of the boys and girls counting softly at first as if far away, gradually growing louder until they enter the hall, and marching through the audience mount the platform. They count as they march "raz-, dva-, raz, dva, tri-," ("one-, two-, one, two, three-"). When all are on stage, NIKOLAI stands on a box or tree stump downstage L. The boys and girls, some standing and some sitting, gather around him and sing, NIKOLAI leading.]

Song with Dance, Korobushka, p. 26

[At the conclusion of the song the dancers form into line, the music quickens into a livelier tempo, and the dance is performed at least four times.]

NIKOLAI. This is the period for games and for lunch. After the games we shall divide into groups for there are several things to do. You may go to the kino [cheers], the theater [cheers], or the swings [cheers]. [Bell rings at counter and BABUSHKA calls.]

BABUSHKA [in a singsong manner]. Come, come, nice hot sausages and good fresh bread; nice hot sausages and good fresh bread; come and eat, come and eat [repeating many times].

KATSI. Health belongs to those who eat good fresh bread. Fresh air in the clean parks, great trees to shade you, and pure sunshine will make you healthy.

BABUSHKA. Come, come, nice hot sausages and good fresh bread. [Boys and girls crowd around counter; take food and milk. All sit down to eat, talking and laughing happily. When it is quiet KATSI sings.]

Song, In My Garden Is a Hazel Tree, p. 28

[All join in the chorus, or entire song may be sung by everyone.]

BABUSHKA [wiping her eyes]. A beautiful song but my favorite is another.

NIKOLAI. What is it, Babushka?

BABUSHKA. "Flow, River, Flow."

NIKOLAI. Sing it for us, Babushka. [BABUSHKA sings it. All may hum with her.]

Song, Flow, River, Flow, p. 27

[After song there is a great commotion at back of hall. DIDO and BIDO come running down through aisles, whooping. They tumble into somersaults, make faces at the boys and girls, and generally provoke laughter. Then they face audience and begin to sing a few strains of "My Friend," p. 30. They do not sing it together for DIDO sings in a high voice quickly, and BIDO in a low voice slowly. Each is annoyed at the other but will not stop, singing louder and louder until NIKOLAI intervenes.]

NIKOLAI. What are you trying to do, split our ears?

[DIDO and BIDO *continue.*]

NIKOLAI [*shakes them slightly*]. Wait, wait a moment, I want to ask a question. [*They finally stop singing.*] What are you singing?

CLOWNS [*together*]. A song about my friend.

NIKOLAI. Oh, it is the same song but it does not sound the same because you are not singing it the same way.

CLOWNS [*together*]. Same song.

DIDO. My way is best.

BIDO. My way is best. [*They continue saying this several times, louder and angrier.*]

NIKOLAI [*intervening*]. But you can't sing like that; nobody can enjoy it.

DIDO. I began first. It is my right to sing it.

BIDO. I began at the same time. It is my right to sing it.

NIKOLAI. It is evident that you cannot both sing your song at the same time. It is also evident that you cannot decide which shall be first. [*Turning to girls and boys.*] We shall have to decide.

[*Girls and boys cheer.* CLOWNS *scowl and turn their backs to each other.*]

NIKOLAI [*explains situation to group*]. Dido and Bido each wish to sing. By chance they choose to sing the same song at the very same time, but not the same way. What happens? It is a jumble. We cannot enjoy the song for Dido sings fast in one key and Bido sings slowly in another key. They grow angry, both refuse to stop, and we are denied hearing the song. Result, chaos, and no one benefited. Dido and Bido, who were friends, are now enemies. We who liked them both are irritated. No one is satisfied. There must be a way to settle the matter, but how?

ANTON. Send them away.

MARINA. Then we won't hear the song.

MYHASH. They must take turns.

ALL. Take turns, take turns.

ELSA. But who will begin?

VASILI. They must draw lots.

ROSANDA. But that is only chance; it does not settle the matter.

NIKOLAI. No, it does not settle the matter. We must think of something that calms their anger, for no clear thinking comes when black looks and angry hearts are troubled. They must settle it themselves.

ANTON [*walks between them and points*]. See how funny they look scowling.

MARINA. Make them look at each other. [*All laugh and say, "Yes, make them look at each other."*]

[NIKOLAI *turns* DIDO *and* BIDO *around; they look at each other scowling at first, gradually look sheepish, smile, then laugh loudly. Everyone laughs.*]

DIDO. You may begin.

BIDO. You may begin.

[*They continue bowing and asking each other to begin.* NIKOLAI, *fearing another outburst of anger, intervenes.*]

NIKOLAI. Dido and Bido, we shall set the key and the time and you can both sing. Everyone will listen. Out of chaos comes order; we go from anger to good fellowship, each one winning, no one losing, the best good for all, and all for the best good.

[DIDO *and* BIDO *sing; boys and girls join in chorus.*]

Song, My Friend, p. 30

[*As song ends, girls and boys divide; one group forms on left with* DIDO *and* KATSI, *the other group on right with* BIDO *and* NIKOLAI.]

[ANNA *enters left crying lustily. In her hand is a tin cup of berries. Only group on L. of stage listen to her. Others are occupied with* BIDO *and* NIKOLAI.]

KATSI. Well, well, what is the matter?

ANNA. I've lost my mother [*crying*].

KATSI. Where is she?

ANNA. I don't know. [*Others crowd around her.*]

KATSI. We shall help you. Tell us all about it.

ANNA. Today is rest-day, so, early this morning we came out here, mother, little sister, brother, and I. All morning we played together. Then mother and I took brother and sister to the kindergarten playground. After that we walked in the forest; mother stopped to rest while I gathered some berries. I must have gone too far and turned into another path because I cannot find the place where mother is resting.

KATSI. What path did you take to the forest?

ANNA. The path from the kino.

KATSI. Ah, yes. Now we must help you and your mother to find each other. [*Turns to group which crowds around* ANNA *downstage L.*] What is the first thing to do?

ROSANDA. Go to the forest on the path from the kino.

MYHASH. Not at first; her mother may have left the path.

ELSA. Take her to the gatekeeper.

[*While they are thus occupied,* MOTHER *enters R. She is sobbing.* NIKOLAI, BIDO, *and group surround her.*]

MOTHER. My child, my child, Anna, where are you? Oh, oh, oh!

NIKOLAI. What is the matter?

MOTHER. Trouble is upon me. Dark shadows cross my path. Why, oh why —

NIKOLAI. Tell me, what has happened?

MOTHER. My daughter has been taken away, away, oh, oh!

NIKOLAI. Don't weep. Wait a moment. [*To boys and girls*] What shall we do?

MARINA. We must help her.

MYHASH. First we must know what has happened.

ELSA. Find out what she means.

VASILI. Yes, what is she talking about?

NIKOLAI [*to* MOTHER]. Tell us all about your trouble.

MOTHER. Early today we came to the park, my three children and I. All morning we were together; then I took the little children to the playground. Anna and I walked in the forest until I was tired. Anna went to pick berries for me and I cannot find her. She has been stolen. [*Begins sobbing again*]

NIKOLAI. She could not be stolen. She is safe in this park. [*Turns to boys and girls*] What shall we do?

ANTON [*from group surrounding* ANNA]. Let us take her to the Bureau of Information.

CHORUS [*from group surrounding* MOTHER]. Yes, yes, hurry.

[*Groups surrounding* ANNA *and* MOTHER *separate as* KATSI *leads* ANNA *toward center of stage and* NIKOLAI *leads* MOTHER *toward center of stage.* MOTHER *and* ANNA *see each other.* ANNA *rushes into* MOTHER'S *arms while boys and girls cheer. All circle* ANNA *and sing.*]

Song, Anna's Rosy Cheeks, p. 31

[ROSA *and* IVAN, *in Ukrainian costume accompanied by others, if possible, enter R. All greet them.*]

NIKOLAI. Where are you going now?

ROSA. To the theater; we are singing and dancing there.

NIKOLAI. Can you dance for us, here?

IVAN. Yes, if someone can play for us or sing.

ROSANDA. What is the song?

[IVAN *and* ROSA *hum tune of* "Hopak."]

GIRLS *and* BOYS. Yes, we know that.

Song, Hopak, p. 32

[*All sing song.* IVAN *and* ROSA *and other dancers begin the Hopak. At end, all may whirl or* IVAN *and* ROSA *may end their dance, then others repeat it. At end of dance, bells ring off stage.*]

NIKOLAI. The programs are beginning at the kino and at the theater. At the kino is the picture "*Garmoniya*" (The Accordion Player). At the theater you will see Ivan and Rosa and all the Ukrainian dancers, also the jugglers.

DIDO [*stage R.*]. I go to the kino. Who comes with me? [*Part of group says, "I do."*] Then come here. [*Group goes to him.*]

BIDO [*stage L.*]. I go to the theater. Who comes with me? [*Another group says, "I do."*] Then come here. [*Group goes to him.*]

NIKOLAI [*at center*]. And I go to the swings. Who comes with me? [*Rest of group says,* "I do."] Then come!

[NIKOLAI *starts off marching to the count as at beginning* — "*raz-, dva-, raz, dva, tri-,*" ("*one-, two-, one, two, three-*"). *Boys and girls shout farewells,* "Goodby, see you next rest-

day," *etc.* DIDO *circles stage, exits L.;* BIDO *circles stage, exits R.* NIKOLAI *leads his group through audience. Curtains close, leaving* BABUSHKA *and* KATSI *cleaning up at the counter.*

CURTAIN

At the Frontier — Poland and Czechoslovakia

by STELLA MAREK CUSHING

PLACE and TIME: The boundary line between Poland and Czechoslovakia at harvest-time, late June.

SCENE: The background shows blue sky, foothills of the Carpathian Mountains in the distance, nearby the golden grain piled into sheaves, a few rocks and low fir trees. Upstage, directly in the center, is a low well. The boundary line is in the middle of the stage, extending from the well to the footlights. A stone may be placed as a marker. Also upstage at each side may be low platforms hidden by shrubs or rocks.

CHARACTERS:

JAN (Yan), Polish guard
JINDRA (Yeen'-dra), Czechoslovak guard
WOJTEK (Voy'-tek), boy leader of Polish peasants
Polish Peasant Girls
   HANUSIA (Ha-noo'-shya)
   BRONIA (Bro'-nya)
   STASIA (Sta'-sya)
Polish Peasant Boys
   PIOTR (Pyau-tr)
   BARTEK (Bar'-tek)
VACLAV (Va'-tslaf), boy leader of Czechoslovak peasants
JOSEF (Yo'-sef), the fiddler
Czechoslovak Peasant Girls
   RUZHENA (Roo'-zhe-na)
   JIRKA (Yeer'-ka)
GRANDFATHER
KAZIMIERZ (Ka'-zi-myairzh), boy leader of Polish Sokol delegation
LUDMILA (Lood'-mee-la), girl leader of Czechoslovak Sokol delegation

("J" is pronounced like "y", "r" is rolled, and "a" is pronounced as in father.)

GENERAL SUGGESTIONS: This play is produced easily, as each group may be selected from a different class; also, the singers and dancers may be drawn from different classes and rehearsed separately. It is most effective if only violins are used to carry the tunes, which will also give violin students excellent experience. Perhaps for the dances, and to lead the last song, it may be necessary to use a more experienced violinist, or a pianist. The guards, Jan and Jindra, are simple folk but their philosophy is worth noting. Considerable humor may be put into these characterizations. Great care must be taken to see that the border is not crossed until the stage business requires it. This play is suitable for an out-of-door festival in which case the dialogue should be somewhat shortened. Very large groups of students and adults may be used, especially in the delegations.

MUSIC: (*See* Unit V: Trips Abroad — Poland and Czechoslovakia, p. 34.)

COSTUMES: (*See, The National Geographic Magazine.* Poland, April, 1932, plates 3–8; March, 1933, plates 1–8, pp. 325–342; Czechoslovakia, February, 1921, pp. 114–155, June, 1927, plates 1–16; January, 1933 for Sokol pictures.)

INTRODUCTION (*To be printed on program or spoken as a prologue before the curtains open*): The scene for our play is at the frontier of Poland and Czechoslovakia. It is the time of harvest and also the day when great delegations are crossing the boundary from Praha, or Prague, as we call it. They are going to Krakow for a Sokol congress.

The word Sokol means "falcon." About eighty years ago in Prague while the Czechs were still under Hapsburg rule, this organization was formed for the purpose of providing a means for social intercourse, for physical prowess, and for the moral betterment of its members. It became very popular in all the Slavonic countries and was the organization that gave to the Slavs the spiritual, mental, and physical courage which helped them in their struggle for liberty.

We see fields of grain extending for mile upon mile without any apparent division at the boundary line. Here the peasants live peaceably on both sides of the border, fraternizing as neighbors, and sowing and harvesting their wheat with little thought of political intrigues and national hates and jealousies. In imagination we can see even the frontier guards drawn into the friendly circle, showing how it may be in the future when frontiers are not barriers and the people of the world live in peace.

[*Just before curtains open a song is heard.*]

Song, Clanking Spurs, p. 34

[*As curtains open, a group of Polish peasants is seen L. They are resting from their work of harvesting the grain. Some are drinking water at the well, some are lying on the ground. Upstage, extreme L.,* JAN *is standing facing the group.* JINDRA, *in similar position, is standing downstage R., with his back to singers who occupy only Polish side of stage. After song, without any pause, fiddler begins music of "Krakowiak." Six or eight couples dance as others sing.*]

Song with Dance, Krakowiak, p. 36

WOJTEK. It is time to go back to the fields. The sun is high in the heavens and we have much work to do before night. The grain is ripe for harvesting. It must be gathered today. Tomorrow the clouds may turn their barrels upside down upon us.

HANUSIA. It will not rain tomorrow for tonight the moon is full. No storm dares to look at the full moon.

WOJTEK. You are right, I had forgotten that.

STASIA [*looking off*]. The wheat is like a field of gold with the sun shining upon it.

BRONIA. It is graceful, dancing in the breeze.

PIOTR. Have you noticed how full and heavy is the cup at the end of each stalk?

WOJTEK. It will be a rich harvest this year.

PIOTR. When the wheat and rye are gathered the grain will be brought to father's mill to be made into flour.

STASIA. Then we shall make the flour into loaves of bread.

HANUSIA. The baker will put it into his great oven.

BRONIA. Then we shall eat it. [*All say* "um." *Horn blows off stage L.*]

WOJTEK [*looks off*]. Father is waving us back to the fields. It is the signal to go. [*All rise but one boy.*]

BARTEK [*yawning*]. I think that I shall rest awhile. It is very pleasant here in the shade.

WOJTEK. You are a lazy one. [*Appeals to others*] What shall we do with him?

BOYS. Do? [*Several boys move quickly to take hold of him but he jumps up and runs off. Others laugh. Horn blows again. All say goodby to* JAN *and exit L.*]

[*The guards,* JAN *and* JINDRA, *walk upstage to center, turn, walk together downstage, turn away from each other, walk upstage, turn, walk downstage, turn, this time toward each other, apparently see each other for the first time, salute.*]

JAN. Ah, Jindra.

JINDRA. Good day, Jan.

JAN. And how fare you in your country?

JINDRA. Very well, and how is it in Poland?

JAN. Good, my friend. The harvest shows good yield.

JINDRA. Then the winter will be a pleasant one with enough food for all.

JAN. Yes, the wheat, corn, oats, and rye have all been spared from drought or too much rain.

JINDRA. Your village will make a great festival.

JAN. Yes, it will be a merry time. We shall carry the sheaves of wheat to the priest to be blessed. The girls will make wreaths for their hair.

JINDRA. And you will dance and sing the whole night through.

JAN. Why not? This is the time to be happy. Now tell me, what of the Czechoslovak harvest?

JINDRA. The same as yours, my friend. Does not the same sun shine, the same rain fall, and the same wind blow on your country and mine?

JAN. You are right, Jindra. Does not the same God bless both harvests?

JINDRA. There is no division up there.

JAN. The earth has no line drawn upon it to say, — This earth will grow our wheat; that will grow your wheat! A wagon of dirt from your country and one from mine would be just the same.

JINDRA. Yes, they are the same. It is only we who are different.

JAN. Are we so different?

JINDRA. Aren't we? [*They stand closely together and peer into each other's faces.*]

JAN. You have two eyes; I have two eyes. Mine are blue; yours are brown.

JINDRA. But blue or brown, they are eyes to see [*they look again*]. Your mustache is light; mine is dark.

JAN. But they are both beautiful — see how long mine is!

JINDRA. See how long mine is! [*They peer into each other's faces again.*] Then we are not so different. We are friends.

JAN. That is because every day while we walk back and forth guarding the boundary we talk together.

JINDRA. That is how we know each other. For three months now we have been friends.

JAN [*reflects*]. Jindra, when I first came here I did not like you.

JINDRA. No? It was because you did not know me. [*They throw their arms around each other's shoulders and begin walking upstage along the boundary line. They turn, face audience, and sing.*]

Song, Andulko, p. 39

[*At end of song, voices are heard outside and they quickly move away from each other, taking rigid positions downstage R. and L. Enter* CZECHOSLOVAK PEASANTS *carrying scythes and sickles led by* VACLAV *and* GRANDFATHER *laughing and talking about being thirsty, hot, eager to rest, etc. They drink at well; some pretend to wash their faces, sit down, recline, or stand beside the well. Some open kerchiefs containing bread and ham and share with the others.* JINDRA *relaxes and greets his friends.* JAN *moves off stage. The fiddler begins music and all sing.*]

Song, No Is My Answer, p. 41

VACLAV [*wiping his face with a colored handkerchief*]. No more work today. We shall make this a holiday.

RUZHENA. Soon all the grain will be gathered into great sheaves left to dry ready for the threshing.

VACLAV. How many hectares of wheat have we finished today?

JOSEF. Seven hectares; and tomorrow we shall harvest my father's fields.

RUZHENA. And the next day ours will be gathered.

Then we shall have a festival at our house. Father has ordered the gypsies to come and play for us.

VACLAV. Good, we shall celebrate the harvest with singing and dancing. I shall be your partner for the Beseda. [*All tease* RUZHENA.] But now no more work. The Sokol delegations are coming from Praha to the great Sokol congress in Krakow. We must greet them.

JIRKA. I should like to go to one of those meetings.

VACLAV. Ask your father to take you next year.

JIRKA. What is it like, Vaclav?

VACLAV. It is something fine and noble. It is like a great army, but not of soldiers, it is an army of brothers. You know how we do our exercises? How carefully our leader trains us? Think of our group, then think of ten thousand men doing one of our patterns on a great field and you have a picture of what it is like.

JIRKA. It is almost more than I can see.

VACLAV [*turning to the guard*]. And now, Jindra, what news do you guard the frontier?

JINDRA. We are expecting the delegations today on their way to Krakow for the Sokol congress.

VACLAV. I know. We have just been talking about them. We work no more today. We wait here to greet them. I am proud to be a Sokol.

ALL. Yes, yes! So are we!

GRANDFATHER [*coming forward*]. When I was ten years old, here in our village, Dr. Tyrsh, the founder of the Sokols came to talk to us. He told us that to be good Sokols we must keep our bodies healthy and strong, our minds alert and eager for knowledge, and our lives clean and honorable, that by such training we learn to live nobly for the good of our land.

VACLAV. Grandfather, you have been the leading teacher of Sokol in our village. Tell us again what it means.

GRANDFATHER. Sokol is the word for the bravest bird that flies; it also means hero. In healthy bodies there is no room for disease, in clean minds there is no room for deceit, in high character there is no room for decay. In a nation of Sokols there can be no treason, indifference, or cowardice. [*The young people are impressed by this speech.*]

VACLAV. Grandfather, we do not forget your words. We shall greet the delegations with cheers, with singing and dancing.

JOSEF. Why not a song now as we wait? [*Plays a few strains of* "Trumpeter, Blow." *All sing.*]

Song, Trumpeter, Blow, p. 45

GRANDFATHER. Yes, these old songs are always best. They have come from the hearts of our people. They must never die.

JIRKA. Let us dance the Beseda.

ALL. Yes, the Beseda.

Song with Dance, Beseda, p. 46

[*As last figure is finishing, enter L.* JAN *and* POLISH PEASANTS. *They are greeted by* CZECHOSLOVAK PEASANTS. *Everyone is very jolly; some drink at well, there is much conversation, badinage back and forth, laughter, whistling — anything to make it seem natural. Soon singing is heard at back of hall. Enter* POLISH DELEGATION *through auditorium onto Polish side of stage, singing as they come. They do not march — rather saunter down aisles led by* KAZIMIERZ *and mount steps to platform.*]

Song, Clanking Spurs, p. 34

KAZIMIERZ [*to* JAN]. We are Sokols from Krakow. We are here to welcome the delegation from Praha.

JAN. I have permission to allow you to cross the frontier when they come. [*Turns to* JINDRA.] Am I right?

JINDRA [*salutes*]. I have been told that a delegation from Krakow will be allowed to cross the frontier today. [*They form a group on the boundary line upstage.* CZECHOSLOVAK PEASANTS *crowd to center stage very friendly.*]

VACLAV [*to* KAZIMIERZ]. I am a Sokol, too. That means that we are brothers.

KAZIMIERZ. And clasp of hands makes us friends. [*They clasp hands over the boundary.*]

CZECHOSLOVAK PEASANTS. Good morning! *Na zdar!* (Health to you!)

POLISH DELEGATION. Thank you! Good morning! Good morning!

[*From back of hall a fiddle is heard playing* "Ah, Lovely Meadows."]

Song, Ah, Lovely Meadows, p. 42

[*Enter* CZECHOSLOVAK DELEGATION *through auditorium onto the Czechoslovak side of stage, keeping time to the music. When they reach stage they pause until song is ended. Meanwhile,* CZECHOSLOVAK PEASANTS *come forward and join in song. When song is ended all cheer, wave kerchiefs, saying* "Na zdar!" CZECHOSLOVAK PEASANTS *move upstage;* POLISH PEASANTS *likewise, leaving downstage free for the two delegations.* KAZIMIERZ, *leader of the Polish delegation and* LUDMILA, *leader of the Czechoslovak delegation meet at the border line.*]

KAZIMIERZ. It is our honor to welcome you to our country, Poland. We are glad to meet you here and to escort you to our beautiful city of Krakow. The congress of Sokols would not be complete without delegates from Praha where the Sokol was born.

LUDMILA. As we left our golden city the sun was shining on the windows of the castle where our President lives. It was like a smiling farewell message from one who believes that all people of Slavic blood should live as brothers. The Sokol teaches that. We are glad to receive your welcome.

VACLAV. Our home is in the frontier village beyond the trees. These are our fields where we have been working. Here is a well with clear water. Rest here a little.

LUDMILA. Have we time?

KAZIMIERZ. Yes, we must wait for others to come.

LUDMILA. Good, then we shall rest. [*Members of the* DELEGATION *remove their knapsacks; some drink at well, others sit down, all mingling except* POLISH PEASANTS, *who are grouped closely upstage. The two guards are at rigid attention upstage by the well.*]

VACLAV [*to both* DELEGATIONS]. While you wait here, let us all join together in a song.

WOJTEK. Or a dance.

KAZIMIERZ. Something we all know.

JOSEF. Shall it be a polka?

ALL. Yes, yes, a polka!

JOSEF. Then in honor of our hosts I shall play one of their songs. [*He starts the tune.*]

POLISH PEASANTS. Hurrah!

CZECHOSLOVAK PEASANTS. Bravo!

CZECHOSLOVAK DELEGATION. Bravo!

POLISH DELEGATION. Bravo!

Song with Dance (Polka)* Hurry Up, Fellows, p. 37

[JOSEF *plays. At first the members of the* POLISH DELEGATION *choose partners from the* CZECHOSLOVAK DELEGATION. *They cross the border as they dance. The guards move downstage but at extreme L. and R. Then the* CZECHOSLOVAK *and* POLISH PEASANTS *choose partners and dance disregarding the border.* JAN *and* JINDRA *walk toward center as if to interfere with the crossing, but finally cannot resist the music. They take each other and polka with the rest back and forth across the border, remaining downstage where they can be seen. Gradually everyone stops dancing except the guards who continue gaily as curtains close.*]

CURTAIN

---

* The Polka is the most popular step in the folk dances of many European countries. It takes on the characteristics and temperaments of the people. As danced by Slavonic peoples it has more verve and action than when done by other countries; it might be called a hop polka step, beginning with the count "and" of the preceding measure.

Count "and." Hop on right foot.

Count 1. Step on left foot.

Count "and." Bring right foot to left.

Count 2. Step forward on left foot.

Count "and." Hop on right foot.

(Repeat measure with opposite foot.)

Position A. Same as for Peasant Waltz.

Position B. Same as for Modern Waltz (in these two positions girl begins with opposite foot).

Position C. Boy takes girl's left hand in his right. Partners face each other, arms straight toward back. Both begin Meas. 1 with outside foot. On Meas. 2 begin with inside foot, back to back, swinging arms forward in a semicircle.

Hristos Se Rodi

Christ Is Born

by STELLA MAREK CUSHING

PLACE and TIME: A peasant's home in Palanka, Yugoslavia — a village near the town of Nish — on Christmas Eve, the sixth of January.

SCENE: Home of the Lazarevich family, furnished simply. The walls may be light, as if whitewashed. Upstage center is a door, closed; downstage R., a door, open. To R. of center door is a small, high window. At L. is a stone fireplace with a fire burning. Near the hearth is a basket or box in which is a burned log. Downstage R. there is a table large enough to seat the family when they are eating. There are several benches and stools around the large table. Downstage L. on a small table is a manger scene. Under the window is a wide bench or seat covered with an oriental rug. Bright shawls or pieces of embroidery or tapestry may adorn the walls, with copper and brass trays, bright bowls or pitchers on mantel and shelves under window. An ikon is on the mantel. A low candle burns in front of it.

CHARACTERS:

GRANDFATHER LAZAREVICH (Lä-zä'-rĕ-vĭch) — called Deda (Dĕ'-dä)

FATHER LAZAREVICH — called Tata (Tä'-tä)

MOTHER LAZAREVICH

Children of the family

NADA (Nä'-dä), 18 years old

DUSHAN (Dōō'-shän), 16 years old

MILOSH (MĬ'-losh), 12 years old

MARA (Mä'-rä), 10 years old

STANKO MARINOVICH (Stän'-ko Mä-rĭ'-no-vĭch), neighbor's son, the *Polažajnik*, meaning "first footer"

RANKO (Rän'-ko), 18 years old

DANA (Dä'-nä), 12 years old

MARYAN (Mär'-yän), 16 years old

Young People for Processional

("R" is always rolled; z as in "azure")

GENERAL SUGGESTIONS: This play should be given with quiet dignity and reverence. The simple rites, such as placing the log on the fire scattering the straw, lighting the candle, etc., should be observed in a ceremonial manner. Because so great a responsibility for carrying the play devolves upon the mother, it is important that a student of considerable poise should take this part. If none is available it might even be desirable to choose an older student or adult. Her actions at end of scene must not be hurried. When the young people greet Deda, they should kiss his hand.

MUSIC: (See Unit VI: Trips Abroad — The Southern Slavs, p. 50.)

COSTUMES: (See, The National Geographic Magazine, January, 1928, pp. 48, 51, 52, 60, 83, plates 1, 3, 7–10, 12, 16; September, 1930, plates 4, 5, 7, 8, 13, 15, 16, pp. 271, 290–293.)

Since the procession is seen only through the windows, complete costumes are not necessary; capes, shawls, woolen and fur caps are sufficient.

INTRODUCTION (To be printed on program or spoken as a prologue before curtains open): At this season the Christian world is celebrating the birth of the Christ-child. We are glad that at least once a year in almost every corner of the world millions of people are united as they sing the angels' song, "Glory to God in the highest, and on earth peace, good will toward men."

Many carols and customs of other lands are familiar to us, but we have known little of the ways in which our neighbors in the Balkans observe Christmas. Today we are privileged to discover the charm and beauty of ancient customs still observed there.

It is Christmas Eve in Palanka, Yugoslavia, a village nestling in a fertile valley, surrounded by glistening snow-clad hills. It is the sixth day of January, for, according to the Greek church, the eastern Slavs observe Christmas thirteen days later than the western world.

We shall visit the Lazarevich family in their home as they sing their lovely carols and follow the simple rites of the season.

[GRANDFATHER sits near the fire in a large chair. MILOSH and MARA are sitting on the floor, stage center. MILOSH works on a small cradle; MARA is wrapping a cloth around a doll. MOTHER sits on the wide bench grinding coffee. NADA stands beside her holding a bright vest in her hand as if she had been sewing. All are singing as curtains open.]

Carol, Peace To All, p. 52

[When carol is finished NADA goes to GRANDFATHER while MOTHER works at shelves and goes back and forth to kitchen.]

GRANDFATHER. It makes me happy to hear you sing this carol. It is the one I like best of all. Well I remember, as a boy, learning this carol and many others from my grandmother.

MILOSH. It must be very old if your grandmother knew it.

GRANDFATHER. It is much older than that. For centuries it has been sung in our land.

MARA. How long is "centuries," Deda?

GRANDFATHER. Far longer than you can count, little one. Let us sing it again, this time with sweeter tone and steady count. [All sing it again; MOTHER pauses in her work.]

NADA [thoughtfully]. Often have I wondered what the shepherds thought as they were quietly watching their sheep that night when they saw the great light in the sky.

MILOSH. What was the great light?

GRANDFATHER. It was a star, perhaps, or a great comet in the heavens; no one really knows.

MILOSH. We call it a star in our songs and stories.

GRANDFATHER. Yes, a star or a light; it does not matter. All we know is that some great light shone and guided the shepherds.

MARA. The shepherds must have been very cold that night as they watched their sheep. Was there snow on the ground?

NADA. No, in the land where Christ was born the winter is not like ours, cold and snowbound. It is warmer there. [NADA returns to help MOTHER; takes cloth from bench.]

MARA [goes to DEDA]. See, Deda, now I have the babe wrapped in swaddling clothes ready for the cradle.

MILOSH [takes cradle to DEDA]. And the cradle is finished. Look, Deda, is it a good manger for the Lord Jesus?

GRANDFATHER [examining it]. You have made it well. Already you are a good carpenter like the Christ-child who worked in His father's shop.

MILOSH. When I am a man I shall build great churches. In every church I shall put a cradle.

MARA. And I shall place a babe in swaddling clothes in every cradle. [MILOSH places cradle in front of manger. MARA places babe in it. MOTHER and NADA unfold cloth.]

NADA. Our table will look very beautiful, Mati.

MOTHER. Yes, draga (dear), we are using our best embroidered cloth.

NADA. I am glad that we save it for our feast days.

MOTHER. It is good to save it for Christmas; Easter; Slava, our Patron Saint's day; and Svadba, our Wedding Day. Some day it will be used for your Svadba.

NADA [blushing]. I wonder what neighbor's son will be our Polażajnik.* I like our custom of having a neighbor send his son to be our guest for the holiday and to be the first to set his foot on our threshold after midnight on Christmas Eve. Do you think that Stanko will be our Polażajnik?

MOTHER. I have heard that Stanko Marinovich will be the "first footer." Does that please you?

NADA. Yes, Mati.

MOTHER. He is a good boy. He seems not to be lazy and he is good in his studies.

NADA. He talks of going to a school of agriculture for two years where he can learn better how to care for his father's field holdings, vineyards, and orchards.

MOTHER. It is well for the young to learn new ways. [There is a great commotion and stamping of feet outside; the children run to the door.]

FATHER LAZAREVICH [outside center door]. Open, open the door.

DUSHAN [outside]. We have brought the log for the fire. [MILOSH opens center door. FATHER and DUSHAN enter carrying a large log. They stand in center.]

FATHER. Mati, did you ever see such a badnjak (Christmas log)? Never was a better one brought to our home.

MOTHER. Every year it seems to be a better one.

GRANDFATHER [comes to look at it]. It is a stout badnjak and will easily last through the holiday.

DUSHAN. With enough left to light the fire next year.

MOTHER. Milosh, bring the old log from the woodbox. [MILOSH runs to the woodbox.]

FATHER. The new log must be lighted from the old one.

[MILOSH carries a small piece of burned log.]

MILOSH. I shall place it first on the fire. [He does so.]

MOTHER. Milosh, do not burn yourself.

MILOSH. No, Mati, I am careful.

MARA. How quickly it catches the flame.

FATHER [goes to fire]. Now, Dushan. [They lift log and count as they place one end on top of old log.] Jedan (Yě'-dän), dva, tri, — there, it will last for three days with enough left to light the new log next year.

GRANDFATHER. It is a good custom, my children.

MILOSH [goes to DEDA]. Why do we always save the old log?

MARA [goes to DEDA]. What does it mean?

GRANDFATHER. The custom has been given to us from ancient times. It is a symbol of sacred warmth and of the eternal fire ever burning, like the fire of our faith burning steadily in our hearts.

[There is a knock on the center door. MARA and MILOSH rush to open it.]

STANKO [a neighbor, out of breath]. I have good news, good news! Just now in the village square I saw two carts drawn by four oxen. The carts are filled with boys and girls from the town of Nish. They have come for the Christmas festival in the church.

FATHER. Did you know any of them?

STANKO [excitedly]. Yes, your cousins, Ranko, Dana, and Maryan. That is why I came running to tell you.

---

* It is the custom in sections of Yugoslavia for a household to send one of the sons to be the neighbor's guest during the Christmas holidays. He is the first to step across the threshold after the midnight hour. It is a symbol of the friendliness which exists between the two families.

GRANDFATHER. They come to bless our household at Christmas.

FATHER. We shall know if all is well with our family at Nish. Stanko, will you remain and greet our cousins?

STANKO. Thank you. I am to be your *Polažajnik*. It was my wish, and my father has given me permission to come to your house to bring you our good wishes.

GRANDFATHER. Then stay, as it is almost the midnight hour.

STANKO. Thank you, Deda, it is my pleasure. [*NADA goes to table; STANKO moves gradually over to NADA.*]

MOTHER. Father, Dushan, there is hot water in the tank beside the stove. You must make yourselves ready for our guests as no one comes unwashed to the table on Christmas Eve. [*Playfully*] Dushan, I shall examine your ears and hands.

DUSHAN. Yes, Mati, on Christmas Eve I shall not tease you. [*They exit door R.*]

MILOSH [*runs to MOTHER*]. Mati, I would like to run to the square to meet our cousins.

MARA [*runs to MOTHER*]. And I, too, would go, Mati, please.

MATI. It is cold. [*Takes shawl from bench*] Let me wrap my shawl about you.

MILOSH [*takes coat from bench*]. I shall take father's great coat. [*They run out center door.*]

MOTHER [*following them to door*]. Do not fall on the crusted snow. [*Watches them, then goes to GRANDFATHER. They observe STANKO and NADA and are pleased.*]

STANKO. Nada, are you glad to see me?

NADA [*nods*]. I am glad that you are our *Polažajnik*.

STANKO. I have brought your household some of the finest wheat flour, and for you, Nada, the largest ripe olives from our best grove.

NADA. For a long time I have been making you a new vest. It is finished, and Mati says I have made it well.

STANKO. Nada, if I go away to school, you will wait for me?

NADA. I shall wait, Stanko.

[*They are interrupted by singing off stage. They go to window.*]

Carol, The Holy Season, p. 52

MOTHER. It is the procession on its way to the church, but they do not pass our door.

GRANDFATHER. They are going for the service at midnight.

MOTHER. If my sister's children are coming here we shall wait and go to the church for the early morning service.

STANKO. Some are coming this way.

NADA. It is Dana and Maryan and Ranko.

[*Singing of procession is still faint. FATHER and DUSHAN enter from door R., as MILOSH, MARA, RANKO, DANA, and MARYAN enter center door. All greet them. They go first to GRANDFATHER, then to MOTHER, FATHER, DUSHAN, NADA, etc.*]

GRANDFATHER. Welcome to our household.

RANKO [*center*]. My father sends greeting to you. We have brought you gifts of rye and corn. [*He holds them high.*]

FATHER. We are grateful.

MOTHER. And my sister, your mother?

DANA. She is well; we bring you her love.

GRANDFATHER. Our house is blessed.

MARA. Come, Dana, and see the babe in the manger. [*DANA crosses over.*]

MILOSH. And see the cradle I have made to hold the babe.

DANA. Father has carved us a new Josef and three little lambs for our manger. [*The children group around manger.*]

DUSHAN. Ranko, this is Stanko, our *Polažajnik*. He is our neighbor and we are good friends.

STANKO. I have been sometimes to Nish with my father's oxen to carry our goods to the market. It is a large town.

RANKO. Yes, the railroad from Belgrade to Salonika goes through Nish. [*GRANDFATHER and FATHER are near the fire.*]

STANKO [*to FATHER*]. I have forgotten my stick. I must have it to strike the sparks.

FATHER. It will soon be the midnight hour; go quickly.

STANKO. I shall, I shall.

[*All say "Goodby" or "Hurry, Stanko." DUSHAN and RANKO join FATHER and GRANDFATHER.*]

NADA. Shall we finish preparing the table?

MOTHER. Yes, Maryan and Dana may help. [*MARYAN and DANA go to table.*] First the cake. [*NADA brings cake from shelf and places it in the center of table.*]

MARYAN [*giving MOTHER a basket*]. Mother sent honey, mushrooms, nuts, and cakes.

MOTHER. They will add to our feast. [*Takes things from basket.*]

DANA [*as MARA comes to table*]. Mm, the cake smells good.

MARA. I am hungry after so many days of fasting.

MILOSH [*near fire*]. I am always hungry. [*All laugh at him.*]

DANA. We, too, have fasted for forty-five days.

NADA. The sweets will taste good for we have eaten nothing but bread, beans, peas, and potatoes.

MOTHER. The fasting does no harm for a little while. And the feast will taste better. Grandfather will cut the cake at the New Year.

GRANDFATHER. Yes, it is my honor. Each of us shall have one piece.

NADA. And we shall leave one piece for the stranger.

RANKO. Mother says always one piece for the stranger who may come hungry to our door on New Year's Day.

NADA. Mati, it is the best *Chesnica* (Ches'-ni-tsa) we have ever had, the very best Christmas cake.

MOTHER. Each year, my daughter, is better than the last.

MARA [*bringing fruit*]. Here is the fruit, Mati.

DUSHAN [*bringing nuts*]. And the nuts.

MILOSH [*bringing apples from fireplace*]. Here are the apples.

MARYAN. Here is the honey I brought.

MOTHER. We shall surround the cake with the fruit, which is for the children. [*They do so.*]

DUSHAN. The nuts are for the birds. [*They place the nuts.*]

MARA. They, too, must be remembered at Christmas.

GRANDFATHER. And tomorrow morning the cows and the sheep, the goats, hens, and geese shall all have extra food.

FATHER. No one is forgotten on Christmas Day; everyone must be fed.

DUSHAN. I am hungry; and you, Ranko?

RANKO. It was a cold ride over the hills.

MARA. I am hungry, too. Are you, Dana? [*DANA nods.*]

MOTHER. First the straw must be brought.

MILOSH. I shall bring it. [*Runs out center door.*]

NADA. Shall I bring the soup and bowls? [*MOTHER nods and NADA and MARYAN exit door R. NADA and MARYAN return and stand quietly near table. MILOSH enters with bundle of straw.*]

MOTHER [*takes it and goes to manger in the corner*]. Once more we celebrate the birthday of the Christ-child. There was no room for Marya and Josef at the inn but the cattle welcomed them saying, "Come, let the Child be born among us; our breath shall keep him warm."

FATHER. Tonight we make of our home a manger. Christ is born again in our hearts.

[*MOTHER and children scatter the straw. NADA and MARYAN put soup and bowls on table. All but GRANDFATHER kneel before the manger and sing.*]

Carol, Kyrie Eleison, p. 51

MOTHER. Come, Deda, Tata, everyone take your places. [*MARA and MILOSH help GRANDFATHER, who limps. He sits at the head of the table, FATHER opposite him. The children sit on both sides. MOTHER stands at one corner of table*]

234

and pours soup into the smaller bowls. All exclaim over soup, how good it smells, tastes, etc. Bread is piled high; all the children eat ravenously and ask for more. Real soup, bread, and honey should be used.]

NADA. Mother, you are not eating. You only serve us.

MOTHER. I am glad to serve you. It is my duty and pleasure. I shall not break my fast until after the midnight hour.

MILOSH. Then tell us a story.

MARA. A legend.

ALL. Yes, a legend.

MOTHER. What better legend could I tell you than a true story about the brave gusla players who portrayed in song and story the wondrous epics of our glorious past.

The Gusla Player

In days long ago our people were not free. For five hundred years under Turkish oppression our history, our customs, and even our language were in danger of becoming forever lost. Even the names of our heroes and the glorious deeds of the past might not be told. Also, travel was hard over rough mountain trails and narrow valley passes. There was danger, too, for the soldiers of our conquerors watched the trails. Those living in the mountains knew little about the plainsmen. Those in the valleys could never meet their mountain brothers.

They were dark days until wandering bards began to appear in the land, gusla players, wending their way from mountain village to valley town, rousing the people with songs of glory, restoring their pride, and kindling their hope for freedom.

Do you ask how they were able to travel thus when for others it was forbidden? The guards thought that they were of no importance. They were only poor wandering minstrels. Surely a gusla player could do no harm singing and playing on his instrument of a single string.

How little the rulers knew that it was these bards who kept our people united. They sang of our proud race, they recited our glorious past, they told of Stefan Nemanya, one of the first of our great kings; of his son St. Slava, our patron saint; and of the greatest warrior of all, Kralyevich Marko. They told what was happening to our brothers in the north and west; they brought news from afar off. Lagging spirits revived, hearts were again filled with courage, souls fired with zeal.

On such a night as this a bard might come. A home was honored by his presence.

That was all long ago, but we do not forget the gusla players of old, the wandering minstrels of other days. Tonight, on this Christmas Eve, we pause to do them honor. As we observe our ancient customs let us remember that, but for them, our heroes might have been unknown, our past might have been forgotten, our soul might have died.

ALL [*exclaiming, each one saying something different*]. Thank you. A good story! How brave were the gusla players.

MOTHER. Now I light my candle. [*Goes to fire and lights it.*] It is the symbol of the Christ-light. I place it here in the window to light the stranger who may pass by. Are there not many legends about the Christ who came disguised to the door?

MARA. Sometimes he came as a poor child.

MILOSH. Or a hungry man.

MOTHER. Might he not come to bless our home this night?

GRANDFATHER. No one would deny anyone entrance on Christmas Eve.

FATHER. Mother, you must not forget the bowl of dried peas and beans.

DANA. This morning Mother let me throw the peas and beans.

RANKO. And I scattered the straw.

NADA. Let me throw the peas and beans.

MOTHER. Do you remember the words?

NADA. Have you not taught me?

DUSHAN. All of us know what to say.

GRANDFATHER. It is time that they begin the custom. Let each speak a line.

[NADA, DUSHAN, MARA, and MILOSH *gather in the middle of the room, their backs to each other, each one facing a corner.* MOTHER *stands in the center of them with a bowl of peas and beans. As each one speaks he turns to his corner of the room and throws a few of the beans to that corner.*]

DUSHAN. May there be plenty in the lands to the North.

MILOSH. May there be plenty in the lands to the East.

MARA. May there be plenty in the lands to the South.

NADA. May there be plenty in the lands to the West.

MOTHER. And may the bounty of our Lord be upon us throughout the year.

FATHER. May this house be blessed.

GRANDFATHER. May all homes have peace and plenty. [*A clock strikes twelve. All stand quietly until the last stroke.*]

GRANDFATHER. *Hristos se rodi* (Hrĭs'-tus sĕ ro'-di). Christ is born!

ALL. *Va istinu se rodi* (Vä ĭs-tĭ-nu sĕ ro'-di). Indeed Christ is born.

[*From a distance joyous singing is heard.*]

Carol, Twelve o'Clock Is Striking, p. 55

[*Young people on stage go to window and door.*]

RANKO. It is the procession returning from the church. [*All watch until carol ends.*]

STANKO [*enters*]. *Hristos se rodi!*

FAMILY. *Va istinu se rodi.*

STANKO. I am the *Polazajnik*, the first footer. I have come — the first to step upon your threshold on the day the Lord was born.

GRANDFATHER. *Zdrävo*, Stanko. Welcome again to our household. It is good for a member of the Marinovich household to become our guest for the holiday.

FATHER. I welcome you, also.

MOTHER. And I.

ALL. And I.

FATHER. Then, Dushan, you shall go to our neighbor's house and be their *Polazajnik*, their first footer.

DUSHAN. I am honored to be their *Polazajnik*. Tonight I am a man. [*Exits center door.*]

STANKO [*goes to fire followed by* NADA. *He strikes the log at each phrase with his heavy stick*]. So many sparks, so much good fortune, so many calves, so many lambs, so much health, so much joy. And may the year be fruitful.

ALL. May the year be fruitful.

GRANDFATHER [*stands between* STANKO *and* NADA]. There are many customs which we observe in memory of the night when Christ was born. They live forever. Keep them in your hearts, my children; cherish them, observe them, for in them you find our store of riches. Sing, sing the carols that tell of our simple faith.

MOTHER. Let our songs echo throughout the ages.

STANKO. Let us go to join the carolers.

ALL YOUNG PEOPLE. Yes, let us go. [*They put on cloaks and capes and exit center door.*]

MILOSH. May we go, Mati?

MARA. Please, Mati.

MOTHER. No, it is late and you are weary. You shall watch from the window. [*They go to window. Singing begins.*]

Carol, What Light Is That, p. 54

[*The procession comes nearer and moves slowly past window. In procession a boy at the head carries a banner with "Hristos Se Rodi" on it. Two boys are carrying a cradle. A girl carries a star on a stick. Several carry branches of fir tree; there are also boys dressed as the wise men and shepherds. Carol may be sung twice. As singing of processional dies away,* MILOSH *and* MARA *yawn.* GRANDFATHER *is sitting in his chair by the fire.* FATHER *stretches out on the bench near the window.*]

MOTHER [*to children*]. It is time for you to go to your beds. We must waken early that we may go to the service at the church. I shall not sleep. This night I keep my all-night vigil beside the Christ-child as Mary did so long ago. *Laku noč* (Lä-kōō noch), Goodnight.

MARA and MILOSH. *Laku noč*, goodnight. [*They exit R.* MOTHER *extinguishes all the candles except the one in the window and one in front of the ikon. Lights dim. Softly the carolers sing in the distance, "The Holy Season." Outside the window in the moonlight,* NADA *and* STANKO *are standing together.* MOTHER *lays a shawl over* FATHER, *who is sleeping.* GRANDFATHER *dozes in his chair, the light from the fire upon him.* MOTHER *then goes to manger and kneels in meditation. As carol is ending, curtains slowly close.*]

CURTAIN

Street Scene in Hongkong

by STELLA MAREK CUSHING

PLACE and TIME: In Hongkong, present year on the Ninth Day of the Ninth Moon.

SCENE: The background may be two-story buildings along back of stage with high cliffs rising in the rear above them, or it may be a plain cloth curtain. Projecting from the buildings are long cloth or paper signs bearing the names of merchants, and signs describing merchandise for sale.

CHARACTERS:

TOY MAN, who beats small drum

FORTUNE TELLER, who rattles bamboo sticks in a round can

BARBER, who strikes cymbals

Three boys

  HWA SHING (Hwǎ Sheeng') meaning China prosperous

  NON SHEN (Nŏng Shĕng') meaning Dragon born

  HSIAO LING (Shyow Leeng') meaning Little heel

Old man

  LI CHAO (Lee Cheow') meaning Superior One

Boys with kites

Girls with lanterns

Townspeople

Vendors	Noises by which they may be recognized
Cloth Merchant.....	musical top
Mending Man.......	hits hollow pipes strung on pole
Sweet Cakes Vendor..	rattles small wooden mallet
Goldfish Man.......	blows bird whistle
Flower Vendor......	blows toy horn
Puppet Vendor......	hits small triangle
Spice Vendor.......	tinkles little bell
Metal Vendor.......	pounds on metal
Soothsayer........	strikes gong
Spun Sugar Vendor..	blows whistle

GENERAL SUGGESTIONS: This scene should be very busy and noisy at the beginning. Some people are in a hurry, others walk slowly. Chinese do not shuffle. Some may walk, others trot. The vendors carry their wares on trays held around their necks by ribbons or tapes, or they carry their heavy wares in bags or baskets hung on long poles held across their shoulders. Some may push two-wheel carts. Study pictures of street scenes for other suggestions. (See, *The National Geographic Magazine*, June, 1927, pp. 702, 705. Also read the articles in that number.) Li Chao wears a false beard and wig. The Barber cuts and snips, but toward the end he stands in front of Li Chao and pulls off wig and beard.

Other properties are small kites in shape of dragons, fish, and birds. Lanterns are large, round, and red, and should be lighted if possible. Red lanterns are always carried in processions. Flashlights may be used inside red tissue or cellophane paper. If stage is deep enough, some lanterns may be hung on the buildings. Christmas tree lights may be used very effectively inside these lanterns and lighted when lantern procession enters. (For correct lanterns, see, *The National Geographic Magazine*, February, 1932, p. 140.)

MUSIC: (See Unit XVIII: Trips Abroad — China, p. 208.)

COSTUMES: (See, *The National Geographic Magazine*, June, 1927, pp. 652-662, 689-706; April, 1932, pp. 510-519.)

INTRODUCTION (*To be printed on program or spoken as a prologue before curtains open*): We are traveling westward today, having sailed across the Pacific, finally reaching Hongkong, called the Harbor of Fragrant Streams. The city is built in a series of fascinating terraced streets reaching from the water's edge to the sheer face of the cliffs some half mile beyond the harbor. At night it is a fairyland of color as every house is festooned with brilliantly-lighted lanterns. The city also overflows into the harbor for thousands live in houseboats or *sampans*. It is a busy place to which we are going, and we shall enjoy watching the Chinese, mingling with them as they are busy about their work, or pausing to observe, as we do, the procession of boys with their kites and girls carrying lanterns. It is the Ninth Hour of the Ninth Moon in Hongkong. Already the vendors are calling their wares. We can tell who they are by the sounds they make. Let us leave our steamer by the Star Ferry and join the throngs in the busy streets.

[*After* INTRODUCTION, *the voices of the vendors begin immediately. As soon as noises are loud, curtains open.* TOY MAN *enters R. and sits L.* FORTUNE TELLER *enters L. and sits R. Cries and noises of vendors are loud as each passes across stage two or three times. The* TOWNSPEOPLE *are buying wares. The* BARBER *enters L. and sits in center cleaning his instruments. Cries gradually die down as music begins.*]

Song, The Street Vendors, p. 208, sung by Barber, Toy Man, Fortune Teller, and all Vendors

[*Everybody sings first stanza and the chorus for all stanzas. Each vendor sings his own stanza, then all repeat first stanza. After song is ended all leave L. except* FORTUNE TELLER, BARBER, *and* TOY MAN. HWA SHING, NON SHEN, *and* HSIAO LING *enter R. carrying kites.*]

FORTUNE TELLER. It is Hwa Shing, Non Shen, and Hsiao Ling. You are wearing coats of silk. Today, then, is a holiday.

HWA SHING. It is the Ninth Day.

NON SHEN. It is the Ninth Day of the Ninth Moon.

HSIAO LING. And the Ninth Hour is the Children's Hour.

TOY MAN. Ah, yes, all the children will go to the field for kite-flying.

HSIAO LING. I have made my kite like a flying fish with horns.

HWA SHING. Mine is a dragon with a long tail.

NON SHEN. Mine is a fiery ball like the sun.

FORTUNE TELLER. It will be a long procession.

NON SHEN. Everyone will be there.

HSIAO LING. We go now to join others at the school.

HWA SHING. It is almost the Ninth Hour. Come. [*They exit L.*]

BARBER. When I was a boy my kite was always the finest.

TOY MAN. There is no merit worthy of such boasting.

FORTUNE TELLER. One seeing is better than a thousand telling of it.

[*Music of "Kites Are Flying" is heard. Boys enter L. carrying kites of all shapes and sizes made of thin gaily-colored paper, some with silhouettes of rabbits, toads, or birds. Girls enter R. Boys hold the kites high, turning them so that audience may see shapes and figures. Following them are all the vendors,* showmen, etc., who were on stage at the beginning. As soon as all are on stage they sing both verses.]

Song, Kites Are Flying, p. 210

HWA SHING. Today the wind is right to send our kites high.

NON SHEN. Whose kite shall fly the highest?

CHORUS. Mine, mine shall.

HSIAO LING. They will almost reach the sun as it is setting.

CHORUS. It is the Ninth Hour of the Ninth Moon.

[*They begin singing again, same song, and exit R., holding kites high.*]

TOY MAN. I shall follow and watch their kites mount the sky.

FORTUNE TELLER. I, too, shall see which one reaches the setting sun. [*To* BARBER] Do you come with us?

BARBER. No, I must work. [*Begins to sharpen tools.*] Only sharp tools make skilful work.

TOY MAN. But there are no customers.

BARBER. There will be.

[TOY MAN *and* FORTUNE TELLER *exit L.* BARBER *sharpens instruments.* LI CHAO *enters R. His hair is long and he has a beard. He goes to* BARBER, *who is already sharpening razor and scissors.*]

BARBER. Shall I cut your most honorable head?

LI CHAO. Not my honorable head, but my honorable hair.

BARBER. And shall I trim your most honorable beard?

LI CHAO. Cut it off.

BARBER [*surprised*]. Cut it off? You have asked me to trim it, but never to cut it off! [*During following conversation* BARBER *works — snipping, lathering, shaving.*]

LI CHAO. My son is returned from America. He hardly knew me with this beard. When he went to America I did not have a beard. Off it must come if I am changed so much.

BARBER. And is he changed?

LI CHAO. Living in another land, changes must come. He speaks in a foreign tongue, lives in a strange house, high and narrow. He is much changed.

BARBER. Has he prospered?

LI CHAO. Yes, but when a man's affairs are to prosper he must remember the proverb of Confucius, "Rich without pride, poor without flattery." It is a matter of purpose to honor and glorify our ancestors. Now my son comes back to pay respects to his ancestors and to teach his wife our ways.

BARBER. Does she not know our ways?

LI CHAO. She is the daughter of Ling-Po. She has never lived among us.

BARBER. Ling-Po and his wife went to America when they were young.

LI CHAO. Yes, and they have never returned. Ling-Po was my friend. I am glad that his daughter is now one of us.

BARBER. If she has always lived in a strange land she must be ignorant of our ways. But you know the old saying, "It is better to remain ignorant than to know what is incorrect."

[BARBER *has finished shaving and is now trimming hair. He stands in front of* LI CHAO *while removing beard, likewise when removing wig.*]

LI CHAO. She has yet much to learn. She has not learned to rise at dawn to pay her respect to me by offering me a cup of hot tea.

BARBER. And does she not bring tea to her husband?

LI CHAO. Not yet.

BARBER. She is a most unfilial daughter-in-law.

LI CHAO. She will learn.

BARBER. And now the eyes, the ears, the nose?

LI CHAO. Everything.

[*With elaborate motions and great ceremony the* BARBER *using a small syringe or atomizer appears to clean out* LI CHAO's *eyes, ears, and nose. When finished* LI CHAO *pays* BARBER, *shakes himself, and exits R., seeming to feel like a new man.* BARBER *puts his tools away and exits R. Lights dim. Music of "Lanterns Glowing" begins. Lanterns on houses light up. Boys enter R. Girls enter, if possible, from side door on floor of auditorium and mount stage by center or side steps, or from stage L. They are carrying large, red, lighted lanterns. They take places at back of stage holding lanterns high. Boys sit or kneel in front of them, holding kites low. All* VENDORS *and* TOWNSPEOPLE *enter and take positions.*]

Song, Lanterns Glowing, p. 211

[*In each verse as they sing "higher, lower," lanterns should dip and heads nod.*]

[CURTAINS *close as song ends.*]

At Home in Japan

by STELLA MAREK CUSHING

PLACE and TIME: Japanese home at the present time on *Tanabata* — Festival of the Stars — the Seventh Day of the Seventh Month.

SCENE: A room in a Japanese home (*see illustration on* p. 186). There are two entrances, R. goes to outside gate, L. goes to other part of house and garden. At center, upstage, is a raised alcove, called *Tokonoma*, the place of honor in respect and reverence to the Emperor. Here, in every Japanese home, hangs the most beautiful scroll, the best print, picture, or ornament of beauty. There are several large, plain, silk cushions on the floor on which the people sit. There are no chairs or tables, only one or two serving stands about a foot high. The background, cushions, costumes, and flowers must harmonize to create an atmosphere of quiet charm and beauty.

CHARACTERS:

GRANDFATHER, O-jii-San (O-gee-Sän). (Only when spoken to San, meaning honorable, is used.)

GRANDMOTHER, O-ba-San (O-bah-Sän)

MOTHER

TERU (Të-roo), maid

HANAKO (Hä-nä-ko), daughter

Children of the family
  Boys: TOSHIO (To-shĭ-o)
        HIROSHI (Hĭ-ro-shĭ)
  Girl: KIKUKO (Kĭ-koo-ko)

UNCLE

AUNT

Children of Uncle and Aunt
  Boy: MAKOTO (Mä-ko-to)
  Girls: HARUKO (Hä-roo-ko)
         YUKIKO (You-kĭ-ko)

KICHI (Kĭ-chĭ), gardener

(There is no marked accent in the Japanese language. In pronouncing the above names there is a slight stress on the first syllable.)

GENERAL SUGGESTIONS: The idea for this play was given to the author by a group of Japanese friends who presented a typical scene of home life in Japan. Those who saw it gained a deeper appreciation of their charm and poise and felt a sense of obligation to these friends for such an interpretation of Japanese culture. Participants should be small in stature and capable of acting with meticulous care and precision. The humor is quiet, the action subdued, lending an atmosphere of dignity and restraint. When the children bow they should kneel, place their hands on the floor, and lay heads on their hands. (*See, The National Geographic Magazine*, April, 1936, p. 442.) When adults enter they stand and bow, bending over and rubbing the legs above the knees. During the tea ceremony everyone is sitting or in a squatting position. Then they bow low but do not place hands on floor. The songs may be sung by a special choral group in front rows of auditorium or behind the scenes. The setting and all properties should be simple and, as far as possible, authentic. (For flower arrangement *see, The National Geographic Magazine*, March, 1933, p. 287.)

MUSIC: (*See* Unit XVI: Trips Abroad — Japan, p. 183.)

COSTUMES: (*See, The National Geographic Magazine*, February, 1932, pp. 132–160; March, 1933, pp. 278, 279, 287, 314, 317, plates 1, 4, 5, 6, 7; April, 1936, plate 5, pp. 442, 443, 445.)

INTRODUCTION (*To be printed on program or spoken as a prologue before the curtains open*): We invite you to go with us to Japan, but not to the busy streets of Tokyo, nor to the great industrial district around Osaka, nor to the Temples of Nikko or Nara. Rather do we take you to a home in Japan where we are privileged to observe the respect that boys and girls show to their elders, to see the quiet charm and beauty of Japanese home life, and to watch the family going about their regular and special duties of the day. It is the Seventh Day of the Seventh Month, celebrated as *Tanabata*, the Festival of the Stars. Old customs are still observed and the ancient legend is always told of Tanabata, Goddess of Weaving and Hikoboshi, the herd boy. Intermingling with these traditional customs, observed since earliest times, are the everyday happenings of school and play which are very much like our own. Thus we realize how modern civilization is linked with the past, and how closely knit is the world in which we live.

[GRANDFATHER *and* GRANDMOTHER *sit on cushions at right of Tokonoma. At extreme downstage* HANAKO *is sewing on bright silk. At center L. upstage* TERU *is rocking a baby which is fastened to her back. The baby may be a large doll.*]

[*After* INTRODUCTION *has been read, curtains open slowly and* "Lullaby" *follows immediately.* TERU *or choral group begin to sing,* TERU *rocking the baby on her back to the rhythm of the music.*]

Song, Lullaby, p. 183

[*As the* "Lullaby" *is finished,* MOTHER *enters L. and looks at babe.*]

MOTHER. My son sleeps well now. Your song has lulled him to slumber.

TERU. Shall I rock him still more?

MOTHER. No, there are other duties for you. Carry him to the garden. Let him sleep under the shade of the bamboo tree.

GRANDFATHER. The wind sighing through the branches will be his slumber song.

GRANDMOTHER. The fragrance of the lilies will sweeten his sleep.

HANAKO. And the fountain water will freshen the air about him.

MOTHER [*to* TERU]. Return here when you are certain that he will not be disturbed. There is much to do before our visitors come. [TERU *exits L.*]

GRANDFATHER. At what hour do you expect my son and his family?

MOTHER. O-jii-San, honorable father, my brother's servant told me they would be here by mid-afternoon. It is a long time since they left us, but the country air has been good for the children.

GRANDMOTHER. I have told Teru to serve the sweet cakes on my best plate and to use our oldest china.

MOTHER. It is all prepared. The lacquer trays are ready. There are but a few more things to do. [*Goes to* HANAKO; *examines her work.*] You have learned the new stitch well. You must leave it now. The flowers have not

yet been arranged for the Tokonoma. Today it is to be your honor to do it.

HANAKO [*laying aside her sewing*]. Do you think that I know well enough to arrange the flowers for Tokonoma?

GRANDFATHER. You have had the best teacher in the city. No one knows better than your Grandmother.

GRANDMOTHER. When I was a young girl Ikenobo taught me. He even prepared flowers for the Emperor.

[TERU *enters L.* HANAKO *brings the flower tools, low table, and vase downstage R. and her cushion to sit upon.*]

MOTHER [*to* TERU]. The flowers for Tokonoma are in a jar in the outer room. [TERU *exits L.*]

HANAKO. O-ba-San, honorable Grandmother, you will watch and help me?

GRANDMOTHER [*getting up, bringing her cushion*]. You will need no help, but I shall watch.

GRANDFATHER [*rising*]. It is nearly time for the children to return from school. I shall wait for them at the gate. [*He exits R.;* TERU *enters L. with flowers. She gives them to* HANAKO, *who begins to arrange them.*]

MOTHER [*to* TERU]. Our visitors are expected within the hour. The path must be swept well and sprinkled with water to show our welcome.

GRANDMOTHER. Have the pine branches been placed beside the doorway?

MOTHER. They have been placed in front of the gold and black screen in the entrance hall. [*To* TERU] When the path is sprinkled, prepare the fruit and vegetables to welcome the Lady Moon when she rises tonight in the heavens. [TERU *and* MOTHER *exit L.*]

[HANAKO *carefully prepares her flowers. They may be iris, azaleas, peonies, lilies, orchids, mock orange, pine branches, or bamboo branches — whatever the season affords, but the number used should be three, five, or seven and so arranged as to form a symbolic triangle.* HANAKO *sings or choral group sings.*]

Song, Cherry Bloom, p. 184

GRANDMOTHER [*examining flowers as song ends*]. You have remembered to arrange the flowers in a triangle.

HANAKO. You taught me to arrange them this way. The tallest flower or branch represents heaven, this one [*pointing to flower at left*] is for the earth, [*pointing to flower at right*] and this one is for man. You have always told me that the numbers three, five, and seven are lucky ones. Why is it so?

GRANDMOTHER. It is an old custom. We believe that these numbers bring us good fortune. Every November we celebrate the birthdays of all girls who are three and seven, and all boys who are five. When cakes are arranged on a plate always there are three, or five, or seven. When flowers are arranged usually they are grouped thus — it has been so for ages past. As you work, whatever you do you will find yourself preparing food or flowers with the lucky numbers in mind. It is our custom.

[HANAKO *has now finished flowers. She puts her tools away and places the vase of flowers on a low stand in front of Tokonoma.* GRANDMOTHER *moves back to her original place.* MOTHER *and* TERU *enter L. with fruit and vegetables.* GRANDFATHER *enters R. with* KIKUKO, TOSHIO, *and* HIROSHI. *The children bow to* MOTHER *and to* GRANDMOTHER *and* HANAKO, *then run to* MOTHER, *L.*]

MOTHER. You are hot and tired. Why did you hurry?

TOSHIO. We thought that our Uncle would be here.

KIKUKO. When will they come? I am anxious to see Cousin Haruko San and Yukiko San.

HIROSHI. And I to see Cousin Makoto.

GRANDFATHER. How impatient are the young! Only with age comes patience and wisdom.

MOTHER. While you are waiting help me arrange the Lady Moon plate. I shall let you choose.

TOSHIO. Everything must be round, for the Lady Moon is round.

MOTHER. Yes, we begin with a round plate. [*The children assist* MOTHER.]

KIKUKO. And all the fruits must be round.

HIROSHI. Here are the dumplings for the center.

TOSHIO. And cherries and plums.

HIROSHI. Tomatoes and onions.

MOTHER. We shall place it where Lady Moon may see it tonight as she shines down. [*She gives plate to* TERU, *who exits R.*]

KIKUKO [*goes to Tokonoma*]. Who has arranged the flowers for Tokonoma today?

HANAKO. Mother allowed me to do them.

GRANDMOTHER. Hanako has arranged them well.

KIKUKO. When I am as old as you, Hanako, I shall have the honor.

HANAKO. The years will slip away and you will soon be grown.

[TERU *enters R.*]

TERU. The honorable visitors have come. [*She turns and bows them in.*]

[*Enter R.* UNCLE, AUNT, MAKOTO, HARUKO, *and* YUKIKO. *All bow three times.*]

GRANDFATHER. We are honored by your visit. *Dozo o Su wari nasai* (meaning, Please honorably deign to place yourself). [*All bow.*]

UNCLE. It is honor for us to be welcomed. [*All bow.*]

GRANDMOTHER. I trust your health is good. [*All bow.*]

UNCLE. Thank you, we are all well. [*He sits beside* GRANDFATHER *center, in front of Tokonoma.* AUNT *sits beside* GRANDMOTHER *and* MOTHER. *Children gather together R.* HANAKO *and* TERU *exit L.*]

MOTHER. The children have gained in health by your visit to the country.

AUNT. They have spent all the days playing in the sunshine.

[*The ceremony of serving tea is a ritual in Japan. (See, The Romance of Japan by James A. B. Scherer, pp.* 108–111.) *For this play only the simplest custom is observed.* HANAKO *and* TERU *enter L.*, HANAKO *carries a small lacquer tray on which are two pots containing tea and water. She places it on floor in front of* MOTHER. TERU *carries a larger tray on which are cups, without handles, and saucers. She places tray on floor beside* MOTHER, *who begins to pour tea.* TERU *exits L. returning with another tray of cups and saucers which she also places beside* MOTHER. HANAKO *serves the adults,* TERU *the children. Since the adults are sitting together,* HANAKO *remains in a kneeling position as she serves the tea.* TERU *waits until all cups are filled then takes tray to children.* HANAKO *and* TERU *bow low each time before serving tea as each one served also bows.* HANAKO *serves in the following order:* GRANDFATHER, GRANDMOTHER, UNCLE, AUNT, *and* MOTHER; TERU *serves the visiting children first.*]

UNCLE [*setting cup down, rising and coming downstage where he now sits*]. Come, children, sit beside me and tell me what you have been learning today in school. [*All gather around him.* HANAKO *and* TERU *remove tea cups and exit L.* HANAKO *returns and sits near* AUNT.]

TOSHIO. I have learned enough characters so that now I can write you a letter.

UNCLE. Tomorrow I shall look at your papers.

KIKUKO. Today we played volley ball — and our side won.

HIROSHI. Every day we play baseball during the noon hour.

TOSHIO. I am learning how to pitch from a boy who used to live in Chicago. He has taught me how to swing my arm before throwing the ball. [*Illustrates.*]

HIROSHI [*runs to L., returns at once with a ball*]. See my ball, Uncle.

UNCLE [*examines it*]. What is this name on it?

HIROSHI. It is signed by the greatest ball player in the world. I saw him play when he came over here. It is Babe Ruth.

MAKOTO. I saw him play, too. What a big man he is!

HARUKO. In the country we had gymnastic drills with flags every day.

YUKIKO. I like the drills best when we do them to music.

KIKUKO [*to other girls*]. Do you play volley ball, too?

GIRLS. Yes, it is fun!

[*Offstage L.* KICHI, *begins to sing* "Oshima Bushi," p. 186. *He continues softly during following conversation*].

UNCLE. What else did you learn today?

TOSHIO. We were studying about the Island of Oshima.

HIROSHI. There the great volcano gushes forth fire.

MAKOTO. Some day we are going there on a pilgrimage.

TOSHIO. Old legends say that a great god dwells there. He sends up smoke and lava in his terrible anger.

HIROSHI. Our people used to sacrifice themselves to the great god.

UNCLE. Yes, the Island of Oshima is a sacred place. There is an old song about the fiery god of anger who lives in the blazing volcano.

TOSHIO. Do you know the song, Uncle?

UNCLE. Yes, I have sung it many times. [*Listens to* KICHI *singing.*] That is "Oshima Bushi" I hear now. Who is singing it? [*All listen.*]

GRANDFATHER. It is Kichi, the gardener.

UNCLE. Does he sing often?

GRANDFATHER. Yes, he is happy in his work.

HIROSHI. Will you sing "Oshima Bushi" for us?

MAKOTO. Then we can learn it.

UNCLE. It is a song for men. When you are grown you will learn to sing it. But I like Kichi's voice. It is clear and he sings with feeling.

GRANDFATHER [*to* TOSHIO]. Ask Kichi to come nearer so that we may hear his song. [TOSHIO *exits L., singing stops.* TOSHIO *returns with* KICHI *who stands bowing and smiling in doorway.*] We have been talking about your song. Today the children were studying about the Island Oshima. Let us hear your song again.

[KICHI *bows again and begins to beat out the drum rhythm with his hands while singing the song.*]

Song, Oshima Bushi, p. 186, sung by Kichi

[*After song,* GRANDFATHER *thanks* KICHI, *who bows and exits L.*]

GRANDMOTHER. Many people have come to the city for Tanabata.

GRANDFATHER. All the town is decorated for the Festival of the Stars. At every house the swaying bamboos with gay sashes and silk belt-cords are stretched between the branches.

AUNT. On them hang many poems, cards, and prayers.

HANAKO. We have hung ours near the gate. Every girl is making an eager wish for sunshine today and for a clear night.

HIROSHI. O-jii-San, honorable Grandfather, will you tell us the story of Tanabata?

KIKUKO. Tell us of the Goddess of Weaving and the shepherd boy as we make an eager wish for sunshine.

MAKOTO. It is the seventh day of the seventh month.

HARUKO. Tell us the legend.

ALL CHILDREN. The legend of Tanabata.

GRANDFATHER [*rises and moves forward; children crowd around him.* MOTHER, HANAKO, *and* TERU *sit L.* UNCLE *sits beside* GRANDMOTHER *and* AUNT, *slightly to their right*]. This is the story of Tanabata.

In ages past the beautiful Goddess of Weaving lived in the Land of the Stars. Her name was Tanabata. She worked every day at her loom while she watched the looms of Earthland and inspired all maidens to be very industrious. Everywhere could be heard the busy sound of looms and the pleasant chatter of happy people. The Emperor of Heaven, father of the Goddess of Weaving, was glad to see his daughter so industrious but he wished also to give her greater happiness.

One day Hikoboshi, a shepherd lad caring for his sheep near the banks of the Heavenly River, came to the home of the Goddess of Weaving, and soon they were married. In their happiness duties were forgotten. The sheep wandered unguided over the hills of Heaven and the loom in the Land of the Stars was idle. So on Earthland — shepherds forgot their sheep and looms became covered with spider webs — thrift was gone — the beautiful art of weaving was almost forgotten. Then indeed was the Emperor of Heaven full of wrath. Sternly he said that Tanabata and Hikoboshi must part; the shepherd must go back to his scattered herds, the Goddess of the loom must return to her neglected task. Their sorrow was so great that the Father God relented a little and decreed that once a year on the seventh day of the seventh month they could meet on the banks of the Heavenly River. So, if the rain does not fall and overflow the banks they meet for a day. That is why every girl wishes for sunshine on the seventh day of the seventh month, so that the Goddess of Weaving and the shepherd boy may be together for a day. That is the legend of Tanabata.

CHILDREN. Thank you, O-jii-San. Thank you, honorable Grandfather. [*All the children bow.*]

[TERU *enters L.*]

TERU [*to* MOTHER]. The little son has wakened from his sleep.

MOTHER. Bring him to us here. My sister will see how he has grown. [TERU *exits L.*]

AUNT. When I left the city he was but three months; now he is almost six months old.

UNCLE [*to boys and girls*]. Let us go into the garden to play.

BOYS. Shall we play baseball?

UNCLE. If you wish. Gather your friends and I shall be the umpire.

TOSHIO. Let us go to the field where there is more room. [*To* HIROSHI] Get the bats and masks. [HIROSHI *runs out L.*]

KIKUKO [*to girls*]. We can play volley ball in the garden.

YUKIKO. We can show you some of the flag drills we know.

[*The girls bow to the older people and exit L.* TERU *enters L. with baby; takes him to* MOTHER. AUNT, MOTHER, *and* HANAKO *admire him.* HIROSHI *enters L. with two bats, a mask, a ball, and any other equipment needed. His arms are quite full. He and the other boys are so intent upon the proposed game that they almost forget to bow to the older people.*]

GRANDFATHER [*reminding them*]. In your haste, do not forget to pay respect to your family. [*With arms full of equipment the boys stop, turn, bow, then quickly exit R., followed by* UNCLE.]

[*Music of* "Cherry Bloom" *begins. Those on stage or a special group sings.* MOTHER *and* AUNT *watch the baby;* TERU *and* HANAKO *put cushions in place, then form tableau with others as lights slowly dim and curtains close.*]

CURTAIN

Vendemmia

Fruit Harvest in Italy

by STELLA MAREK CUSHING

PLACE and TIME: Outside the packing shed of Signor Orsini's estate, late afternoon in September.

SCENE: The background should represent blue sky, green hills, and terraced vineyards just before sunset when the whole earth is warm and glowing. A flower garden may form a low wall upstage with an opening in the center. Behind that platforms may be hidden.

At L. there is a grape-crushing vat about four feet wide and four feet high made to look like old stone work. Near the bottom of the vat is a spigot or faucet connected with a can or pail inside vat which contains punch the color of grape juice. Upstage R. there are a few benches, large baskets or packing boxes. Upstage R. is a crude cradle in which is a life-sized baby doll wrapped in swaddling clothes. Entrances are from upstage and downstage on both sides. If possible, processions should enter down aisles, through auditorium.

CHARACTERS [*as they appear*]:

AUNT ROSA
UNCLE CARLOS (Kar'-lōs)
Workers on the estate
ELISABETTA (Ā-lees-ä-bet'-tä)
ALFREDO (Äl-fray'-do), overseer
GEMMA (Zhem'-ma)
NICOLA (Nee-cō'-lä)
MARIO (Mä'-ree-ō)
MADDALENA (Mäd-dä-lay'-nä)
SIGNOR ORSINI (Or-see'-nee)
SIGNORA ORSINI
GIUSEPPE (Zhu-sep'-pi), grape-crusher
Fruit-gatherers

GENERAL SUGGESTIONS: This play should be set at a fast tempo except during the singing of "My Bambino" and "The Nightingale." The tarantella should be danced with gaiety and spirit. Aunt and Uncle should be chosen from the best dancers. If the play becomes a community project, these characters should be chosen from the adults who know the dance. Signor Orsini is a noisy blustering character. The procession should not be too dignified; the people greet those in the audience as if they were a part of the festa. If given on a stage, the processions may come from different entrances through the auditorium. This play is also suitable for performance out-of-doors with dialogue shortened. The processions can be most effective if seen coming from a distance from different directions led by musicians playing accordions, guitars, violins, or even harmonicas. It will create great enthusiasm if a real scissors grinder with his machine enters just before the song "The Scissors Grinder."

MUSIC: (*See* Unit XV: Trips Abroad — Italy, p. 170.)

COSTUMES: (*See, The National Geographic Magazine*, April, 1928, plates 20, 21, 24; February, 1930, plates 3–8; September, 1935, plates 4, 5.)

INTRODUCTION (*To be printed on program or spoken as a prologue before the curtains open*): Italy has long been a paradise to travelers. Many enjoy best the beauty of the Bay of Naples as the setting sun glows upon the colored sails in the harbor and upon smoking Vesuvius. Some always return to Capri and the Amalfi Drive. Some linger in the lovely lake country, gaze upon the lofty Alps, or climb among the curious Dolomites. Others wander among the ancient ruins of Imperial Rome. Still others think of Italy as mistress of all the arts and sit in admiration at the feet of her noble painters and sculptors.

The paradise to which we shall go is the fertile valley of the River Arno. There as we observe Nature's generous gifts at harvest-time we honor those who have nurtured the vines and trees in fields, orchards, and vineyards.

Now, as the rich harvest is gathered, we join with the peasants in a festa befitting the occasion. Flowers abound everywhere, — roses, nasturtiums, sweet lavender, heliotrope, carnations, white and purple clover, and the oleander tree. Nature is also generous with the health-giving tomatoes, artichokes, fennel, beans, scarlet peppers, radishes, and squash, while a bountiful ingathering of fruits includes oranges, lemons, figs, pears, red currants, and grapes, red, blue, and white.

Come, now to the garden near the great packing shed on the estate of Signor Orsini and join him, his family, and the workers in the festa, time of rejoicing.

[*After* INTRODUCTION, *the music of the* "Tarantella" *is heard and dancing is well under way before curtains open. Some of the workers are dancing, others looking on.* AUNT ROSA *sits by cradle;* UNCLE CARLOS *stands beside her watching the dancing. At the finish, young people cheer as dancers go to* AUNT ROSA *and* UNCLE CARLOS. *For the dance, musicians on stage or phonograph play any good tarantella.*]

ALL. Bravo! Bravo!

ELISABETTA. Aunt Rosa, did we dance the tarantella better this time? Did we remember what you have taught us?

AUNT ROSA [*thoughtfully*]. Well, it was better. You remembered much that I told you. For the young feet it was good. But you do not know all of the turns and every step. The tarantella must be practiced long before it can be danced well. That is why we who are older dance it better than you do.

UNCLE CARLOS. You must dance until you are breathless and can dance no more. You know the legend of the dance?

ALFREDO. You mean about the tarantola that poisoned the girl?

GEMMA. I know that story. It was at festa, in the midst of gaiety that Ofelia was bitten by a large spider.

ELISABETTA. She screamed and fell to the ground fainting because it hurt so much.

NICOLA. Her father quickly took a knife and cut around the sting.

MARIO. The blood spurted out freely. [*Girls groan and shudder.*]

MADDALENA. Poor little Ofelia. She was so frightened.

GEMMA. Who would not be? The tarantola is poison.

ALFREDO. But her father knew what would save her. He knew a way to get the poison out.

ELISABETTA. He said, "Dance, dance, Ofelia, until you can dance no more! Dance, my daughter!"

NICOLA. Everyone began to sing and her father led the dance. Ofelia quickly rose to her feet and joined him.

MARIO. Faster the music and faster the dance. The other boys cut in.

MADDALENA. And the girls began to dance. Soon everyone was dancing.

GEMMA. Ofelia's feet moved faster than anyone's. Her tears were dried by the wind.

ALFREDO. The pain began to go away. But Ofelia's father kept on with the dance.

MARIO. He knew she must dance until she was exhausted.

ELISABETTA. Finally she dropped to the ground, weary, unable to go on.

GEMMA. But she was saved!

ALL. Ofelia was saved! Hurrah! Bravo!

UNCLE CARLOS. I see, you have learned it well. Your bravo should be for the father who knew what to do.

ALL. Bravo! Bravo!

AUNT ROSA. So, whenever you dance the tarantella, remember the legend and do the steps quickly and with spirit. There are many turns in the dance. [*To girls*] When you turn away from your partner, glance over your shoulder and smile at him, like this [*illustrates*].

UNCLE CARLOS [*to boys*]. And when your partner turns, follow her and snap your fingers in her ears, like this [*illustrates with* AUNT ROSA].

GIRLS. Dance for us.

BOYS. Show us how.

[AUNT ROSA *and* UNCLE CARLOS *dance the tarantella.*]

ALL [*as they finish*]. Bravo! Bravo!

[*Enter L. a group of fruit-gatherers. Everyone on stage greets them heartily.*]

GEMMA. It will be a pleasant night for the festa.

MARIO. Tonight the moon is full. It will shine upon us as we celebrate.

ELISABETTA. And the nightingales will sing their lovely songs.

AUNT ROSA. Sing the nightingale song for me now.

Song, The Nightingale, p. 178, sung as a solo or by special group

[*All sit down. The moonlight shows as lights dim.*]

AUNT ROSA [*romantically*]. It will be a night of beauty and romance.

UNCLE CARLOS. You women talk always of romance. We men shall sing also, and our songs will be merry ones. Alfredo will sing of the grasshopper and the ant.

ALFREDO. I shall sing it now.

ALL. Yes, yes, sing it now.

Song, The Grasshopper and the Ant, p. 170, sung by Alfredo and Chorus

[*As song ends,* SIGNOR ORSINI *enters from downstage L.*]

SIGNOR ORSINI. Aha! Why do you not work? Do you think festa has begun? Have you been singing and dancing all day? Where are the full baskets of fruit? Have you picked the figs from the old orchard? Where are the oranges and lemons? The trees are groaning with the weight of the heavy fruit, yet you stay here to dance.

ALFREDO. It was the rest hour, Signor.

ELISABETTA. We were practicing our dance for the festa tonight.

AUNT ROSA. I was not satisfied with their dance. It needed more finish and sparkle.

UNCLE CARLOS. We must teach the young our ways so that they will not forget.

SIGNOR ORSINI. You dance the hours away while I pay. And my fruits will be ruined if they are not picked. The padre will come to bless the baskets and there will be no fruit in them. Here are some already waiting to be sorted. It must be done quickly so that they do not spoil. The packers wait and you dance. Hurry to your work or no festa tonight.

ALL. Oh, Signor Orsini, no festa — Oh!

SIGNOR ORSINI. Off to your work, quickly, pronti. I say off to your work — no festa until every basket is full. No festa, I say, until work is done.

BOYS. We hurry!

GIRLS. Yes! Yes! [*Boys and girls begin to pick over fruit in baskets.* SIGNOR ORSINI *stamps about talking to himself loudly. Baby begins to cry.*]

UNCLE CARLOS. There you see, the bambino cries at your loud voice.

AUNT ROSA. The poor bambino.

SIGNOR ORSINI. My loud voice! Did you not make more noise with your singing and dancing?

AUNT ROSA. Our singing and dancing! That would not disturb him. Is not the love for it in his soul? It gave him sweet dreams. [*Baby still cries.*]

UNCLE CARLOS. The song made his sleep happy and his cradle was rocked by the swing of the dance, but your voice was like the roll of thunder.

AUNT ROSA [*to baby*]. It was to his ears like the sharp crack of a gun. Hush! hush!

[SIGNOR ORSINI *looks worried.*]

SIGNOR ORSINI. Stop him! Stop him! My wife will hear.

UNCLE CARLOS. Of course she will hear — a mother's ears are sharp when bambino cries.

AUNT ROSA. Hush, little one.

[SIGNORA ORSINI *enters, stage L., hurriedly. She runs to the cradle; picks up baby.*]

SIGNORA ORSINI. Mio caro bambino. Do not cry. [*To* SIGNOR ORSINI] What wakened him?

SIGNOR ORSINI. I do not know.

[*Baby quiets a little.* UNCLE CARLOS *and* AUNT ROSA *enjoy* SIGNOR ORSINI'S *discomfort.*]

AUNT ROSA. It was the sharp crack of a gun.

SIGNORA ORSINI. I heard no gun and I was nearby in the garden.

UNCLE CARLOS. It was a roll of thunder.

SIGNORA ORSINI. There was no thunder. The sky is clear and blue.

SIGNOR ORSINI [*crestfallen*]. It was my loud voice.

SIGNORA ORSINI. Again?

SIGNOR ORSINI [*excitedly*]. I come to watch my people at work and they are singing and dancing. They should be picking the fruit, sorting, and making it ready for the packers. They should be working. The festa is the time for singing. They should . . . [*Baby begins to cry again.*]

SIGNORA ORSINI. Arturo, quiet. Sh, sh, bambino. [*To* SIGNOR ORSINI] Always your tongue is like the sharp sting of a bee. Do not speak in such a loud voice. [SIGNOR ORSINI *looks humble.*] There, mio caro bambino, do not cry. Your mother has come to rock you and to sing to you.

Song, My Bambino, p. 175, sung by Signora Orsini
(The workers hum a soft accompaniment)

[*Lights dim during song. At introduction of song* SIGNOR ORSINI *tiptoes off* L. UNCLE CARLOS *and* AUNT ROSA *exit* R. *When song is finished* SIGNORA ORSINI *walks off stage* R. *with baby; some of the boys remove cradle and follow her. As they disappear,* SIGNOR ORSINI *enters* L. *on tiptoe and looks all around for baby.*]

SIGNOR ORSINI [*in a loud stage whisper*]. The bambino sleeps?

BOYS and GIRLS [*loudly*]. Yes, Signor, of course, Signor. [SIGNOR ORSINI *jumps at their loud voices.*]

SIGNOR ORSINI [*in natural voice*]. Good, now we shall proceed with our work.

GIRLS. And the festa? Shall we have the festa?

SIGNOR ORSINI. Of course, of course.

GIRLS. Will there be a procession? [*He nods*]; and singing? [*nods*], and dancing? [*He replies — "si, si."*]

BOYS [*in a loud chorus*]. And eating?

SIGNOR ORSINI. Si, si.

ALL. Hurrah! Hurrah!

SIGNOR ORSINI. Come now, take your baskets to the shed and return with the cakes and candies we have prepared.

[*The boys move table forward slightly, then exit with the girls stage* L. *From stage* R. *a few pickers enter with full baskets as introduction of music for song begins. They place baskets upstage on each side of table as boys enter carrying pitchers and glasses and girls enter with plates of cakes and candies. They arrange them on table while singing. All make a tableau upstage. Enter* SIGNORA ORSINI, UNCLE CARLOS, *and* AUNT ROSA.]

Song, Tic-ti Tic-ta, p. 176

[*As processions enter, lights in auditorium come on or spotlights follow processions. From door on floor at* R. *enter* ORANGE *and* LEMON PICKERS *and mount stage at center, circle stage to* R., *and leave baskets piled up at stage* R. *As soon as they have mounted stage, enter* FIG *and* OLIVE PICKERS *from door on floor at stage* L. *They mount stage, circle* L., *place baskets at* L., *and form tableau on* L. *Then from back of hall down center aisle the grape procession enters. Everyone carries something; trays or baskets of grapes, water jugs, large baskets carried on a pole by two boys, some have long poles on which are tied huge balloons and large grape leaves. Carts may be drawn by boys. Everything is gaily festooned. They are hailed by all. They mount stage, divide, and circle, some of each group forming effective tableaus on raised*

platforms. *Poles of balloons are put into flag standards or Christmas-tree holders upstage; all form at sides — some people standing, some kneeling, some sitting, everyone gay. Music continues until all are on stage. While procession is gathering,* GIUSEPPE, *with elaborate ceremony sits at the side of the grape-crusher, removes his shoes and stockings, washes his feet in the water in a small basin, dries them with a towel, and waits there until he is ready to crush the grapes.*]

SIGNOR ORSINI [*when all are assembled*]. Welcome to the household of Orsini. All summer you have been working hard, caring for the fruits on tree and vine. You workers from the orchards in the valley, — what have you brought to Vendemmia?

ORANGE and LEMON PICKERS. Oranges and lemons.

SIGNOR ORSINI. And you who have come from the terraced vineyards?

GRAPE GATHERERS. Grapes, grapes.

SIGNOR ORSINI. Now comes your reward. You will be paid in good lira for the hours you have labored. [*Cheers*] Now, Giuseppe, it is time for you to crush the grapes.

GIUSEPPE. Si, si, Signor. [*He steps into the grape-crusher and moves around as if he were crushing the grapes as all sing. If real scissors grinder is used, he enters before song, and works on knives while song is sung.*]

Song, The Scissors Grinder, p. 172

[*As song ends,* SIGNOR ORSINI *takes a glass pitcher. With elaborate ceremony he turns the spigot and the grape juice fills the pitcher. All cheer. He serves some of them.*]

SIGNOR ORSINI. This is a happy festa. Stay, be our guests while the setting sun fades away and the moon shines down upon us. Come, let us have singing and dancing. Maddalena, lead us in the dance.

[*Dancers rise and form into one or several small circles.*]

Song with dance, Maddalena,* p. 174

SIGNOR ORSINI. Always at festa we sing, we dance, also, we eat. [*Cheers*]

[*Many rise now, lights gradually brighten as those with baskets of food, bread, sausages, cakes, or candies move about serving others. Some sit down, others stand as musicians begin refrain of "Tic-ti Tic-ta." All join in singing refrain, some moving about, some swaying to the rhythm of the music as the curtains slowly close, open, close again just before end of song, while people on stage wave to audience.*]

CURTAIN

Dance directions for the Tarantella by Michael Herman

FORMATION: Any number of sets of two couples in squares, partners facing each other.

MUSIC: *See* p. 240. Count one, two, to each measure.

STEPS: Step-hop, running step, skipping step.

FIGURE I.

Meas. 1. Count 1. All step sidewise to the left with left foot and clap hands. Count 2. Hop on left foot and swing right across the left.

Meas. 2. Same as Meas. 1, but beginning with right foot.

Meas. 3–4. Four running steps in place, snapping fingers or striking tambourine.

Meas. 5–16. Repeat Meas. 1–4 three times.

FIGURE II.

Meas. 1–2. Take 4 running steps forward toward partner bending low.

Meas. 3–4. Take 4 running steps backward to place, slowly straightening body and raising hands, snapping fingers or shaking the tambourine.

Meas. 5–16. Repeat Meas. 1–4 three times.

FIGURE III.

Meas. 1–4. Boy of Couple 1 and girl of Couple 2 come toward each other, hooking right arms (elbows), turn once around clockwise back to respective places.

Meas. 5–8. Boy of Couple 2 and opposite girl repeat Meas. 1–4.

Meas. 9–12. Repeat Meas. 1–4, hooking left arms.

Meas. 15–16. Repeat with opposite couples.

FIGURE IV.

Meas. 1–4. Boy of Couple 1 and girl of Couple 2 run around each other, passing right shoulders, and return backward passing left shoulders.

Meas. 5–8. Boy of Couple 2 and girl of Couple 1 do the same.

Meas. 9–16. Repeat 1–8, passing left shoulders going forward and right shoulders coming back.

FIGURE V.

Meas. 1–4. All place hands on hips and face right, with left shoulders to the center of the set. Take 8 skipping steps counter-clockwise.

Meas. 5–8. Turn halfway to left with right shoulders to center. Take 8 skipping steps clockwise back to place.

Meas. 9–10. All stretching left hands toward the center forming a windmill, take 8 skipping steps counter-clockwise.

Meas. 13–16. Turn halfway to left, stretching right hands toward center, take 8 skipping steps clockwise back to place.

---

*Dance directions for "Maddalena"

POSITION: Double circle, partners facing each other, boy in inner circle, back to center.

FIGURE I.

Boy takes partner's left hand in his right, extend joined hands backward, free hands on hips.

Meas. 1. Swinging joined hands forward and swaying boy beginning with left foot and girl with right, partners take 3 peasant waltz steps moving counter-clockwise.

Meas. 2. Swinging joined hands backward and swaying toward each other, partners continue the peasant waltz.

Meas. 3–8. Continue Meas. 1–2.

FIGURE II.

All join hands in one large circle, facing center.

Meas. 9–10. Take 4 running steps toward center and pause.

Meas. 11–12. Take 4 running steps backward and pause.

Meas. 13–14. Repeat Meas. 9–10.

Meas. 15–16. Take 4 running steps backward and resume original position of the double circle.

FIGURE III.

Meas. 1–8. Partners take waltz position, and peasant waltz counter-clockwise around circle.

FIGURE IV.

Same as Figure II.

FIGURE V.

Same as Figure I, partners bowing with a ritard on Meas. 8.

Roundup Camp at Night

A Play for Boys

Built around Unit IX: "Songs the Cowboy Sings"

by ALICE GIDEON WHITMIRE

This is a picture of an actual presentation of the operetta by boys in the William H. Seward School, Chicago. The drop curtain shows western hills and coulees and the horse cavy at the left, and was painted by the boys themselves. The picture gives an idea of the ingenuity of the boys in making their own stage setting, the mess wagon, the stove, camp fire, etc., and their own "chaps" from odds and ends of various materials, including their mothers' old coats, old pieces of canvas, oil cloth, table cloths, window shades, and even tops of tin cans for buttons.

This operetta, based on a colorful phase of American folk life, is designed especially for boys, who can take all the parts, singing, speaking, and dancing, and can make their own scenery, costumes, properties, etc.

SCENE: Roundup Camp.

TIME: Evening, between six and eight o'clock. Riders coming in from drive, in from day herd, others off for first guard, cook finishing up his work. Riders sitting around camp fire.

CHARACTERS: Shorty, Bill, Wagon Boss, Slim, Bud, Sarpy Sam, Greeley, Cook, Jack, Curley Bill, Spec, and others.

Song [*as curtain rises*], The Trail to Mexico, p. 80

SHORTY [*coming in, throwing his bridle down, speaking to* BILL]. Thanks for the use of your horse, Bill.

BILL. Pretty good horse, ain't he?

SHORTY. If star-gazin' and high-tailin'-it makes a good cowpony, he's it. You can keep him in your own string. That horse doesn't know there's any cattle in this country. What's the matter with this outfit, anyhow? Expect us to work with only a few real good horses in the whole cavy? *

WAGON BOSS. And you've got two of the best horses in the outfit; you should be kickin'! Cowboys as well as cowponies ain't what they used to be; takes a top hand to ride top horses!

SARPY SAM. Remember old Ruby horse, — belonged to Rube as long as he was with the outfit — he *was* a horse, do anything and everything had to be done around a cow outfit; could ride him fifty miles on circle in the morning and he'd come in as fresh as ever.

SHORTY. Knew what a cow says to her calf!

GREELEY. Good cutting horse, too. Could weave his

* *See* p. 76.

way into the herd and cut out the beef steers better than any horse I ever knew.

SHORTY. He could cut a prairie dog away from his hole.

BUD. And he was a real rope horse! Anything from a yearling calf to a two-thousand-pound steer. He could hold anything. You could rope a locomotive and he'd try to hold it. Good night horse, too. Find the herd however black or stormy the night. I used to use him for a night horse; used to like to sing when I rode him on night guard.

SHORTY. Sing us a song *now*, Bud. How about the old "Lament." I've heard you singin' that song many a night out under the stars.

ALL. Yes, let's have "The Dying Cowboy."

BUD. All right, here goes.

Song, The Dying Cowboy, p. 78

WAGON BOSS. Talking about good horses — We could use a few good cowhands with this outfit, too; there used to be good cowboys as well as good cowponies. It took top hands, top horses, and a good outfit to weather all the grief and storms on those long trails in the olden days. You fellows don't know real grief or real hard work or real cowboyin', either!

Going up from Texas along the Old Chisholm Trail we were weeks on the trail, driving thousands of cattle. We had to face dust and heat from the hoofs of the cattle, hold them in rain or snow, against winds and lightnin', and ride like fury to start them millin' when something would startle them and they'd rise right up in the darkness and start runnin'. Those were the days of real cowboyin'.

ALL. Yes, the days of the Old Chisholm Trail.

Song, The Old Chisholm Trail, p. 88

BILL. Hey, Jack, on first guard with me? Better be leavin'; can't expect Slim and Curley Bill to stay with the herd after eight. That last day herd from four to eight sure is tough.

JACK. Greeley, you and Spec on second guard? Hope it's rainin' pitchforks when you get out. No luck, though, with that clear sky.

BILL. Always hope you have to stand guard in the rain, Greeley, so you won't forget your promise. Boss, tell the other fellows why Greeley likes the rain so well, especially night guard. [BILL and JACK leave for herd.]

BOSS. Well, you see Greeley was always jobbing the other fellows, until one night they jobbed him so bad he swore off playing tricks on the rest of the fellows. Shorty, you tell them, you were in on it.

SHORTY. One night when Bud and I came in from first guard and crawled into bed — glory be! — we thought we were lying down on a jazz saw. Everything in the world from cactus to bridles had been put under our tarp.[1] We knew who had done it, so we go to Greeley's tepee [1] — he's sleeping so innocently — and we tie his trousers into knots and go back to bed. About two o'clock, Greeley has to get up — he's on third guard. But in the meantime, a storm has come up, blew down his tepee, and when he woke up, it was rainin' pitchforks. So he has to crawl out from under his tepee and put his clothes on in the rain. He starts to put his trousers on but his feet won't go through. So there he stood in a downpour, untyin' the knots in his trousers; Bud and I listenin' and laughin' down in our sleeves. All we heard was Greeley half cryin' and half laughin', sayin': "I'm not jobbing anyone in this outfit any more and I don't want anyone jobbing me."

GREELEY. And so far, I've kept my word, ain't I?

SHORTY. You'd better keep it or we'll all job you, won't we?

ALL [shout]. We will. You'll get yours. You bet you will.

[Under cover of shouting, yodeling and singing start; SLIM and CURLEY BILL, coming in from herd, yodeling and singing "Old Paint."]

Song, Old Paint, p. 86

[Boys on stage play and sing "Old Paint." As they finish, SLIM and CURLEY BILL come on stage.]

SHORTY. Well, I guess that cowboy believed in carryin' his trademarks with him. No mistakin' him for anything else, what with "a-ridin' Old Paint" and "a-leadin' Old Sam."

GREELEY. But guess it pays for a cowboy to carry his trappin's along so he won't have to prove himself every-time he changes ranges, like the stranger had to in "The Zebra Dun." Reckon the stranger was pretty lucky.

SEVERAL. How's that? Let's hear his story.

Song, The Zebra Dun, p. 82

WAGON BOSS. That song makes me think of the old Flyin' U outfit and the roundups they used to hold in the Cimarron country. I'll never forget the last roundup there, just before they started trailin' their last trail herd north to Kansas for shipment. It was their last drive up the Old Chisholm Trail, and for me as well, for the next year the railroad was finished clean down to Santa Fe. I'll never forget it, for it was on that drive that another

---

[1] *Tepee.* A canvas tent shaped like an Indian tepee, large enough only for the cowboy's roundup bed and used only for sleeping. In the old days few cowboys carried a tepee; they slept in the open. But of recent years, especially in Wyoming and Montana where winter snows and cold come early and where the work of the roundup continues into the month of December, the tepee is coming into use late in the fall. It is by no means a living quarters, but has barely space for the cowboy's bed, which consists of a *tarp* (canvas covering) and *sougans* (comforts) thrown on the canvas floor of the tepee. Many a cowboy still prefers to brave the elements in winter as well as summer, so he may still be found on the roundup with only his sougans and tarp between him and the stars.

stranger, Little Joe, the Wrangler,[1] he was called, came ridin' into camp and the boss gave him a job. You know his story — it's told in song — sing it.

Song, Little Joe, the Wrangler, p. 84

JACK. Well, I guess he just changed ranges, goin' out like that, doing his work. He just must have gone to a better land.

SLIM. And I'll bet he's ridin' herd, now, with the best of the cowboys, whatever range he's on.

JACK. Won't be long, Slim, before you'll be changin' ranges and be leavin' for Montana. When the roundup's over he'll be packin' his bed on "Old Sam," and he'll be ridin' his own "Old Paint" and be leavin' until next spring. Goin' to hibernate with the wolfer, Slim?

SLIM. Reckon I will and do a little wolfin' myself.

WAGON BOSS. Well, Slim, we'll have a farewell dance for you. The Old Man today asked if we'd make the Big Spring Ranch by this Saturday night; goin' to give a roundup dance for the wagon.

JACK. Think we'll make it, old pard?

WAGON BOSS. If we hold the herd, don't lose our cavy, or no storms hinder us, we'll camp at Dripping Springs Friday night, twelve miles from the ranch.

GREELEY. Hear the schoolma'am's boardin' at the Big Spring Ranch this year; hear she's a tenderfoot from 'way back East! Slim, you plannin' to corral the schoolma'am this year? [Aside to gang] He always does.

CURLEY BILL. We might as well make up our minds right now not to get a look at the lady. We'll just have to tie a handkerchief around our arm and be a lady ourself. We've been doin' it a long time and probably will for a long time to come, — anyhow until this country gets settled and more ladies come in.

[Boys tie handkerchiefs around arms. CURLEY BILL and SLIM lead, SLIM pretending CURLEY BILL is the schoolma'am. Boys dance square dance to the music of "Leather Breeches"; all keep time. As an alternative the cowboy waltz, "Charlie Knapp," p. 89, is offered; or the waltz may be danced before breaking into the square dance.]

Square Dance, Leather Breeches, p. 91

CURTAIN

DIRECTIONS FOR SQUARE DANCE

MUSIC: Leather Breeches, p. 91.

POSITION: Each set contains four couples, lady to gentleman's left, forming a square. At beginning of music partners greet each other, gentleman bowing and lady curtsying, feet stepping in time to music. Couples take right hands and circle in place, gentleman guiding partner with left hand to her back.

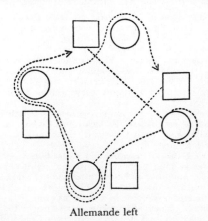

Allemande left

---

[1] *Wrangler. See* the statement defining *cavy*, on p. 76, for the meaning of this word.

I. CALL: "Balance all as pretty as you can,
Swing 'em all round with a left Allemande."

"Allemande left" means to circle "grand right and left." But first the gentleman crosses to left in front of partner, taking right hand of lady of couple to his left and swinging her around once, then reversing his direction and going to his right to meet his partner in a "grand right and left" until he meets his partner again on completion of the circle. While the gentleman is doing this his partner does the same, only in the opposite direction. There should be plenty of feet and elbow movement by gentlemen and quiet shuffling by ladies.

II. CALL: "Meet your partner, promenade eight,
Till you get straight."

When partners meet they circle in place, joining right hands. Then crossing hands, couples slide-hop clockwise in full circle, returning to original place. Couples do not turn as they go around the circle.

III. CALL: "First couple down the center and cast off six,
Swing at the head and swing at the foot;"

First couple, which is the couple at the head of clock position, shuffle down the center of circle between couples opposite them, which "casts off six," circling outside the ring backward to place. When in place swing in place, as does also the couple opposite them.

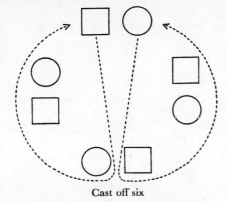

Cast off six

IV. CALL: "Down the center and cast off four,
And when you get home you can swing 'em some more."

First couple shuffle down the center again and "cast off four," circling backward to place, swinging in place as before as does also the opposite couple.

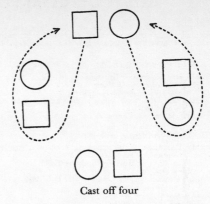

Cast off four

V. CALL: "Down the center and cast off two,
And swing 'em all round, till you get through."

First couple shuffle down the center again and "cast off two," circling backward to place as in "cast off four."

VI. CALL: "All they dance and all they swing,
Allemande left around the ring;"

All swing in place and then around the ring again according to directions as given for "Allemande left" in I above.

VII. Numbers III, IV, and V are repeated, but with second couple casting off six, four, and two. Then the third couple goes through the same figures, and finally the fourth couple. Couples do not change position in the circle, the second couple is always a side couple. The Calls of numbers III, IV, and V are repeated for each couple, merely substituting the words "second couple," "third couple," "fourth couple."

VIII. CALL: "Meet your partner and give her a whirl,
And go right on to the next pretty girl."

After the last "Allemande left" around the ring, when partners meet, instead of promenading together, gentleman swings his partner and then swings each lady at the left, ladies remaining in positions. Swing is done by clasping right hands with left hands to partner's back.

IX. CALL: "When you meet your partner promenade eight,
Till you get straight."

When partners meet final time, they promenade or two-step around circle until they reach their places.

LIST OF CORRELATED RECORDED MUSIC*

The following selections correlate with and illustrate songs and choruses in this book. The unit and page numbers suggest some of the correlations, though there are many others which the teacher will find useful for appreciation and social program studies. A number of songs in this book have been specially recorded, as indicated below and as indicated with the song titles throughout the book.

UNIT I: THE OPEN ROAD

1666 * Country Gardens — Grainger
Shepherd's Hey — Grainger
Minneapolis Symphony Orchestra
Das Lied im Grünen (Song of the Open) — Schubert (7657 — see Unit XI)
Sigrid Onegin (Contralto)

UNIT II: TRIPS ABROAD — SWEDEN

25382-A My Homeland, p. 9 Spring, p. 8 Buxom Lassies, p. 10 Neptune, p. 12
From "Music Highways and Byways"
Lyric Quartet
19923 Oh Vermeland, Thou Lovely — Old Folk Melody
Victor String Ensemble
V-20078 Lördagsvalsen — Waltz
Kinne Kulle — Schottis
Olle i Skratthult's Luffarekapell
35885 The Herd Girl's Sunday — Ole Bull — Three Norwegian Melodies
Lawrence J. Munson (Organ)

UNIT III: STEPHEN COLLINS FOSTER

(From Album C-2, Foster Melodies, 9246-9249)
9246 Ring de Banjo Nelly Bly De Camptown Races (and others)
9247 Jeanie with the Light Brown Hair (and others)
Nat Shilkret-Victor Salon Group

UNIT IV: TRIPS ABROAD — RUSSIA AND UKRAINE

25381-A Ukrainian Folk Songs: In My Garden Is a Hazel Tree, p. 28 My Friend, p. 30 Anna's Rosy Cheeks, p. 31 Hopak, p. 32
From "Music Highways and Byways"
Banduryst Choir
1681 Eight Russian Folk Dances, Nos. 5, 6, 7, 8 — Liadow
Leopold Stokowski and the Philadelphia Orchestra
6514 In the Village — "Caucasian Sketches" — Ippolitow-Iwanow — Prince Igor — Polovetzki Dance — Borodin
Leopold Stokowski and the Philadelphia Orchestra
11443 The Fair at Sorotchinsk — Gopak — Moussorgsky
Cortège des Nobles — Rimsky-Korsakow
London Symphony Orchestra

UNIT V: TRIPS ABROAD — POLAND AND CZECHOSLOVAKIA

Poland
25383-A Clanking Spurs, p. 34 Krakowiak, p. 36 Hurry Up, Fellows, p. 37
From "Music Highways and Byways"
Polish Singing Alliance of America, District 7
1654 Mazurka in F Minor — Chopin
Horowitz (Piano)
16250 Minuet — Paderewski
Ignace Jan Paderewski
Czechoslovakia
25383-B The Goose Girl, p. 39 Trumpeter, Blow, p. 45 No Is My Answer, p. 41 Ah, Lovely Meadows, p. 42
From "Music Highways and Byways"
Jan Hus Choir
1414 Slavonic Dance, No. 1 — Dvořák — Kreisler
Songs My Mother Taught Me — Dvořák — Kreisler
Fritz Kreisler
8694 The Bartered Bride — Dance of the Comedians — Smetana
Polka — Smetana
Minneapolis Symphony Orchestra
11434 The Moldau, Parts 1 and 2 — Smetana
11435 The Moldau, Part 3 — Smetana
Berlin State Opera Orchestra

UNIT VI: TRIPS ABROAD — THE SOUTHERN SLAVS

25381-B Peace to All, p. 52 Kyrie Eleison, p. 51 The Holy Season, p. 52
From "Music Highways and Byways"
Illyria Quartet

UNIT VII: SINGING THE BASS PART

1467 Don Giovanni — Finch Han dal Vino — Act I — Mozart
Don Giovanni — Serenata — Deh vieni alla finestra (Open Thy Window) — Act II — Mozart
Ezio Pinza (Basso)
(See also 1655 and 1729)

UNIT VIII: SONGS OF THE CLASSICAL PERIOD

BACH
1599 Gavotte in G Minor — Bach
Wanda Landowska

8697 Toccata and Fugue in D Minor, Parts 1 and 2 — Bach
Philadelphia Orchestra

HANDEL
1435 Musette and Minuet, "Alcina Suite" — Handel
Philharmonic Symphony Orchestra of New York
1436 Gavotte, Sarabande, Menuet, Gavotte, Tamburino, "Alcina Suite" — Handel
Philharmonic Symphony Orchestra of New York

HAYDN
6634-B Theme and Variations from The Emperor Quartet — Haydn
Elman String Quartet
7080-A Symphony No. 4 in D Major, 4th Movement — Haydn
Philharmonic Symphony Orchestra of New York

MOZART
Don Giovanni — Act I — Mozart (1467 — see Unit VII)
Don Giovanni — Serenata and Open Thy Window — Act II — Mozart
Ezio Pinza (Basso)
1486 The Magic Flute — Overture — Mozart
Philharmonic Symphony Orchestra of New York
11594 Sonata in A Major, Minuetto and Allegretto — Mozart
José Iturbi

BEETHOVEN
Moonlight Sonata — Adagio Sostenuto — Beethoven (6690 — see Unit V)
Ignace Jan Paderewski
14694 Symphony No. 1, in C Major, 4th Movement — Beethoven
Philadelphia Symphony Orchestra
7291 Egmont Overture, Parts 1 and 2 — Beethoven
Philharmonic Symphony Orchestra of New York.

UNIT IX: SONGS THE COWBOY SINGS

1729 Take Me Back to My Boots and Saddle
John Charles Thomas

UNIT X: A MUSICAL TRAVELOGUE THROUGH LATIN AMERICA

25385-A Palapala, p. 108 Adios Te Digo, p. 107 Buy My Tortillas, p. 110
From "Music Highways and Byways"
Rodolfo Ducal (Tenor)
with piano by Irma Goebel Labastille
25385-B Sirup Is So Sweet, p. 103 Yaraví, p. 113 Choucoune, p. 97
From "Music Highways and Byways"
Louise Burge (Soprano)
Rodolfo Ducal (Tenor)
with piano by Irma Goebel Labastille
1339 Tango — Albeniz
Danse Espagnole — De Falla — Kreisler
Fritz Kreisler
21393 El Choclo (Tango Argentino) — A. G. Villoldo, arranger L. Joy
Y Como Le Va (Tango Argentino) — J. Valverde
International Novelty Orchestra

UNIT XI: SONGS OF THE ROMANTIC PERIOD

SCHUBERT
6928 The Hurdy-Gurdy Man Impatience Farewell — Schubert
John McCormack
Moments Musicals, Nos. 5, 2, and 3 — Schubert
Victor Salon Orchestra
7657 Der Erlkönig (The Erl King) — Schubert
Das Lied im Grünen (Song of the Open) — Schubert
Sigrid Onegin (Contralto)
SCHUMANN
Traumeswirren (Dream Visions) — Schumann
Horowitz (Piano) (1654 — see Unit V)
7983 Symphony No. 4, in D Minor, 2nd and 3rd Movements — Schumann
Minneapolis Symphony Orchestra
BRAHMS
11458 Minuet in A Major, Parts 1 and 2 — Brahms
London Symphony Orchestra
8973 Symphony No. 1, in C Minor, 3rd Movement — Brahms
Philadelphia Symphony Orchestra

UNIT XII: HERE COMES THE BAND

20132 Stars and Stripes Forever — March
Fairest of the Fair — March
Sousa's Band
21296 Anchors Aweigh — March
All Hands — March
United States Navy Band
12006 Marche Slave — Tschaikowsky
Boston "Pops" Orchestra

* These numbers refer to the catalog of the RCA Manufacturing Company.

NUMERICAL LIST

BIBLIOGRAPHY

BATES, RALPH, *Franz Schubert*, Appleton-Century.
EATON, ALLEN H., *Immigrant Gifts to American Life*, Russell Sage Foundation, 1932.
FINNEY, THEODORE M., *A History of Music*, Harcourt.
HUBBARD, ELBERT, *Little Journeys to the Homes of Great Musicians*, Wise.
JOFFE, JUDAH A., *My Musical Life* — Rimsky-Korsakoff, Knopf.
SCHOLES, PERCY A., *The Complete Book of the Great Musicians*, Oxford.

AMERICAN COWBOY

LOMAX, JOHN A., *Cowboy Songs*, Macmillan.
SANDBURG, CARL, *The American Songbag*, Harcourt.

ANGLO-SAXON MUSIC IN AMERICA

"The Two Brothers"
CHILD, FRANCIS JAMES, *English and Scottish Popular Ballads*, No. 49, Houghton.
"The Frog Went Co'tin'"
Wit and Mirth, or *Pills to Purge Melancholy*. Juds, London, 1699-1714.
"The Deaf Woman's Courtship"
CAMERON, JOHN, *The Lyric Gems of Scotland*, Second Series, p. 104, Blockley, London.
CHAMBERS, ROBERT, *Songs of Scotland, Prior to Burns*, W. R. Chambers, Edinburgh and London, 1880.
CHAPPELL, *Popular Music of the Olden Time*, Chappell and Company, London.
HULLAK, JOHN, *The Song Book*, Lippincott, England, 1866.
RITSON, *Scottish Songs*, Vol. 2, p. 325, Hugh Hopkins, Glasgow, 1869.
WILKINSON, WINSTON, Manuscript collection, University of Virginia.
"Pretty Sally"
CHILD, FRANCIS JAMES, *English and Scottish Popular Ballads*, Houghton. (See "The Brown Girl.")
KIDSON, FRANK, *A Garland of English Folk-Songs*, Hopwood and Crew, London.
WILKINSON, WINSTON, Manuscript collection, University of Virginia.
"At the Foot of Yonders Mountain"
BUCHANAN, MRS. J. P., Marion, Virginia, Manuscript collection.
Journal of the English Folk-Song Society, English Folk-Song and Folk-Dance Society, London. (See "Come All Ye Little Streamers.")
SHARP, CECIL, *One Hundred English Folk-Songs*, Ditson. (See "Barley Mow.")

CHINA

AYSCOUGH, FLORENCE, *Firecracker Land*, Houghton.
BUCK, PEARL S., *East Wind, West Wind*, Day.
COOPER, ELIZABETH, *My Lady of the Chinese Courtyard*, Stokes.
LEWIS, ELIZABETH FOREMAN, *Young Fu of the Upper Yangtze*; *Ho-Ming, Girl of New China*, Winston.
SEEGER, ELIZABETH, *The Pageant of Chinese History*, Longmans.

CZECHOSLOVAKIA

HESS, FJERIL, *The Mounted Falcon; The House of Many Tongues*, Macmillan.
McBRIDE, ROBERT MEDILL, *Romantic Czechoslovakia*, McBride.
NĚMCOVÁ, BOŽENÁ, *The Shepherd and the Dragon*, McBride.

STEPHEN COLLINS FOSTER

HOWARD, JOHN TASKER, *Stephen Collins Foster, America's Troubadour*, Crowell.

ITALY

CANZIANI, ESTELLA, *Through the Apennines and the Lands of the Abruzzi*, Houghton.
GIBBONS, JOHN, *Afoot in Italy*, Dutton.
LAUGHLIN, CLARA E., *Where It All Comes True in Italy*, Houghton.
NEWMAN, EDWARD M., *Seeing Italy*, Funk.
OLCOTT, VIRGINIA, *Beppo and Lucia, Children of Sunny Italy*, Silver.
UNTERMEYER, LOUIS, *The Donkey of God*, Harcourt.

JAPAN

McNEER, MAY YONGE, *Prince Bantam*, Macmillan.
SCHERER, J. A. B., *The Romance of Japan*, Doubleday.
SUGIMOTO, MME. ETSU, *Daughter of the Samurai*, Doubleday.

LATIN AMERICA

EELLS, ELSIE SPICER, *South America's Story*, McBride.
FRANCK, HARRY A., *South America; Mexico and Central America*; and others in the series "Travels in Many Lands," Owen.
MORRIS, ANN A., *Digging in Yucatan*, Doubleday.
QUIROGA, HORACIO, *South American Jungle Tales*, Duffield.

POLAND

CREW, HELEN COALE, *Under Two Eagles*, McClellan.
HUMPHREY, GRACE, *Poland, the Unexplored*, Bobbs.
KELLY, ERIC P., *Blacksmith of Vilno; Christmas Nightingale; Golden Star of Halich; Trumpeter of Krakow*, Macmillan.
PHILLIPS, CHARLES, *Paderewski*, Macmillan.

RUSSIA

ABRAHAM, GERALD. *Studies in Russian Music*, Scribner's.
MAZER, SONIA. *Masha, a Little Russian Girl*, Doubleday.
WHITE, WILLIAM C., *Made in Russia*, Knopf.
YERSHOV, PETER. *Humpy*, Harper.

SWEDEN

LAGERLÖF, SELMA. *Wonderful Adventures of Nils; Further Adventures of Nils; Mårbacka; Charlotte Löwensköld*, Doubleday.

OLCOTT, VIRGINIA, *Erik and Britta, Children of Flowery Sweden*, Silver.
ROTHERY, AGNES E., *Sweden, the Land and the People*, Chapter Four, Macmillan.

YUGOSLAVIA

ADAMIĆ, LOUIS, *The Native's Return*, Harper.
MERCEIN, ELEANOR, *Sounding Harbors*, Harper.
PUPIN, MICHAEL, *From Immigrant to Inventor*, Scribner.

CLASSIFIED INDEX

ALPHABETICAL INDEX